Three Tomorrows

Three Tomorrows

American, British and Soviet Science Fiction

John Griffiths

BARNES & NOBLE BOOKS
TOTOWA, NEW JERSEY

First published in Great Britain 1980 by
THE MACMILLAN PRESS LTD

First published in the USA 1980 by
BARNES & NOBLE BOOKS
81 Adams Drive
Totowa, New Jersey, 07512

ISBN 0–389–20008–5
ISBN 0–389–20009–3

Printed in Hong Kong

British Library Cataloguing in Publication Data

Griffiths, John, *b. 1934*
    Three tomorrows.
    1. Science fiction, English–History and
    criticism
    2. Science fiction, Russian–History and
    criticism
    I. Title
    823'.0876   PR830.S35

    Macmillan ISBN 0–333–26910–1
    Macmillan ISBN 0–333–26912–8   Pbk

    Barnes & Noble ISBN 0–389–20008–5
    Barnes & Noble ISBN 0–389–20009–3

Contents

Author's Note

I have wherever possible, in referring to books by Western writers, cited paper-back editions fairly recently published in the bibliographical notes to each chapter. Where it seems to me relevant I have also given the date of original publication. In the case of the Russian science fiction I give the title and author's name and year of publication, followed by the letters Btk and a number which corresponds to the number given in the bibliographical section of Russian/Soviet Science Fiction edited by A. F. Britikov and published by the Academy of Sciences and Institute of Russian Literature, Pushkin House, Leningrad 1970. Details of translations are given where known.

Introduction

When I completed the first version of this book a decade ago the worlds of science fiction were the oyster of the amateur literary explorer. A few sketch maps had been drawn, one or two routes more carefully charted by such pioneers as Kingsley Amis,[1] Marjorie Nicolson,[2] Roger Lancelyn Green,[3] J. O. Bailey,[4] Damon Knight[5] and Patrick Moore.[6] In the intervening ten years that unknown territory has practically been trampled underfoot by the following hordes of academic settlers.[7] Scientific expeditions, statistical expeditions, survey parties, aerial maps of every comma and co-ordinate have come pouring forth with as little resemblance in style or excitement to those early charts as a satellite photograph to the Mappa Mundi. Where have all the dragons gone? Surely detail and accuracy did not have to spell the death of excitement?

The publisher who first commissioned this work was taken over by a continental firm and went on to become very profitable by concentrating on the coffee table. So the cheque (modest) went into the bank, the MS into the lost-causes drawer in my desk (rather full), and the subject matter to the back of my mind. When, in the summer of 1978, the present publishers, thanks to the persistent faith of my friend Derick Mirfin, asked me to disinter the MS, I found myself confronted by so many maps and signposts as scarcely to know which way to turn. Whereas in 1969 I had been quite clear that I had something to contribute, what justification could there now be for yet another scrap in this well marked paper-chase? Paradoxically, it was my very absence from the field for so long which encouraged me to think there might be a useful purpose to be served by a book such as the one I had originally conceived. The technique that I had found useful in writing about foreign countries[8] had been to visit them on occasions separated by eight to ten years.

While this could not make one master of the minutiae of their development, it did give a bifocal perspective which made significant changes stand out in sharp relief. I found that on several occasions such changes had escaped the notice of those who had lived in daily contact with their settings. Could the same technique be applied to science fiction?

I had originally set myself a cut-off date for new material of July 1969 when Man's first landing on the moon seemed about to end an era of speculation and begin one of exploration. Coming back to science fiction after a decade it still seems to me to be a turning point – indeed the terrain on the gentle slope below me now seems in marked contrast to the steep climb up the scarp. The first thing I noticed was that the ground before me was positively swarming with academics of all kinds and descriptions, from those well-equipped for showing new paths to what Ballard has called a 'Lumpen Intelligentsia' scurrying energetically about, bleating strange noises. Into the sometimes irritatingly cosy world of enthusiastic reader and writer of SF, almost deliberately exclusive, had intruded all the exasperating waspishness of the professional academic in-fighter. While the directions called by some were clear and easy to understand and accept, others appeared to converse only in a meaningless gobbledygook. What on earth, for example, did this mean? 'A Mantric quality is achieved as the author injects these characters with zones of associative fantasy and immense withdrawals into a non-verbal quietism, beyond and without the power of words.'[9]

The dangers of such misleading cries were well recognised by one of the editors of *Foundation,* who wrote: 'This use of language is ultimately nakedly aggressive and territorial – as if by describing SF in specialist academic terminology the don could somehow assimilate it, make it look like his property, with the subconscious analogy of repainting a stolen car and putting new licence plates on it.'[10] Against this formalistic approach had to be set the no less confusing informality of a forced matiness, a conscious trendiness, of critics determined to show that they were at home in a world of proletarian literature where intellectual precision might be mistaken for bourgeois decadence. What could I make of a critic capable of dismissing those more traditional writers who drew strength from 2,000 years of common culture as 'bringing with them whole trains of associations, all the baggage of a high culture which has increasingly become a dead weight'?[11] Scorn seemed to be poured on any work which was not cloaked in obscurity, peppered with jargon and committed to view the world through the blinkers of political dogma – usually, though by no means always, of the extreme left.[12] Would not an amateur entering into this Babel add to the confusion, particularly his own?

I was further deterred by the extent of the ground to be covered. Far from diminishing, the amount of SF published seems to have grown. For example, in little over six months between June 1974 and February 1975 the relatively impoverished, and therefore necessarily selective, Science Fiction Foundation at the North East London Polytechnic had acquired 128 full-length SF novels published in 1974–5. Even though about one-fifth of these were reprints of works I might have been expected to have read already, at the rate of one novel published every two working days and with no allowance for short stories, criticism or foreign-language works, let alone SF in other media, it would be impossible to acquire a comprehensive acquaintance even with the whole field. Yet my hypothesis, that science fiction could tell us certain things about social trends and about the role of science in the development of different societies, would not allow me to concentrate on a single more manageable sector. Not only would I need reliable guides but would have to be quite narrow in my definition of the type of science fiction which would meet my needs. But the amateur is working in isolation, without benefit of the reading and opinion of colleagues, so how is he to select his material? I suggest that random selection and personal whim, if exercised in sufficient quantity, are statistically as likely to produce a typical cross-section of the genre as any more calculated system of selection. For pre–1969 work, when there was in any case very little academic or published guidance to the field, this is the method I have used. For work published in the subsequent decade I have benefited from the advice of a number of members of the SF foundation at the NELP, to whom I am indebted. In the limited time available for updating this work I have not been able to obtain every title they recommended but did read the great majority, as well as continuing to make freelance selections of my own. Making the usual proviso about the dangers of generalising from the particular, then, I think I have encountered a sufficient cross-section of Western SF to provide a significant sample and to form a reasonable basis for opinion.

Where Russian science fiction is concerned I am greatly indebted to Alan Myers, Britain's leading authority in this field, not only for guidance and comments to supplement my own research but for the loans of as yet unpublished articles and in particular of his felicitous translation of *Snail on the Slope* [13] which saved me from floundering in the peculiar complexities of its Russian text. Advice, of course, can be ignored, misunderstood or unverified, so none of my advisers can be held responsible for any errors and omissions in the text. I cite in the text only those books I have read, and the same is true for virtually all the additional works given in the notes to each chapter. While this limits the scope of reference it seems the only way to give the reader a fair measure of the size and range of the sample on which I base my opinions.

Limitations on space also had to exercise their discipline and I have, therefore, excluded cinema and television SF, as I know little about these media.[14] I have also avoided reference to the numerous SF magazines since the regiment of anthologisers has ferreted out most of the interesting material for presentation between more widely-spaced paper covers. There are, in any case, no Russian equivalents with which parallels could be drawn, though there are two SF annuals *Fantastika* and *NF.* I have generally confined myself to Russian science fiction, both pre- and post-revolutionary, rather than drawn on the wider communist empire. Though there is now much SF published in the satellite states and in particular in Hungary, their regimes, and the philosophy associated with them, have been imposed by external force rather than established over six decades following a successful internal revolution. There is thus likely to be a subtle difference in the relationship between writers and rulers in states whose literary philosophy is an imperial imposition when compared to a country in which such philosophy is part of the motivating force behind the whole power structure.

Moreover I do not read Hungarian, Czech or Polish. My regret is that this limitation precludes any extensive reference to the remarkable work of the Pole, Stanislav Lem. I believe its characteristics stem more from his Polishness than from his politics, and since he himself specifically rejects any special role for science fiction [15] and even rejects the Russian Tarkovsky's film treatment of his novel *Solaris* [16] I feel I can leave him aside with a clear conscience.

My selection is therefore personal but it is, I hope, broadly representative of the SF of three countries – Britain, the United States and the Soviet Union – and is examined in the light of my experience working in those countries and of my acquaintance with their three very different languages.

So much for the raw material, but what of the methodology? In the light of what assumptions and theories do I examine it? It is not now necessary to argue the existence of a relationship between literature in general and social attitudes in general. Ever since Professor Karl Mannheim's illuminating demonstration of their interdependence[17] it has been axiomatic that thought – or rather its verbal expression – can best be understood in its social context. Because ideas are not spontaneously generated we can explore the relationship between vested interests and the ideas they espouse. The corollary that, from a sufficiently substantial and homogeneous body of thought or knowledge-based literature, insights may be gained into social attitudes has been much less often considered. I believe science fiction constitutes such a body of literature for reasons which I will try to explain. First of all, when examining the relationship we usually examine the light thrown by *current* social trends on *current* literature. The exercise is intended to give us greater understanding of what *is* happening *now*. Science fiction, on the other hand, is concerned, even when the narrative is set in the past, with what *may* happen in the *future*. It is, therefore, concerned more with people's expectations than with their experiences. The accelerating pace of change affects our expectations, fearful or hopeful, of tomorrow and this in turn markedly affects the way we behave today. The SF writer's expectations of tomorrow and the day after, in so far as they are likely to be fulfilled, may give a warning, however brief, of the way the world will probably go.

The second distinguishing feature which makes SF such good literary litmus paper is not so much that it is written by a special sort of person as that it is usually read by a special sort of person. Nor is the reader special by virtue of mere demographic definitions, though certain sections of the general population are disproportionately, even dominantly, represented among science fiction readers. There are far more men than women, though this is rapidly changing with the widening concept of women's social roles; readers are in the 15–25 age-group rather than the 25–50 one, though the fanzines are run mainly by those in the 30–40 age-group. The SF reader is special by virtue of the fact that he is willing to approach the work in a particular way. As Brian Stableford has said in a perceptive essay on the mass-marketing implications of SF: 'The label "Science Fiction" does not simply tell a would-be reader something about what a book contains. It also tells him something about *how it should be read.*'[18]

If, as Roland Barthes contends, the 'I which approaches the text is already itself a plurality of other texts', then for SF that plurality is at least a largely common denominator. [19] The *same* magazines, the *same* stories and novels will have been read by the follower of SF to a far greater extent than is possible with the classical texts which are progenitors to the rest of contemporary fiction. The science fiction reader is one who has not only said 'I still have my sense of wonder' but one who is willing to be forced to look outward rather than inward, however unpleasant the image revealed. He prefers not to gaze endlessly into his own emotional entrails in the way demanded by the modern psychological novel. He is still prepared to be excited, rather than awestruck and overwhelmed, by the infinite variety of the universe.

Stableford in his *Notes Towards a Sociology of SF* applies to SF the three socio-literary categories of literature devised by Hugh Dalziel Duncan (namely: maintenance, which reflects the assumptions of society; restorative or escapist, which gives a negative or mirror image of the distressing aspects of society; and directive, which is the attempt of an intellectual élite to impose a pattern or direction on society). [20] He considers SF to be a poor anticipator of social events and therefore not likely to prepare us for change. [21] I do not myself regard prophetic accuracy as an essential or even an important ingredient of SF (see chapter 1), but I do think its capacity to recognise the germ of future development and enlarge upon it from different angles and in fanciful ways is important. Science fiction presupposes in its readers a willingness to consider possibilities rather than fact, to hypothesise however bleak the prospect. It is in this very directive mode that SF gives the clearest glimpse of the future. I would, however, endorse Stableford's view that the special nature of SF is such that consideration of a substantial cross-section of the genre will tell us more about the society of its readers than detailed analysis of single outstanding works or even of the works of particular outstanding authors alone, though this may help.

The essential difference between SF and other forms of literature is, of course, that we are dealing with *science* fiction. In some respects the very term seems to suggest a contradiction. How can the known and the make-believe be part and parcel of the same creation? As Robert Pirsig says in his own exciting attempt to reconcile the two worlds of reason, manifest in technology, and the mysticism of spiritual experience, 'The whole purpose of scientific method is to make valid distinctions between the false and the true in nature, to eliminate subjective, unreal, imaginary elements from one's work so as to obtain an objective, true picture of realities.' [22] Yet to suppose that scientific method is contradictory to the purposes of fiction is to misunderstand both – there can be, after all, true lies.

Because science aims to obtain objective truth, scientific ideas – beliefs if you like – ought to be ones in which we can trust as a matter of fact rather than opinion, beliefs which are not subject to doubt as are the beliefs of the religions which science has displaced. But ironically the very scientific method which should lead us with certainty creates a multiplicity of doubts (see note 21). There are no immutable answers in science, only questions and hypotheses embracing more of the observable evidence. Scientists, as Thomas Kuhn says, are 'puzzle solvers', not problem solvers. [23] As he points out when writing about what he calls 'normal', that is, elucidatory, science: 'Nor do scientists normally aim to invent new theories and they are often intolerant of those invented by others. Instead normal-scientific research is directed to the articulation of those phenomena and theories that the paradigm already supplies.'

Science, then, is not usually so much about discovery of the unknown, the unexpected, as about the confirmation or the elaboration of the known. Similarly, much SF is simply a set of variations on established themes or literary paradigms, and equally rarely do its practitioners come up with a new paradigm. When they do, one has to ask: is it an original creation – in so far as in a social context anything is the original creation of an individual – or is it simply the literary reflection of a parallel or impending breakthrough in the 'real' world? Until the mid-1960s Russian SF writers, most of them scientists, were kind enough to behave as scientists might be expected to behave, rather than with the intuitive irrelevance and illogicality of creative artists. They would accept the official datum unquestioningly and elaborate upon it. But scientists are constantly coming up with surprising discoveries because of the operations of basically unsurprising 'normal' science. These discoveries, even when crystallised by genius, are essentially the product of a collective activity of a carefully ordered and logically developing nature. So even the Russian science fiction writer will sometimes surprise himself and his readers.

Science fiction is not like other writing about science; it looks forward where other kinds usually look back, speculates where others consolidate. The scientist,

> by the very nature of his textbook-orientated education, the fact that his progress and success depends on the acceptance of given ideas, is as narrow, rigid and dogmatic as the orthodox theologian, and more than those brought up in other non-scientific disciplines. Yet this collective rigidity is the very instrument by which the anomalies essential to the discovery of new paradigms and progress are thrown up.[24]

By contrast, the writer, though to a greater or lesser degree derivative, has been influenced by a selection from a common pool of unrejected culture so vast that every selection is inescapably different, and every writer's conditioning therefore different. The SF writer is in effect bridging these two distinct conditioning processes (though, often with Russian writers, the science can inhibit the imagination). The good SF writer is essentially a creative artist first, but a creative artist who knows or understands and sympathises with one or more fields of scientific thought.

When a revolution takes place in any science, or indeed in any society, new perspectives are suddenly visible.

> During revolution scientists see new and different things when looking with familiar instruments in places they have looked before. It is rather as if the professional community had been transported to another planet where familiar objects are seen in a different light and are joined by unfamiliar ones as well.[25]

When a new paradigm is discovered the scientist can be said to be working in a new world. The literary devices of science fiction are the instrument by which the writer creates a hypothetical paradigm so that his reader may consider the possibilities and implications of the new world to which he, too, has been translated. The science fiction writer, in a world where even groups of scientists (physicists and geneticists for example) can scarcely understand each other, sets himself up as a kind of cosmic translator between different ways of seeing the world, not just today's but tomorrow's world. In this book, by looking at a wide variety of SF stories, we shall try to see what tomorrow may have in store.

Notes

1. Kingsley Amis, *New Maps of Hell* (first pub. 1961; New English Library, 1969).

2. Marjorie Nicholson, *Voyages to the Moon* (New York, 1949).

3. Roger Lancelyn Green, *Into Other Worlds* (New York: Abelard-Schuman, 1957).

4. J. O. Bailey, *Pilgrims Through Space and Time* (New York: Argus, 1947).

5. Damon Knight, *In Search of Wonder* (Chicago: Advent Publishers, 1956).

6. Patrick Moore, *Science and Fiction* (Science Fiction Book Club, 1958).

7. For more recent criticism of and guidance to SF my choice is necessarily arbitrary and by choice short:
Brian Aldiss, *Billion Year Spree* (Weidenfeld, 1973); D. H. Tuck, *Encyclopedia of Science Fiction and Fantasy* (Chicago: Advent, 1974); Thomas Clareson, *SF: The Other Side of Realism* (Bowling Green, Ohio, 1971); Samuel R. Delany (ed.), *Quark/I* (New York: Paperback Library, 1970); *Foundation*: the regular (fairly!) SF review of the Science Fiction Foundation at NELP.

8. John C. Griffiths, *Afghanistan* (Pall Mall/Praeger, 1967), and *Modern Iceland* (Pall Mall, 1969).

9. From a review in *Foundation 11* from which the following is a further example:

> No doubt the infinite hypocrisies he senses and evinces in his prose-poem are far less elegant and more explicit in the Siberia of fact. Even so, being formed in the cracked mould of the capitalist ethos, M. Le Clézio has found a style for the mystery he seeks to corrode away. He is well experienced in the existential canon, with perhaps Camus and Barbusse as heroes, Genet and Robbe-Grillet as influences, and the Gallic penchant for masochistic rationalism being a compulsively used tool. Yet, given the existentialist's screaming inconclusiveness, the denial of absolutes, the metaphysical/menstrual quality of such thought worlds, the values which drop out and crystallize at the end of the book are known to us all: Freedom, Love, Privacy, Peace and Dogs, in whatever order.

10. Also in *Foundation 11.*

11. Another review, ibid.

12. For a lucid and admirably brief account of this particular approach to literature see Terry Eagleton, *Marxism and Literary Criticism* (Methuen, 1976). This may be the point honestly to admit that my own liberal prejudices make it impossible for me to accept the *total* validity of the marxist approach – though I by no means reject it all. For this reason any detailed argument about the positions adopted by Adorno, Althusser, Benjamin *et al.* would seem fruitless in the present context.

13. Arcady and Boris Strugatsky, *Snail on the Slope* (Leningrad: Btk 501, 1966). A translation by A. Myers is due at the time of writing to be published by Bantam.

14. Philip Strick, *Science Fiction Movies* (Octopus, 1976), is suggested as a useful introduction to the subject.

15. 'I do not segregate SF from the rest of literature, which is why I don't think it should bear the burden of any different duties or roles from normal literature', from an interview in *Foundation 15*.

16. Ibid.

17. Karl Mannheim, *Ideology and Utopia* (Kegan Paul, 1936), mostly written 1929–30. This may seem to deny the singular contribution of the individual artist but Mannheim himself was at pains to dispel this misconception:

> In such cases it is customary to speak of a forerunner and of his role as a pioneer and to attribute this individual's achievement, sociologically, to the group to whom he transmitted the vision and in whose behalf he thought through the ideas. This involves the assumption that the *ex post facto* acceptance of the new view by certain strata only lays bare the impulse and the social roots of the outlook in which the forerunner already participated unconsciously, and from which he drew the general tendency of his otherwise indisputably individual accomplishment. The belief that the significance of individual creative power is to be denied is one of the most widespread misunderstandings of the findings of sociology. On the contrary, from what should the new be expected to originate if not from the novel and uniquely personal mind of the individual who breaks beyond the bounds of the existing order? It is the task of sociology always to show, however, that the first stirrings of what is new (even though they often take on the form of opposition to the existing order) are in fact oriented towards the existing order and that the existing order itself is rooted in the alignment and tension of the forces of social life.

18. *Foundation* 11.
19. Roland Barthes S/Z, (Cape, 1969).
20. *Foundation* 15.
21. Ibid.

The commonly quoted hypothesis that it may serve to insulate readers against the shock and stress of rapid environmental change is made dubious by the observation that hardened science fiction fans are notoriously conservative with respect to the content of the *genre* itself. If reading science fiction does not prepare people for change within science fiction itself, can it really prepare them for environmental change?

The record of science fiction in anticipating social problems is extremely poor. All the fears that haunt contemporary images of the future were invisible in science fiction until they became matters of concern in the real world. This observation is rather damaging to the hypothesis that science fiction prepares people in any way to meet these anxieties as they arise. A case may still be made out for a continuing directive effect, however, because of the way that these issues were taken up and 'fed back' by science fiction. Science fiction, by and large, does not simply reflect these anxieties but *amplifies* them and locates them within a system (or a set of systems) of priorities relating to future-orientated actions and questions of moral responsibility to future generations. It is this set of priorities (or these sets) which stand out as ideas and sentiments maintained by science fiction. Though the view of contemporary man and his ecological and social situations is basically critical and frequently pessimistic, the moral imperatives presupposed by the priority systems maintained by science fiction are steadfastly opposed to intolerance, cruelty and materialism.

22. Robert Pirsig, *Zen and the Art of Motorcycle Maintenance* (first pub. 1974; Corgi, 1978).

If the purpose of scientific method is to select from among a multitude of hypotheses, and if the number of hypotheses grows faster than experimental method can handle, then it is clear that all hypotheses can never be tested. If all hypotheses cannot be tested, then the results of any experiment are inconclusive and the entire scientific method falls short of its goal of establishing proven knowledge.

What shortens the life-span of the existing truth is the volume of hypotheses offered to replace it; the more the hypotheses, the shorter the time-span of truth. And what seems to be causing the number of hypotheses to grow in recent decades seems to be nothing other than scientific method itself. The more you look, the more you see. Instead of selecting one truth from a multitude you are *increasing the multitude.* What this means logically is that as you try to move toward unchanging truth through the application of scientific method, you actually do not move toward it at all. You move *away* from it! It is your application of scientific method that is causing it to change!

23. Thomas S. Kuhn, *The Structure of Scientific Revolutions* (Chicago: IEUS, 1962).
24. Ibid.
25. Ibid.

1
What is science fiction?

Science fiction can be found in many guises, none of which by itself constitutes the true image. Indeed, in each of the eight categories in which genuine SF stories may be found the majority definitely do not meet my definition of the genre. An elaborate attempt to define SF does not now seem particularly helpful, but some description of what kind of stories we shall be discussing is necessary if only to set reasonable limits to the ground to be covered.

That type of narrative I shall suggest is genuine SF will be found in stories of very different stamp: the prophetic; the story of the single false premise; the adventure story or space opera; the mystico-religious tale, or what I like to term metaphiction; fantasy; the instructional narrative; speculative fiction; and satire.[1] It is not, however, sufficient pedigree for an SF story to claim ancestry in any one of these categories and C. S. Lewis is right to warn us of the danger of careless categorisation – though I do not accept his strictures on those who claim that SF is in itself a literary genre.[2] Yet in a sense Lewis was setting up an Aunt Sally. It is undoubtedly wrong to lump together the diverse kinds of writing he describes and just call them SF but that does not mean to say that there may not be a distinguishable body of work, definable as SF, which has characteristics not possessed by any other body of work.

Several of the types of story already listed are mistakenly taken to constitute the totality of SF. The wildest claims for the uniqueness of SF are usually made on the grounds of the scientific achievements predicted by its practitioners and of their prophetic accuracy. The classic example usually cited is Arthur Clarke's anticipation of communication satellites.[3] If the claim to prophetic accuracy is to be made the qualifying factor then it is at least equally arguable, for example, that Newton could claim priority over Clarke in envisaging satellites in his *The System of the World,* a popular version of the third book of the *Principia,* published in 1728. The Russians would certainly regard the speculative writings of K. E. Tsiolkovsky towards the end of the nineteenth century, with their details of sealed cabins having their own air purification systems and rocket propulsion using liquid fuels to give more energy than solid, as having the best claims to have forecast space travel in general, indeed if not to have fathered it. The list of claims is almost endless, as we shall see later in this chapter and again in the next, from Mark Twain's forecast of television – which he at least had the linguistic grace to call the telelectroscope – in 1898, to that of Dr Rose's heart–lung machine in Frank Quattrocchi's *He Had a Big Heart.*[4]

Conveniently forgotten are the many instances when the SF prediction has been proved wide of the mark. However, these prophetic claims are seldom mocked at by the apologists for SF, some of whom regard prediction, provided it conforms to specific rules, as fundamental.[5]

It is not the business of a science fiction writer to record matters of contemporary fact or scientific truths which have already been discovered. It is his business to take what is already known and, by extrapolating from it, draw as plausibly detailed a portrait as he can manage of what tomorrow's scientists may learn . . . and of what the human race in its day-to-day life may make of it all.[6]

To accept the definitions of the extrapolists is to equate SF with no more than technological forecasting – a skill in fact professionally practised by a number of SF writers and a claim actually made by one of them.[7]

Are they right, however, in thinking that the prophetic element of SF is the important one? If it is, it is only so in passing. Science fiction may, like the great increase in adult games, toys and play-things, be a useful psychological crutch to enable people to adapt by anticipation to such extensive and frequent man-made changes in their environment as have hitherto only had to be bridged over several generations. But the fact that in a thousand forecasts SF gets ten specifically right is not surprising or important. Its role in conditioning people to expect more fluid terms of reference in *general* about the future is, as we shall see, another matter.[8]

J. W. Campbell is perhaps getting nearer the role of the prophetic element in SF when he says, 'The major problem of science fiction is to predict the probable *consequences* of certain *suggested* [my italics] changes in the technological systems by which man lives.'[9] Although here the correct emphasis is placed on consequences and on the tentative nature of the changes involved, it is still not right, I think, to consider this a major part of science fiction's role.[10] Asimov's attitude to this problem is undoubtedly the right one. In 1956 he first published a story about exploration on Mercury.[11] When the story was republished in 1965 he drew attention to the fact that the scientific content was now known to be wrong. At the time the story was first published it was believed that Mercury always kept one side away from the sun but by the time it was republished this was known not to be true. But Asimov refuses to alter his story 'merely for the convenience of astronomers'.[12]

At the other extreme from the extrapolists we have the single postulate school. Damon Knight perhaps puts their case most succinctly:

> A science fiction writer may pick his premise according to taste – that pigs fly, or that Napoleon never became Emperor, or that the planets are eggs laid by a giant bird – but he must then, by the rules of the game, develop his story with rigid logic and without violating known fact, except when the violation itself constitutes the basis of the story and a plausible explanation is furnished.[13]

But if we accept Damon Knight's definition, does *The Picture of Dorian Gray* or *Alice in Wonderland* then become science fiction? In neither of these stories is there any attempt to justify or explain the trick by which their real/unreal worlds are entered. This is true also of many contemporary tales masquerading as SF.

Often the single postulate school is in fact doing little more than present its excuses for telling an adventure story. In many such stories all we have is travel to Jupiter instead of Tartary, to an empire on Mars instead of in Peru.[14] For many writers SF is not a departure into a world of unfettered imagination but an escape into the comforts and fetters of a convention totally without imaginative challenge – save in the occasional trifling detail – and is as stereotyped as the Western. It is probably no coincidence that in so many of these space Westerns, particularly those of Murray Leinster, the prospecting theme is common. But there is certainly no need to be unduly scathing about this type of story. In so far as Lewis is right and SF is just the modern version of the morality play or myth of earlier times, then it is only to be expected that the morality play of our own century, the Western, should itself be translated into science fiction terms. Perhaps part of the current appeal of science fiction is precisely that it is a genre in which an heroic adventure story can still unashamedly be written.[15] It is noticeable that many of these stories have an almost mystical touch or affinities with medieval notions of chivalry.

Moreover, the adventure story approach can be so well tackled as to be something more. My own favourite example is Robert Heinlein's *Glory Road*, a tale much mocked by modern critics for not being what it never sets out to be.[16] A device – a magical couch – is used to translate the hero and heroine to an alien planet, and in that sense the tale is not strictly SF. The story is written in the racy, slightly flippant style of the good adventure yarn. In it there is some very keen observation of the human condition and indeed a good analysis of what adventure and the spirit of adventure are all about. There is thoughtful analysis, too, of the effect of pride. But if this were all it would just be a good adventure novel. The fact is that having used his device to effect his translation Heinlein then gives his new world a coherence and consistency in a wealth of detail which, although the story borders on the fantastic or magical, makes it a genuine SF adventure. It obtains its effect, as one character remarks, by 'the commonplace mixed with the wildly different'. It deliberately denies logic because 'logic is a way of saying that anything which didn't happen yesterday won't happen tomorrow'. We are enticed instead to indulge in a kind of literary lateral thinking, as, for example, when the apparently invincible monster Igli is defeated by being made to eat himself from the feet up, in a manner reminiscent of the tales of Greek mythology.

Too often, however, in reading adventure SF one is forced to agree with C. S. Lewis's complaint against many writers of science fiction:

> Why did you lure us on like this,
> Light year on light year, through the abyss,
> Building (as though we cared for size!)
> Empires that cover galaxies,
> If at the journey's end we find
> The same old stuff we left behind,
> Well worn tellurian stories of
> Crooks, spies, conspirators, or love,
> Whose setting might as well have been
> The Bronx, Montmartre or Bethnal Green?[17]

Lewis, however, goes on in the next verse to demand an almost mystical justification for writing science fiction. Certainly, the relationship between science fiction, mysticism and fantasy needs to be examined if we are to reach a more stringent definition of science fiction. Lewis himself says, 'I'm no scientist and not interested in the purely technical side of it.' It is hard in fact to escape the impression in reading his famous trilogy that the whole exercise is mounted as a Christian allegory couched in the terms of a literary entertainment.[18] He himself disclaims any didactic purpose. He would, in fact, probably agree with the Asimov character who says, 'Modern fantasies are very sophisticated and mature treatments of folk motifs. Behind the façade of glib unreality there frequently lie trenchant comments on the world of today. Fantasy in modern style is, above all, adult fare.'[19] Yet whatever its purpose, it is hard to deny that the Lewis trilogy comes closer to being acceptable as science fiction, by however precise a definition, than to fantasy.

Much contemporary fantastic literature is directed by the marketing men at the same audience as they seek for SF and this, I think, adds to the confusion between the two. Fantasy may perhaps be defined as that type of story whose development is arbitrary and whimsical. Although it may seem easy in theory to draw a distinction between science fiction and fantasy, between science and magic, in practice it usually proves difficult to discern the borderline between them – as indeed it sometimes is to define the division between magic and any new field of knowledge, such as extrasensory perception. Lewis's supposition that science fiction is 'a story where the mere pattern of events is all that matters'[20] is not a helpful distinction when in the same breath he equates this pattern with that of myth. Nor is it the rationalisation of myth in modern terms and its logical presentation which turn a story into SF. The insistence on logic by itself sets us on a false trail. Tolkien's Hobbitt books or Mervyn Peak's *Titus Groan*[21] are perfectly logical and coherent, yet neither could ever for a moment be taken as anything other than fantasy.

Fantasy too, are those matter-of-fact seemingly logical stories with a step-by-step build-up to a fantastic and unsubstantiated climactic twist. Classic among these is Arthur Clarke's *The Nine Billion Names of God*,[22] but there are many imitators. Stories of this type are turned into fantasies by the arbitrariness of their pay-off line.[23] The most ambivalent of all writers in this hinterland is probably Ray Bradbury. Bradbury sees with the real mind's eye of a child. Where Dickens had the child's penetrating observation of the real, Bradbury reveals the child's far more important world of 'true unreality'. But with this particular approach the greater part of Bradbury's work, and in particular the many stories he writes concerning children, falls under the classification of fantasy. When Bradbury writes a genuine science fiction story, as in *Fahrenheit 451*, he does so with something of that hypersensitivity which one expects in the good fantasy writer.[24]

In his SF the conflict between materially comfortable science-based stereotypes and the uneasy freedom in which mind and spirit flourish is the main theme. His aim is to protect us from our mania for technology, to make us see, through acts of imagination, that too great a realism and materialism is leading inevitably to our destruction. By creating a sense of revulsion in the reader, Bradbury persuades him to reject the purely technological values the author despises. It is not always easy in several of his stories to draw a dividing line between science fiction and fantasy,[25] and this blurring of the distinction typifies the better quality science fiction/fantasy writing.

Two other occasional inhabitants of this no man's land who may perhaps be ranked with Bradbury in skill and imagination are Kurt Vonnegut and Theodore Sturgeon. Kurt Vonnegut's *Cat's Cradle*,[26] with its delightful pseudo-religion of Bokononism, develops a splendidly fantastic satire. Despite the fact that the central scientific idea – that a particular form of ice (Ice Nine) is capable of changing the molecular structure of all matter with which it comes into contact and hence eventually 'freezes' the whole world – does not itself play a very significant role, it is arguable that without this central concept the story in all its carefully ordered wildness could not have developed.

Similarly, Theodore Sturgeon's *Killdozer*[27] is a most exciting and carefully written tale which turns on the central 'fantastic' idea that a piece of machinery can be possessed of and animated by an evil spirit. The possessed machine then tries to destroy the small handful of isolated construction workers whose tool it is, and a fascinating struggle between men and animate machine unfolds. (The animate machine is a theme we shall examine more fully later.) I would myself accept both these stories as science fiction if only because while reading them one is in no way conscious of any element of fantasy and because the key idea is not just assumed but explained.

That is not to say that a tale of fantasy cannot be perfectly acceptable to the reader, but what distinguishes it from science fiction is that all the while he is reading he is aware that it is a tale of the impossible rather than of the, however remotely, possible. He is conscious of being involved in a symbolic exercise rather than in a reflection, albeit distorted, of reality.

It is I think this confusion between science fiction and fantasy which frequently leads to the accusation, with all its scornful implications, that science fiction is 'escapist' literature. It is far from this, for at its best it deals with reality, or rather an infinite number of possible realities, which may even be singularly unpleasant. Escapist modern literature is surely that great army of novels set in the academic seclusion of dons' households, or in hospitals and common rooms, which reflect a reality so distorted as to be more 'unreal' than many of the worlds of SF. In fact SF deals with a far more real world, measured in terms of its outward points of reference, than the modern psychological novel concerned only with looking inward. It may be, as Amis says, that science fiction is not escapist in itself but rather the cause of escapism in its addicts. Many people who read it may well be attracted by the fact that within the science fiction story the individual, often without any scientific or technical qualifications whatsoever, is apparently able to effect events and influence his own destiny, whereas in real life the increasingly complex nature of science and technology renders it virtually impossible for him to influence the outcome of such events. In a world in which we suffer from too much knowledge and too little comprehension, SF can give the temporary illusion that the ever widening gap is in fact narrowing and can be bridged.

But if in our definition of SF, myth, magic, fantasy and escapist literature must often be excluded, so at the other end of the spectrum must that of unforgiving realism. It is not the function of SF to provide a vehicle for formal scientific or technical education in its narrowest sense – the imparting of information – or to render us numerate either in the precise or general meaning of that term.[28]

I doubt whether many of the readers of SF have sufficient knowledge or critical faculty to decide whether an ingredient of a story is science or fiction and if science how accurate. Certainly we are not required by SF to view things in terms of numbers, either in the equations of celestial mechanics or the formulae of organic chemistry, although these, with greater or lesser accuracy, may be sprinkled throughout a Western SF story for the sake of verisimilitude. It is usually in the Russian story that the detailed scientific argument conducted in symbolic form other than language is considered proper. However, I think it *is* a role of SF to suggest that certain attitudes, situations and behaviour may be given added meaning and precision by considering them in the light of the knowledge extant or possible in one of these scientific fields.

It is in failing to recognise this distinction that so many would-be writers of science fiction fall into the abyss of dullness, for which of course they have some very distinguished precedents.[29] This type of science fiction was put in its proper place by George Hay when he wrote, 'There is nothing more appalling than the tale, still very much with us, where the hero, stunner in hand, holds up his narrative for two pages while he explains the logical development of computerised double entry book keeping, or whatever.'[30]

The difficulty with SF is that since the setting is usually totally alien or speculative no pre-knowledge can be assumed in the reader and everything has therefore to be explained from scratch. If after all a knowledge of double entry book-keeping were necessary to understand the plot of a conventional novel it *would* be necessary to explain its niceties to most of us.

There is a difference between the Western science fiction story 'lecturing' to the lay reader to justify the evolution of the plot and the much more direct teaching purposes of the Russian science-fiction story, but even in the Western version these encapsulated mini-lectures within the text frequently form a stumbling block to the flow of the narrative. That is not to say that there are not a number of fascinating parallels between the serious hypotheses put forward in contemporary scientific work and the same kind of speculation within science fiction stories. The fact that these latter have often anticipated the actual laboratory work does not I think invalidate our earlier dismissal of the prophetic role of SF as a major one.

Biological communications with the use of exo-hormones, and ESP;[31] learning by protein injection, and the instant knowledge of many SF stories;[32] the study of tachyons, theoretical particles that can move faster than light, and stories of communication beyond the light barrier or escape from the limitations of relativity; the work of Kosmolinsky and Dushkov on the rapid deterioration and subsequent recovery of mental performance in men isolated and confined in small chambers, and the many stories studying the initial shock of space isolation;[33] work at the Russian Academy of Sciences demonstrating cadmium sulphide crystals growing stronger when light is shed on them, and the SF stories using crystals and light for material changes;[34] these are but a few of the many parallels I have come across in the course of my reading.[35] Nor is the traffic all one way. Early in 1969 reports were published in the United States on experiments in group conflict using a boys' summer camp as a laboratory. By restricting admission to boys of the same age, the same social background, and the same educational level the experimenter provided himself with an extremely homogeneous group of human test animals. Divided into groups and pitted against each other by the disguised psychologists, conflict grew fairly quickly and was only resolved by the need for common concerted action against contrived outside emergency. It is hard not to believe that this experiment might have been prompted by a whole range of SF stories on this theme and in particular perhaps of that classic of youthful animal behaviour, Golding's *Lord of the Flies*.[36]

The science fiction writer does not, of course, have to hit the scientific nail on its fictional head. Take the case of Ice Nine, referred to earlier. Until recently ice was known to exist in eight different forms, numbered from Ice One to Ice Eight, each of which is the most stable phase at a particular combination of temperature and pressure – ordinary ice at atmospheric pressure is Ice One. In 1963 Vonnegut described the properties of a fictional ninth form of ice, Ice Nine. This was blue-white and had a melting point of $114 \cdot 4°F$ and was also capable of nucleating and so crystallising all the water in the world – with the inevitable disastrous consequences. Fortunately for mankind Vonnegut's speculation, while perfectly legitimate, bore no resemblance whatsoever to the Ice Nine later discovered with very different properties and reported in the *Journal of Chemical Physics*.[37]

Western writers run the whole gamut from the scientifically very precise to the totally dotty.[38] The Russian writer, on the other hand, does not seem to be so plagued by this problem. He considers it a perfectly proper role for a science fiction story to convey scientific information, and he enjoys in any case a public much more given to the serious reading of science on a popular level. Moreover, science and scientists are usually treated more reverently than in the West. In 1959, when I was working in Moscow, a Russian friend gave me a book called *Celestial Mechanics*,[39] which contains a degree of complexity, particularly in the mathematics, which would certainly not be taken up as ready bedside reading by an English-speaking public. It was assumed that I should naturally find it intelligible and entertaining and I admit to pretending this was so.

It would be wrong to attribute too much importance to the Russian predilection for scientific fact. Limited choice is a far more significant factor. Works of fiction obtain a much smaller share of the country's print output than in the West, though print runs are usually enormous by our standards. Since it is necessary for the fiction writer to demonstrate his ideological orthodoxy by frequent injections of propaganda, one way to avoid the tedium of Marxist polemics is to stick to reading purely factual works. We shall see later whether Marxist scientific shibboleths of the post-war period – Lysenkoism in biology,[40] the suspicion of cybernetics, a science not really blessed until the 24th Party Congress in 1970 – are reflected in the permitted literary and political no man's land of science fiction. However, it is interesting to note that these two sciences are the main vehicles for social criticism in Solzhenitsyn's play *Candle in the Wind* written in 1960.[41]

Over-emphasis on the scientific in the science fiction story lays the writer open to two dangers. One, which seems to be overlooked by many writers about science fiction, is that the scientific accuracy which they predicate as essential for their story while accepted as such today may a decade hence be a scientific fallacy: scientific truth is a rapidly moving target. The second danger is quite simply that even by contemporary standards the science may be wrong.

Does this mean that the science has in fact no role to play in the story? That the term science fiction is such a paradox as to be nonsense? Or at least that this particular genre ought to be called by some other name, such as possibility fiction, context manipulation fiction? Or, as Damon Knight seems to think, is it sufficient to redefine it as *speculative* science fiction? If this is the case then in what way does SF differ from scientific speculation, a story involving a universe in a continual state of expansion differ from a reasoned exposition of the theory of an expanding universe?

Is it that the theory is usually only concerned with a possible phenomenon, the story is concerned with the effect that such a phenomenon, assumed possible, would have on human beings – or beings at least?

Such is Ivor Evans's view:

Typically it refers to possible, if improbable, advances in science or technics or to such unprecedented natural phenomena as fissure eruption or a new and malignant germ. Yet it is not essentially concerned with such advances or catastrophes; its real interest lies in their effect upon human beings or other intelligent creatures.[42]

Yet this distinction is not always entirely valid. The essential difference is rather that while the expounder of straight theories seeks to convince, the SF writer, by entertaining, hopes to persuade. The one relies on the evolution of an accepted process of logic, the other on challenging accepted logic.

I do not think, therefore, that insistence on the speculative nature of the scientific content of the story is really any more helpful in reaching a definition than the contrary insistence on the prophetic accuracy of that scientific content. However, it is certainly true that many science fiction stories have a useful role in reminding us that even the scientific community has its blind spots, and is unable to accept certain phenomena such as levitation, telepathy, clairvoyance, which it usually refuses to treat objectively and scientifically, as a proper study for scientists.[43]

It seems arguable that as far as the science constituent is concerned SF might equally be called knowledge fiction, for it is concerned with the impact of contemporary knowledge and its extension into the future on human behaviour. The science fiction writer is saying to his reader, 'If you take such and such a thing or things as known then might not the following consequences emerge?'

SF might, if you like, more properly be called datum fiction. This is not to concur with that school of thought which says that the science fiction writer is permitted only one supposition however outrageous; for 'datum' fiction requires the supposition or suppositions themselves to be perfectly acceptable to the reader. It derives its plausibility, in part, from the fact that the reader lives in a world undergoing a knowledge explosion, in which new theories and facts are constantly being propounded and discovered and almost as constantly being proved wrong or incomplete. All that the reader requires is that the suppositions he is asked to make shall fit reasonably into the current state of this general pattern of flux.[44]

A substantial part of SF is satirical in aim and, even if frequently *set* at some future date, is primarily concerned to make us examine the present. One of the characters in 'The Evitable Conflict' says, 'It is the obvious which is so difficult to see most of the time. People say "it's as plain as the nose on your face". But how much of the nose on your face can you see, unless someone holds a mirror up to you?'[45] The same point was made a little differently two centuries earlier by Swift when he described satire as a mirror in which the beholder sees every face but his own; Stapledon uses a similar approach in

Sirius: 'In making me you made something that sees man from clean outside man, and can tell him what he looks like.'[46] Clifford Simak quite overtly claims that one of the principal roles of SF is that it encourages us to re-examine our ideas, institutions and beliefs to see if they have outlived their usefulness, to see whether they are still relevant and valuable to us now. But to say that the intention of science fiction is frequently satirical is not to admit that all the satire which claims to be science fiction is such.

The same considerations hold good for many stories of a moral or philosophic nature. Again SF may have a valuable contribution to make in this field but the moral is not the essential SF ingredient. In an interesting essay in the *New Scientist*,[47] Paul Johnson seeks a new moral philosophy for a dynamic society, which is presumably to say a moral philosophy which takes account of the increasing rapidity of change. A number of good science fiction stories do this and it is interesting to look at those where the hero is subjected to an apparently incongruous succession of totally unrelated events, to each of which he has to adapt himself if he is to survive either physically or spiritually. The particular form of moral expediency which has come to be known as political pragmatism is not uncommon in science fiction and in so far as science fiction is largely dedicated to challenging the validity of all fixed standards it may be argued that it provides just the sort of moral philosophy which Johnson was apparently seeking. Is SF then a kind of fictional humanism, or fictional metaphysics or even, as one writer has suggested, 'eschatological romanticism'? A moral may be implicit in an SF story as in any other. In such a case as Lewis's trilogy the desire to make a moral or philosophic point is clearly the overriding motive for *writing* the story. But SF is not *read* for moral improvement, which is just as well since its different practitioners take many moral standpoints and in the majority of cases none at all.

We shall see in Chapter 2 that science fiction was probably not possible until a society which had whole-heartedly accepted the new religion of science was in being. Can we then find a satisfactory definition of science fiction at all? There certainly are one or two which do not appear to exclude any science fiction of however distant a relationship. For example, Asimov writes in the introduc-⇐ tion to his *Mysteries*: 'SF is a literary response to scientific change, and that response runs the entire gamut of the human experience. Science fiction, in other words, includes everything.'[48] Michael Moorcock in his edition of *SF Stories from New Worlds* says that it is 'a wish to say something about the human condition. This is what good science fiction concerns itself with. . . .'[49] But this is much too vague and indeed surely the objective of almost any work of fiction. Such definitions are scarcely helpful in that they include virtually all forms of fiction, as Asimov at least admits.

There are a number of definitions by SF writers which seem to come nearer to embracing all the types of story at which we have briefly looked, but they still tend to cast the net too widely. Theodore Sturgeon's – 'A science fiction story is built around human beings, with a human solution, which would not have happened at all without its scientific content' – seems to be in the right direction, apart from its undue insistence on the role of humanity within this context.[50] Or again, Amis, in, for him, a rather long-winded way, 'Science fiction is that class of prose narrative treating of a situation that could not arise in the world we know, but which is hypothesized on the basis of some innovation in science or technology, or pseudo-science or pseudo-technology whether human or extra-terrestrial in origin.'[51] Apart from his insistence that these situations could not arise in the world we know, this definition seems, as does Sturgeon's, to encompass the greater part of the genre with which we are dealing.

But of all the writers who have attempted to describe this particular field in which they were working, none I think has put it better than Olaf Stapledon as long ago as 1930 in the preface to *Last and First Men*:

> But if such imaginative construction of possible futures is to be at all potent, our imagination must be strictly disciplined. We must endeavour not to go beyond the bounds of possibility set by the particular state of culture within which we live. The merely fantastic has only minor power. Not that we should seek actually to prophesy what will as a matter of fact occur; for in our present state such prophecy is certainly futile, save in the simplest matters. We are not set up as historians attempting to look ahead instead of backwards. We can only select a certain thread out of the tangle of many equally valid possibilities. But we must select with a purpose. The activity that we are undertaking is not science, but art; and the effect that it should have on the reader is the effect that art should have.[52]

But while acknowledging that the criteria of art must certainly apply to SF we still have to ask what ingredients, if any, distinguish this particular corner of the story-teller's art from any other; to what particular discipline of selection should its writers submit? In SF it is not enough to ask how will people behave if they are frightened, excited, disgusted, and so on. In the SF story you must much more specifically ask how they will behave if these emotions are caused by some factor outside our current everyday experience. In nine cases out of ten, of course, the answer is exactly as if they were affected by some conventional contemporary stimulus. The test of SF, therefore, is not so much an emotional one as intellectual. SF is a measured study of hypothetical changes in environment and of Man's reaction to them. It is in a sense only fiction concerned with an environment which happens to be at the mercy of rapidly accelerating scientific and technological change.

So far we have only warily circled round the problem of making a definition of SF for this study, now we must make our own, doubtless arbitrary, definition: 'A science fiction story is one in which the suspension of disbelief depends on the plausible development of a central technical or scientific idea or ideas.' It is a story because, as Stapledon very properly reminds us, this is primarily art, fiction to entertain and enlighten and only secondarily fiction of a particular kind. We shall come later (chapter 8) to examine Amis's proposition of the idea as hero in SF. For the purpose of our present definition we accept it and insist only that the idea be of a technical and scientific nature. In defining scientific we will go along with Robert Hooke when (in 1663) he implored his fellow natural philosophers to 'improve knowledge of all natural things'.[53] In other words we will accept that the idea can be any part of 'a systematic body of verifiable knowledge' – not verifi*ed*, but verifi*able*. And finally we note that critical to the success of the whole venture is the plausible development of those ideas. I shall make no further attempt to justify this definition other than to point out its convenience for my purpose but I will however in the following chapter go on to examine the evolution of the genre which could bring it to a point where stories matching this definition have come to be written which are quite distinct from any other form of contemporary fiction.

Notes

1. If I may further illustrate my general thesis without at this stage having to justify my examples in detail, I would say that in the prophetic

category Heinlein's *Stranger in a Strange Land* is SF and that Wells's *The Shape of Things to Come* is not; the premise in Vonnegut's *Cat's Cradle*, that a single substance could have a chain reaction changing everything to ice, makes it science fiction, while that in *The Picture of Dorian Gray* does not; the exploits of *Dr. Who* are SF adventure, those of *Superman* are not; *Canticle for Leibowitz* or *Dune* is metaphiction, the *Scientologist's Book of Dianetics* is not; Bradbury's *The Day it Rained Forever* is SF fantasy, Mervyn's Peak's *Titus Groan* is just fantasy; Hoyle's *The Black Cloud*, or any one of a multitude of Russian science fiction stories, is instructional SF, *Robinson Crusoe* is not; Asimov's *Foundation* Trilogy is speculative SF and Plato's *Republic* is not; *1984* or *Player Piano* are SF satires and *The Battle of the Books* is not.

2. C. S. Lewis, *Experiment in Criticism* (Cambridge University Press, 1961).

> They talked as if it were a homogeneous genre. But it is not, in the literary sense, a genre at all. There is nothing common to all who write it except the use of a particular 'machine'. Some of the writers are of the family of Jules Verne and are primarily interested in technology. Some use the machine simply for literary fantasy and produce what is essentially *märchen* or myth. A great many use it for satire; nearly all the most pungent criticism of the American way of life takes this form and would at once be denounced as un-American if it ventured into any other. And finally there is a great mass of hacks who merely cashed in on the boom in science fiction. . . . You can if you wish, class all science fiction together; but it is about as perceptive as classing the works of Ballantyne, Conrad and W. W. Jacobs as 'the sea story' and then criticising that.

3. Leonard Lockhart in 'The Lagging Profession', *Analogue Science Fact and Fiction* (1960), has written a delightful story making fun both of this claim and of the intricacies of patent law. Arthur Clarke himself is cast in the role of principal character. The nub of the story is in Clarke's comment, 'As I understand it then, if a man is way ahead, he cannot obtain a patent because he cannot carry out the invention. Then, at the time he is able to carry out the invention, it is too late to obtain a patent.' Arthur Clarke, in his *Profiles of the Future*, gives many examples of 'chance discoveries' and the essential irrelevance of mere prophecy to SF.

4. Frank Quattrocchi, *He Had a Big Heart* (Fantasy House Inc., 1955). It is a bold man who will deny the possibility of any particular fiction story's prediction. Some of those who have done so have been made to look rather foolish. For example a Dr F. R. Molton in an astronomy textbook published in 1930 stated unequivocally that science fiction stories about inter-planetary travel were totally impossible and that anyone knowing the physical forces involved would know them to be so!

5. For example, J. W. Campbell, Introduction to *Prologue to Analog* (Panther, 1967).

6. Frederik Pohl, *Slave Ship* (first pub. 1957; Four Square, 1963); Fletcher Pratt in Hugo Gernsback, *Ralph 124C 41 Plus* (1950) – quoted in *Science Fiction Through the Ages 2* (Panther, 1966) – puts it thus:

> The very method employed in the book, that of supplying the people of the future with technical inventions which are the logical outcome of those currently in use or logically developed from currently accepted principles has become fundamental in science fiction. Indeed, it may be said to constitute the very art. . . .

7. I cannot agree with G. Harry Stine in *How to Think a Science Fiction Story* (New York: Street & Smith, 1961) when he says that extrapolating these curves 'is downright serious stuff, not fantasy, because the trend curve says that something is going to happen. Consideration of all the varied aspects of this is a proper, legitimate and professed job for science fiction.'

8. Nor is the argument much affected by the nature of the prophecies referred to, though Professor Hans Eysenck suggested that it was in a *New Scientist* article on 26 June 1969. One supposition, put forward by Asimov in a BBC television interview in 1970, is that the big changes are relatively easy to foresee but the unforeseen ones are much more important, influential and difficult to anticipate. Radio broadcasting was not difficult to predict, soap opera was. It is probably fair to say that given some indication of a social need and of the growth of the technology involved in meeting that need it is not too difficult to forecast major changes. Amis, on the other hand, has argued (*New Maps of Hell*) that it is *not* the *un*foreseen consequences of scientific development with which we should concern ourselves but precisely those trends which can be so easily extrapolated. Yet rather contradictorily Amis regards one of Wells's chief contributions to SF as being that he 'liberated the medium from dependence on extrapolation.'

9. J. W. Campbell, Introduction to *Analog 3* (Panther, 1968).

10. Some writers have suggested that SF is a valuable way of being able to prophesy doom and disaster, without irritating the reader. See *New Scientist* 26 Feb 1970, review of Desmond King-Hele, *The End of the Twentieth Century?* (London: Macmillan, 1970).

11. Isaac Asimov, 'The Dying Night' in *Mysteries* (Panther, 1969).

12. Ibid., Preface.

13. Damon Knight, Preface to *A Century of Science Fiction* (Pan, 1966). Cf. Christopher Anvill, 'Not in the Literature', in *Analog 3* (Panther, 1968), or Philip Dick, *The Man in the High Castle* (Penguin, 1965).

14. To pick two examples which are certainly no worse than many others; James Blish in *The Virgin Planet* (Mayflower, 1966) appends a long pseudo-scientific and unconvincing footnote to justify his taking his hero to a planet entirely peopled by women. Although the usual space-opera clichés of birds instead of horses and so on are liberally sprinkled about the

text it is just another adventure story. Avram Davidson's *Rork* (Penguin, 1969) might as well be set in Africa.

15. This type of story can be well done as in *Gunner Cade* (first pub. 1952; Four Square, 1966) or *Outpost Mars* (first pub. 1961; Four Square 1966), two novels by Cyril Judd, the pseudonym for Judith Merril and Cyril Kornbluth; or more recently as in Frederik Pohl's *Gateway* (Gollancz, 1977), and Bob Shaw's *Orbitsville* (Gollancz, 1976).

16. Robert Heinlein, *Glory Road* (Four Square, 1965). This is run a close second by Charles Harness's *The Paradox Men* published in various versions between 1949 and 1953 (New English Library, 1976). In this story he buckles his swash with some fine insights and a graphic analogy of the duality of a space /time continuum using the hoops of a gyroscope. In the Heinlein vein also are Jack Vance's stories such as *The Dragon Masters* (Panther, 1967) and *Star King* (Panther, 1968). A less favourable view of Heinlein is taken by Tom Shippey: '*Glory Road* is weak because of the absence of constraints on the hero, and the feebleness with which turns of the plot are rationalised.' For another critical approach to Heinlein see the article in *Foundation* 7 by Peter Nichols.

17. Quoted in Ivor Evans (ed.), *Science Fiction Through The Ages 2* (Panther, 1966).

18. C. S. Lewis, *Out of the Silent Planet* (first pub. 1938; Pan, 1952), *Voyage to Venus* (first pub. 1943; Pan, 1953), *That Hideous Strength* (first pub. 1945; Pan, 1955).

19. Prentis in Isaac Asimov, 'Kid's Stuff', in *Earth Is Room Enough* (Panther, 1960).

20. C. S. Lewis in his Introduction to the novels of George MacDonald (Bles, 1946).

21. Mervyn Peak, *Titus Groan* (first pub. 1946; Penguin, 1968).

22. Arthur Clarke, *The Nine Billion Names of God* (first pub. 1953; Corgi, 1966). In Clarke's story the two Western experts sent to Lhasa to computerise the prayer wheel are sceptical of the Tibetan belief that when the nine billion names of God have been 'said' the world will end. As they ride away they look back at the sky and see that 'overhead, without any fuss, the stars were going out'.

23. Avram Davidson's 'Or The Grasses Grow' in M. Kornbluth (ed.), *Science Fiction Showcase* (Mayflower, 1968), is another mystical ending of the world translated into Red Indian terms and Philip José Farmer *Night of Light* (Penguin, 1972) gives a skilful exposition of the road to Damascus, an interesting mixture of religious allegory and scientific explanation.

24. Ray Bradbury, *Fahrenheit 451* (first pub. 1954; Corgi, 1957). The title of the story indicates the temperature at which paper burns.

25. E.g. Ray Bradbury, *The Silver Locusts* (Corgi, 1956), a collection of short stories.

26. Kurt Vonnegut, *Cat's Cradle* (Penguin. 1965).

27. Theodore Sturgeon, 'Killdozer' in *Spectrum 3* (first pub. 1945; Pan, 1966).

28. In *Prologue to Analog* (Panther, 1967), Campbell's proposition is that 'Science fiction is, very strictly and literally, analogous to science facts. It is a convenient analog system for thinking about new scientific, social and economic ideas – and for re-examining old ideas.' This may be something that can be done in science fiction but it is not of itself a definition of science fiction.

29. Jules Verne, has been described by Ivor Evans in *Science Fiction Through The Ages 2* (Panther, 1966) as a mere geographer rather than a story-teller, using his fiction simply as a vehicle for conveying fascinating scientific information. Certainly H. G. Wells in *The Shape of Things to Come* (first pub. 1933; Corgi, 1967) uses what was subsequently to become a very popular Russian technique. The dream experienced by Dr Raven is a device to try to introduce, justify and make palatable what turns out to be a very dull political treatise. *The Shape of Things to Come* is today boring to read, precisely because it is so speculative without being fictional. When Wells is content to abandon both polemics and technical justification he writes what is still some of the most entertaining work in the genre.

Amongst modern British practitioners of the realist school Professor Hoyle distinguishes himself. In *The Black Cloud* (Penguin, 1960) an intelligent cloud of gas which is approaching our planet has to be persuaded not to do incalculable damage. The story is full of little formulae and equations on the lines of Russian SF. It contains a kind of scientific showing off which although it may have been thrown in to convince the reader of the authenticity of the story can have meant little to any but a few of Hoyle's astronomical and mathematical colleagues. Stories like *A for Andromeda* (Corgi, 1963) and *The Fifth Planet* read in parts more like tracts than novels, particularly where the thoughts and behaviour of the characters are concerned.

30. George Hay (ed.), *Disappearing Future* (Panther, 1970).

31. *New Scientist* (June 1969), 'Study of Unconscious Interpersonal Communication by exo-hormone'.

32. Dr Samuel Barondes, Albert Einstein College of Medicine Yeshiva University, *New Scientist* (6 Feb 1969).

33. Kosmolinsky and A. Dushkov, *Aerospace Medicine* (Priroda, 1969) no. 4, p. 124.

34. Carried out at Russian Academy of Sciences in the late 1960s.

35. Consider this passage from Charles L. Harness's *The Rose* (first pub. 1953; Panther, 1969):

The prism is rotated very slowly into a tiny beam of light. Part of the beam is reflected and part refracted. At exactly 45° it seems, by Jordan's law, that exactly half is reflected and half refracted. The two beams are picked up in a photo cell relay that stops the rotating mechanism as soon as the luminosities of the beams are exactly equal.

Compare this fictional experiment with just such an experiment designed as a test of quantum theory and reported in the *New Scientist* (10 Oct. 1969):

Imagine an ideally semi-transparent mirror that reflects exactly half of the light falling upon it and transmits the other half. If a single quantum of lights hits such a mirror then, as we know from experimental evidence, it can be either transmitted or reflected. In practice, however, we cannot predict which of these two possibilities will actually occur. The fact that we do not know any mechanism that causes the light quantum to 'choose' one way or the other may merely indicate that physicists still have much to learn. The other possibility, suggested by quantum theory, is that there is no causal mechanism, that randomness is a basic feature of nature, that laws of chance alone decide where the light quantum will go. Closely related to this statistical viewpoint is the axiom that quantum processes cannot be predicted exactly – or, applied to our example, that it is impossible to predict with more than 50 per cent accuracy whether the light quantum will be reflected or transmitted.

An unconventional test of this axiom is suggested by reports that certain people can guess future events, ranging from the outcome of a die throw to the death of a relative, with amazingly high accuracy. Suppose we arrange an experiment in which every second a light quantum reaches a semi-transparent mirror, and we ask a human subject each time to guess in advance whether the light quantum will be reflected or transmitted. If the axiom discussed above is correct then the subject, no matter how hard he tries, should obtain close to 50 per cent correct guesses. If, on the other hand, subjects could be found who scored consistently higher, in test runs sufficiently long to overcome chance fluctuations, this would indicate that the axiom is wrong. I believe that the experiments I shall report indicate that the axiom is indeed wrong. This implies that quantum theory does not give, at least for systems that include human subjects, a complete description of nature.

As it is somewhat difficult to observe single light quanta accurately and to prepare an accurately semi-transparent mirror, I used a different quantum process in my experiments – the spontaneous decay, under emission of an electron, of strontium-90 atoms. I placed a small sample of strontium-90 near an electron counter (a Geiger-Mueller tube) so that the counter registered the arrival of an average of 10 electrons per second. For this situation the axiom implies that it is impossible to predict when, for example, the next electron will be registered. To check the axiom, the human subjects were asked to guess the arrival time of the next electron, with respect to the momentary position of an electronic four-position switch rotating at the rate of one million steps per second.

But while the scientist was using the experiment quite properly to test a specific hypothesis, Harness was in fact using his fictional experiment to launch an elaborate and highly imaginative piece of cosmic fictional metaphysics.

36. William Golding, *Lord of the Flies* (Faber, 1968).

37. *Journal of Chemical Physics*, XLVIII, 2362.

38. Some speculations are very wild. Late in 1969 an amazing book by Eric von Daniken, *Chariots of the Gods* (Souvenir Press, 1969), quite seriously tried to set out to prove, through the most bizarre collection of supposed items of archaeological and religious evidence, that this planet was visited some 8000 years ago by beings from outer space who fertilised some of the inhabitants and then departed. One particularly hilarious example is the illustration from a Mayan temple which the author claims shows an astronaut in a rocket!

39. Ryabov, *Celestial Mechanics* (Moscow: Foreign Languages Publishing House, 1959); but see James Blish's 'Future Recall', an essay in George Hay (ed.), *The Disappearing Future* (Panther, 1970), for a warning of the dangers of inaccurate science in SF.

40. Z. A. Medvedev, *The Rise and Fall of T. D. Lysenko* (Columbia University Press, 1969).

41. A. Solzhenitsyn, *Candle in the Wind* (Bodley Head/OUP, 1973).

42. Ivor Evans (ed.), *Science Fiction Through The Ages 2* (Panther, 1966).

43. In Isaac Asimov's *Belief* (first pub. 1953; New English Library, 1967) such attitudes are not only satirised but a means of breaking them down is suggested. The hero finds that he has the power to levitate but no one in the scientific academic world in which he works will believe him and his insistence, backed by discreet demonstration, is only taken as charlatanry and costs him his job. As one of the characters says:

It was something you couldn't understand and therefore something horrible. You're a physical scientist. You *know* what makes the universe run. Or if you don't know, you know someone else knows. Even if no one understands a certain point, you know that someday someone will know. The key word is know.

(The hero in the end achieves his objective by so placing himself in the audience at a distinguished scientist's lecture that only the lecturer can see him. He then proceeds to levitate and pretend that he hasn't, that it is the lecturer's illusion.)

44. It is perfectly proper to regret, with Ballard – 'The Venus Hunters', in *The Overloaded Man* (Panther, 1967) – the necessity for this state of affairs.

It's unfortunate for the writers of science fiction that they have to perform their task of describing the symbols of transformation in a so-called rationalist society, where scientific, or at least pseudo-scientific explanation is required a priori. And because the true prophet never deals in what may be rationally deduced, people such as Charles [the chief character in the story] are ignored or derided today.

But then we are not dealing with prophecy but with science fiction.

45. Isaac Asimov, 'The Evitable Conflict,' in *I Robot* (Panther, 1968).

46. Olaf Stapledon, *Sirius* (first pub. 1944; Penguin, 1964).

47. *New Scientist* (4 Sept 1967).

48. Isaac Asimov, *Mysteries* (Panther, 1969).

49. Michael Moorcock (ed.), *SF Stories from New Worlds* (Panther, 1967), from *New Worlds* 1965 and 1966.

50. Quoted in Preface to Damon Knight (ed.), *A Century of Science Fiction* (Pan, 1966).

51. Kingsley Amis, *New Maps of Hell* (first pub. 1961; New English Library, 1969).

52. Olaf Stapledon, *Last and First Men* (first pub. 1930; Penguin, 1963).

53. But we shall not necessarily exclude his exceptions ('not meddling with divinity, metaphysics, morals, politics, grammar, rhetoric or logic'), and to his list we might perhaps add psychology and sociology.

2
The evolution of science fiction

As the 1969 moon landing marked a watershed in science fiction writing, so the origins of the genre can plausibly be traced to the spate of speculative writing which followed the dramatic discoveries of Galileo and Kepler by which Man first reached out to the moon in any practical way. Not that Cyrano de Bergerac's *Voyages to the Sun and Moon* (1650) or even earlier Bishop Godwin's *Man in the Moon* (1638) and Bishop Wilkins's *The Discovery of a World in the Moone* (1638) can claim to be anything but the most primeval ancestors of modern SF.[1] In a sense these writers are no more writing fiction, as we understand it, in the century before the creation of the novel than was Lucian a further fourteen hundred years earlier. Lucian's *True Histories* does not qualify as science fiction but rather deliberately sets out to be ridiculous and implausible in order to make its point.[2] If no limits are to be set to the absurdities which are acceptable then it is possible to argue, as does George Hay,[3] that the soothsayers of the Roman Empire were themselves SF writers.

Kepler himself turned his hand to fiction, and *Somnium* (1634) is also claimed by some as the earliest example of science fiction. But he makes no attempt to suspend the disbelief, and demons are the means of transportation to the moon. It is hard to say, of course, whether anyone in that earlier age ever believed that he had actually observed demons hauling a human being through space, whereas a present day scientist operating a high-energy particle accelerator might claim to have 'observed' time travel. Kepler does at least go on seriously to examine some of the problems of life in a vacuum, gravitation, and so on. The point about all these early attempts is that the science and the fiction are quite clearly divorced from each other. The narrative has a dual purpose, on the fictional side to make moral and philosophic points, and quite separately, and merely in passing, to make some scientific speculation within the rude mechanics of the story itself. By the time SF reaches full maturity in the 1940s and 1950s the reverse is true and it is the direct social 'comment' which is the passing aside.[4]

We should not put too narrow an interpretation on the element of science even in the earliest science fiction. A major science fiction category, that of the utopia – or dystopia – has a very respectable ancestry. If we are prepared to accept that social and political science may qualify as one of the ingredients in science fiction, then we have to go back at least to Plato's *Republic*. The word 'utopia', coined by Sir Thomas More for his own work, begins to put the stamp of a type on this category of story, though seventeenth-century utopias are frequently philosophic or political discourses rather than stories. The moral is overt and didactic, and does not spring naturally from the mechanics of the story. Francis Bacon's *The New Atlantis* (1626) marks the beginnings of modern utopian science fiction, but what Bacon considers important is that 'The end of our foundation is the knowledge of causes, and secret motions of things; and the enlarging of the bounds of human empire, to the effecting of all things possible'. The role within the story played by technology is a minor one. In *The New Atlantis* we certainly have fresh water distilled from salt, transplant surgery, television, radio and submarines, but all are brought forth as incidental wonders dependent on social and philosophic causes rather than as causal elements of behaviour in themselves.

Another important ingredient for the science fiction of the future had its beginnings in the fantastical travel tales, real and imaginary, unleashed by the great explorations of the sixteenth and seventeenth centuries. Such traveller's tales were little different from the space stories of today: venture into an unknown peopled with imaginary dangers and delights to which the writer's hero reacts.

At the end of the seventeenth century this reaction begins to be studied not merely in terms of character and situation but with a fascinated delight in the practicalities of the protagonists' solutions to the problems they encountered. The obsession with gadgetry to be found in so much SF of the 1930s had as its progenitor such tales as *Robinson Crusoe* (1719), whose interest for the modern reader lies more in the ingenuity of Crusoe's devices than in his moral reflections. Even earlier, in *The Consolidator* (1705), Defoe had shown remarkable prescience in his invented gadgetry. In this satire he talks of a machine with immense wings worked by wheels and springs and powered by 'an ambient flame, which fed on a certain spirit deposited in a proper quantity to last out the voyage'.

Despite, perhaps even because of, the tremendous stimulus and excitement of the new discoveries in astronomy, the amazing voyages of the sixteenth- and seventeenth-century explorers and the general ebullience of the Renaissance, no 'genuine' SF was written until long after the fervour had abated. There was sufficient novelty in the concrete discoveries of science and geography to satisfy the most voracious appetite and sufficient self-confidence to make speculation about the future by men happily absorbed in the present seem a somewhat idle pursuit. It was not until the age of reason that the first fiction of reason could be written.

Whether or not *Gulliver's Travels* is the nightmarish intellectual outpourings consequent upon Swift's devouring of Boyle's *Essay upon Eating Oysters*, it is, in *Part* III at least, science fiction within the definition we have made. [5] It is in style and content a story which would be quite at home in a modern SF anthology. I once used the following passage from the voyage to Laputa, suitably enhanced with electronic music, as the opening passage of a BBC radio programme on science fiction because I hoped to make my point by the listeners' inability immediately to date the piece:

> The sky was perfectly clear and the sun so hot that I was forced to turn my face from it: but all of a sudden it became obscured, as I thought, in a manner very different from what happens by the interposition of a cloud. I turned back, and perceived a vast opaque body between me and the sun, moving forwards towards the island; it seemed to be about two miles high, and hid the sun six or seven minutes. As it approached nearer over the place where I was, it appeared to be a firm substance, the bottom flat, smooth, and shining very bright from the reflection of the sea below. I stood upon a height about 200 yards from the shore, and saw this vast body descending almost to a parallel with me, less than an English mile distant.

Here we have a story using the accepted background of both contemporary fears and contemporary scientific research and discussion in order to put over a message. Moreover, the message is put over as an interesting story. Swift is primarily mocking the pedantic exactitude of some contemporary scientists and since his purpose is not so much to convince as to arouse contempt there is not always the necessary attempt at plausibility.

Nevertheless, anyone familiar with the preoccupations of the Royal Society at the time would have felt the scientific basis for the island's flight and for the bizarre researches of its inhabitants at least to have been a plausible extrapolation from current knowledge of magnetism and gravity. That Swift intended us to disapprove of the experimenters and their absurdities does not diminish the reality of the scene he paints; indeed his genius as a writer sometimes so catches up the reader as to diminish the impact of the satire. Generally speaking, however, with the exception of the un-categorisable genius of William Blake, it is this satirical dystopian trend of Swift's which dominates any writing which might loosely be classified as science fiction for the next 150 years.

The pure fantasists tended to be diverted into the Gothic novel (although Horace Walpole shows a touch of science-fiction thinking in a letter to the Reverend William Mason in May 1774), or into straightforward prophecies. Most of the prophecies, like those of the anonymous writer of *The Reign of George VI 1900–1925* (1763), or of Julius von Voss in *Ini, a forecast of 21st century life* (1810), have not only turned out to be wildly inaccurate, but are not themselves developed with the plausibility necessary to suspend our disbelief.

In America the satirical science fiction approach was put to good use by Washington Irving in *The Conquest by the Moon* (1809). While this is one of those 'just supposing' stories and is primarily satirical social criticism, it can lay claim to be one of the earliest 'alien invasion' stories. It employs what was to become the traditional SF technique of disguising a contemporary situation by setting it at a distance in time and place in order to make us think more objectively about something to which we generally react emotionally. *The Conquest by the Moon* is written as an argument rather than as a tale, but it contains within it a 'let us suppose' story whose purpose is to criticise American treatment of the Red Indians at a time when such self-searchings were rare.

'Neither would the prodigy sailing in the air and cruising among the stars be a wit more astonishing and incomprehensible to us, than was the European mystery of navigating floating castles through the world of waters, to the simple natives'. The BEM (Bug-Eyed Monster) technique, which was also to become an SF tradition, is used in this work to demonstrate how the first discoverers might have looked to the Indians. There follows a plea for tolerance and understanding which is naïve in terms of a Vonnegut or Sturgeon

satire of contemporary America but which is an honourable progenitor of this school of writing. Such satirical heirs to Swift were
exceptional and few works appear before the late nineteenth century which can even remotely be considered to meet the requirements of our mid-twentieth-century definition of SF.

Sir Peter Medawar has argued that there are a number of close
parallels between the contemporary world and the first half of the
seventeenth century; what he describes as a syndrome of dissatis-
faction and unbelief. Medawar suggests:

> Novels and philosophical belles-lettres now have an inward-
> looking character, a deep concern with matters of personal
> salvation and a struggle to establish the authenticity of personal
> existence; and we may point to the prevalence of satire and of the
> Jacobean style of 'realism', a desire variant of unreality, on the
> stage.[6]

It is difficult, however, to go with him all the way in his parallel of
the vigorous Elizabethan and Jacobean eras with our present
decade of doubt, brought about by the applications of science and
technical innovation in a way that was scarcely paralleled in the far
more hopeful seventeenth century. While modern Man's space
travels might lead us to share Bacon's view that 'the opening of the
world by navigation and commerce, and the further discovery of
knowledge [inspired] a total reconstruction of sciences, arts and all
human knowledge . . . to extend the power and dominion of the
human race . . . over the universe', we can no longer look on the
discovery of such 'new worlds' as 'a discovery of all operations and
possibilities of operations, from immortality, if it were possible, to
the meanest mechanical practice'.

Certainly, many of the basic ingredients for science fiction had
appeared in embryo by the early eighteenth century, but even if SF
is taken as no more than a kind of fictional humanism it was clearly
not sufficient for its growth merely to have a widespread inculcation
of scientific 'facts', acceptance of experimental method or the
stimulus of apocalyptic forebodings. These, however tenuously, in
the shape of biblical fundamentalist dogma, the beginning of experimental science in Roger Bacon and DaCusa, the experimental
laboratories of the Renaissance, and the conviction of an imminent
call to final judgement are all influences on medieval literature
which yet produced no science fiction. It was additionally necessary

for the belief to be established, amongst at least a substantial minority, that Man could, through the use of the scientific method and scientific methods, modify his environment and therefore, ultimately, his destiny.

Primitive, and to a lesser but appreciable extent medieval, Man was surrounded by forces he did not understand, and he lived in fear. He invented myths to limit and control these fears. They were a form of rationalisation. But as Medawar says, 'Science fiction is distinguished by its implicit assumption that man can change himself and his environment.'[7] Why then did science fiction not appear, other than occasionally and coincidentally in dystopian form, at least by the middle of the eighteenth century?

It is true that even in the eighteenth century Man's earthly future was seen by the great majority as a finite and relatively limited span of time to be concluded by Armageddon and the separation of the sheep from the goats. This may be one of the reasons why the early utopias were set contemporarily while ours are set in a distant future. The idea of the limit to Man's future began to disappear as there gradually developed a conviction that there was no limit to human inventiveness and ingenuity. This was heralded in the Baconian optimism that 'there is no difficulty that might not be overcome' provided Man will only concentrate his abilities, but it took more than two centuries for this idea to become a popular conviction. It has been argued with the benefit of hindsight by a number of writers, among them Paul Johnson, that, by the end of the eighteenth century, as a result of the industrial revolution this optimistic conviction was really no longer reasonable, and that while 'there could be no argument that the stock of human knowledge was daily increasing and that no imaginable natural catastrophe could halt, let alone reverse the process', the assumption of those who launched the industrial revolution that material and moral progress were in some way linked had come to be challenged.[8] Johnson goes on to put the common argument of the 1960s that 'all scientific advances must be placed, right from the start, in some form of social and moral context'.[9] He has little sympathy for those scientists who have begged us to subject science to some form of moral examination, because 'they have used the language of traditional morality, which is increasingly inadequate to tackle the new concepts of change'[10] – a stricture presumably applicable to the Russian Marxist also using the language of his traditional morality. Such pessimism would have been totally foreign to the eighteenth century, for example, and I suspect that in fact we have now come full cycle again to the more vigorous uncertainties of earlier times. Modern medicine has brought about a great increase not only in longevity but in the capacity physically to enjoy life, an increase which has affected our aspirations, while the prospect of a sudden cataclysmic end to all human life has destroyed the hope slowly engendered through the eighteenth and nineteenth centuries that science and reason would bring about an inevitable millennium.

Perhaps even until 1945 science could be seen as the friend of mankind,[11] but after the explosion of the first atomic bomb its evident capacity to destroy humanity turned it also into a potential enemy. Thus we resurrected the monster of Dr Frankenstein, the devil of Faust – forbidden, uncontrollable and therefore dangerous knowledge. Why then is science fiction, within our chosen definition, really only to be found flourishing in the middle decades of the twentieth century and only in scientifically and technologically advanced countries? If we say we cannot detect genuine science fiction in earlier times, equally we cannot detect it in the literatures of technically undeveloped countries, save occasionally in an imitative way. From the sixteenth century to quite late in the nineteenth, all those capable by virtue of intellect and education of taking an interest in and understanding new theories across the whole field of science were able, if they wished, to do so directly rather than at second hand. There were indeed popularisers like Fontenelle, and popularisation is certainly a necessary ingredient for science fiction,[12] but in a way the age of reason impeded the development of science fiction: explanation being the enemy of speculation.

Today the sheer mass of scientific knowledge is beyond individual comprehension, despite the far higher level of general education. This has created a speculative appetite which cannot be satisfied by active investigation or full-time hypothesising. We have to some extent returned to the situation of the primitive man who required his myths and mysteries as protection against forces which he could neither fully understand nor control. It is during the nineteenth century that we begin to see the development of this particular form of protective myth. As Medawar said in this context of Teilhard de Chardin, 'Intelligent and learned men may again seek comfort in an elevated kind of barminess.'[13]

Already, at the beginning of the nineteenth century, some doubts were beginning to appear. Faust is resurrected in Mary Shelley's *Frankenstein* (1818) and even earlier in 1806 the anonymous author of *Omegarus Syderieria* or *The Last Man,* a so-called romance of futurity, has begun that long chain of post-catastrophic stories leading up through Richard Jeffries' *After London* (1885) to the astonishing output of H. G. Wells in the last five years of the nineteenth century – the period in which he wrote almost all his science fiction as opposed to his later polemical quasi-science fiction.

It is in the concept of *The Future as Nightmare,*[14] of which the post-catastrophists had already given an inkling, that science fiction really begins to blossom. In anticipating Wells's recognition that science and technology were themselves the essential catalysts of social change, Samuel Butler can claim priority in *Erewhon* (1872) in creating the first modern dystopia. Until the nineteenth century every story written which might claim to be science fiction was written for some other purpose, satire, pastiche, comedy of the absurd, and never primarily for the sake of the story itself. You rarely have a sense of a writer saying, 'What would happen if . . .?' only of him saying, 'I don't like what is happening', or 'You should do it my way'.

Although Butler's story is primarily satirical it does use what has since become one of the classic techniques of science fiction. At the time of his writing the controversy arising from the propositions of Darwin and Lamarck had divided society into the scientifically conscious who accepted the theories of evolution then put forward and the fundamentalist who dogmatically rejected them. Butler in concluding his discussion about the impending superiority of machines over Man and indeed Man's replacement by them writes ironically, 'With those who can argue in this way I have nothing in common. I shrink with as much horror from believing that my race can ever be superseded or surpassed, as I should do from believing that even at the remotest period my ancestors were other than human beings.' The 'dragons' of industrial society had been identified but could they be slain? St George, even at the height of imperial assurance, was beginning to show signs of doubt.

Wells was not content to leave his futuristic strictures to ironic implication. In 1902 he gave a lecture to the Royal Institution entitled 'The Discovery of the Future' in which he saw 'the world as one great workshop and the present as no more than material for the future, for the thing that is yet destined to be'. Although there is an element of determinism, this is very different from Amis's later more typical twentieth-century view that the future is 'a sort of black non-existence upon which the advancing present will presently write events'.

Although Wells had not yet abandoned the possibility of science moulding that future for the better, the pessimism, which has run since his day like a black thread through almost all science fiction that is not totally naïve, is already discernible in his writing. Hillegas suggests that *The Time Machine* is the first imaginatively coherent picture of a future worse than the present. But is *The Time Machine* in fact science fiction? SF, we have said, tries to justify its assumptions where fantasy never bothers. When Damon Knight argues that Wells, although not inventing time travel, was the first one to translate it from the realm of fantasy into that of science fiction because the operation of the little white lever translated it from magic to mechanism, one cannot fully agree with him. The device is used no less arbitrarily than the magic of his predecessors, nor does Wells attempt to explain *how* the machine works. What has fundamentally changed is the general level of technical and scientific background knowledge against which the story takes place. To the ordinary intelligent reader of the day it had no longer become totally impossible that such a device as Wells employs could be constructed for time travel. It may be arguable that Kepler's readers, for example, were equally convinced that there was a possibility of their being hauled through space by demons. Perhaps our convictions today or in Wells's time are no more knowledge-based or rational than they were in Kepler's but are just as much a matter of faith – it is only the religion that has changed. But that change is significant, for the new religion postulates that miracles are made at the instance of Man, not by divine, or demonic, intervention. *The Time Machine* can, therefore, properly claim to be a science fiction story not because of any piece of Wellsian exposition but because Wells has recognised, however unconsciously, that the changing nature of his mass audience has enabled science fiction to be written at last.

In 1851 William Wilson in the first work actually to use the term science fiction rhapsodised, 'All known sciences contained within themselves worlds of exquisite poetry. And the more the general mind becomes familiarised with the ever varying interest and fascinations connected with their study the more rapid will become the diffusion and the rise of science.'[15] In fact the reverse was true. It was only with the rise of science and a general knowledge of it that writers were able to exploit for a mass audience the 'exquisite poetry' within it, which as science became increasingly complex was otherwise inaccessible to the lay reader in its mathematical and conceptual obscurity.

It is as an anticipator of science fiction themes that Wells is perhaps at his most remarkable. The super city, the huge advertisement dioramas, children packed off to crèches and child educational refineries all appear in *When the Sleeper Wakes*, *The War of the Worlds* is the alien invasion *par excellence*, and in *Men Like Gods*, when Catskill points out the necessity for pain, hardship and difficulty, we are seeing that nascent Fascism, that standard conservative theme to be repeated so often in subsequent science fiction.[16] Belief is expressed in the emergence of *homo superior*, however painful the circumstances in which he may have to be conceived. The theme is echoed by Forster in 'The Machine Stops'.[17] The evils Wells depicts are essentially the evils of contemporary society and therefore physical evils. Explanations are only given in terms of the physical sciences to the exclusion not only of the social sciences but almost of emotional and spiritual realisation alike. Yet surprisingly Wells openly says that the study of utopias is a proper subject for sociology.

While Britain became the centre for satirical and catastrophic SF, the more simple SF adventure writers were to be found in France, first with the voluminous and steady output of Jules Verne[18] and later with the brothers Rosny. While Wells tried 'to domesticate the impossible hypothesis', J. H. Rosny, Senior, in particular, let his hypothesis range wild and can justly claim to have been (in 1912) the first writer to describe a life form with other than an oxygen/carbon base. It is interesting that apart from a few pioneers like Verne and the Rosnys no real interest in science fiction was shown in France until the mid-1950s. Even now the work of their writers does not compare favourably with British or American science fiction, concentrating as they do on sexual fantasies rather than on true science fiction.[19]

An interesting, even significant, difference between the early science fiction writers and their post-Second-World-War counterparts is that for all the nineteenth-century giants' faith in science their stories usually entail some quasi-miraculous intervention – from comets to the common cold – to solve their dilemma, whereas many modern science fiction writers are content to rely on scientific solutions, or to accept disaster.

Wells's approach, of course, endorses his belief in the supremacy of science over art: the very fallacy against which Stapledon was later to warn the science fiction writer. There was perhaps some justification in M. Roberts's criticism of Wells when he wrote, 'A journey to the moon, and not something like the composition of Beethoven's *A Minor Quartet*, is treated as the greatest achievement possible to man.'[20] Decadence and aesthetic as opposed to rationalist values were seen as inseparable, and it is perhaps not surprising that Wells should have written in the *War of the Worlds* that the Martian invasion 'has robbed us of that serene self-confidence in the future which is the most fruitful source of decadence'. This is a problem which we shall see emerging again in the work of Soviet science fiction writers in the early 1960s. In many ways Wells is more a forerunner of Soviet than of Western science fiction. Certainly Zamyatin, one of the earliest Russian science fiction writers, pays extensive tribute to Wells, and his best known work, *We*, markedly shows his influence. (It in turn was to influence Orwell's *1984*.) Zamyatin admired Wells's development of 'social scientific fantasy' (that is, science fiction) which he considered Wells's great and original contribution. 'As urban fairytales, the scientific romances of Wells were quite naturally based on the iron laws of science. Thus there is no magic in these fairytales but only logic.'[21]

Zamyatin's thesis then goes on to discuss whether the combination of exact science and fairytale and fantasy, as in SF, is not paradoxical. But he decides that it is not, if it is seen as myth, which has always been bound up with religion. The religion of today, Zamyatin says, 'is exact science'. Zamyatin's view of the scientific element, and indeed the view of subsequent Russian science fiction writers, is Cartesian where the Western writer is perhaps more Baconian in outlook.[22] But even Zamyatin is bound by the necessity to have what is in effect a communist world as the only possible future, a restriction which was already beginning to make Wells's twentieth-century pseudo science fiction writing, with its large doses of 'neat' socialism, boring in contrast to his earlier works.

Lenin, writing in 1908, three years after the publication of Einstein's Relativity Theory, made the kind of distinction which ought to have guided (but failed to do so) subsequent Russian science fiction writers.

The 'essence' of things or their 'substance' is also relative, it expresses only the degree of man's power of penetrating into and knowing objects; and even if yesterday this penetration did not go any further than the atom, and today, no further than the electron and ether, then dialectical materialism insists on the temporary, relative, approximate character of all these milestones on the road of knowledge of nature, through the progressive science of man. The electron is as inexhaustible as the atom, nature is infinite but it exists; and only this categorical, unconditional recognition of its existence beyond the consciousness and sensation of man, distinguishes dialectical materialism from relativist agnosticism and idealism. [23]

It would be wrong to attribute the pedantry and educational worthiness of much of latter-day Russian science fiction to an inability to see their subject with as much imagination as Lenin himself. In a story called *Plutonia*, begun in 1913 but not finished until well after the Revolution, Obruschev, while laying down the dictum that a good science fiction novel must be plausible, also insists, both in the foreword and the book itself, that it should be educative. This handicap the majority of his national successors willingly accepted. He derides the work of Verne and Conan Doyle but his own story shows marked similarities to the latter's *Lost World* without being nearly so exciting. It is as much a fictionalised lesson in paleontology as Verne's were in geology and while it can be said to be mercifully free of the propagandising of much later Russian science fiction it frequently falls into that fiction's typical trap of lecturing to the reader.

After the Revolution, SF in the Soviet Union tended to hark back to the Russian utopian writers of the nineteenth century – Prince Mikhail Shcherbatov's *Land of Ophir* (1783), Prince Vladimir Odoyevsky's *Year 4338* (1840) and Nikolai Chernishevsky's *What is to be done?* (1863), are all social blueprints sprinkled with references to technical marvels. The latter was described by Lenin as 'a wonderfully deep critic of capitalism'. [24]

The Russian writer shares, and even exceeds, the Western fascination with gadgetry and technical marvels. Odoyevsky, for example, has airships, synthetic foods and a trans-Himalayan tunnel. Chikolev's *Neither Fact Nor Fantasy* (1895) is an electrical utopia and Rodnik's fragment *The Self Propelled Petersburg–Moscow Underground Railway* (1902) reads more like an engineering proposal than a story. Maxim Gorki (who subsequently became Stalin's literary yes-man) had written, 'science and technology should not be depicted as a storehouse of ready made conventions but as an arena for battle where an actual living man overcomes the resistance of matter and of traditions'. His advice was steadfastly ignored by most subsequent Russian SF writers. The arch-technologist of early Russian SF was K. Tsiolkovsky, whose detailed calculations were almost unreadable, but his big-thinking optimism infected later writers who also took up the utopian themes of the nineteenth century. Alexei Tolstoy in the 1920s (*The Garin Death Ray*), and the superficially orthodox Alexander Belayev until his death in 1941, enlarged upon the theme of Soviet Man as the hero of a scientifically engendered future, albeit in Belayev's stories the settings are not in the Soviet Union and the characters are only derivatively Russian.

Until 1928 the Communist Party did not much interfere in the field of literature. Independent cultural organisations and publishing houses flourished and there was an extensive magazine output of science fiction. Of these Alan Myers says,

> Most were plagiarisms of western products or direct translations, featuring plenty of mad scientists; after the suppression of the magazines in 1930 people looked back on these stories with affection even in the 50s, and contrasted their action-filled pages with the dull contemporary product. There were space operas as well as utopias in a varied SF scene, and most of Belayev's best work appeared between 1925–29. [25]

In 1925 the first Communist Party declaration on literature was a fairly modest bid for overall but non-specific control. But this changed as first the general proletkult movement gave way in 1928 to RAPP (association of Russian proletarian writers) and then to the still more censorious Soviet Writers' Union in 1932 whose increasingly restrictive decrees were enforced by Zhdanov, nicely described by Eagleton as 'Stalin's cultural thug'.

Peter Yershov suggests that it was to escape the horrors and stupidities of the New Economic Policy in the 1920s that Russian writers in this genre retreated to the world of fantasy. Although he does tend to interpret everything he reads in anti-communist terms his explanation is, I believe, partly valid. I shall come to explore its relevance to the reversal of roles in Western and Russian SF in the 1970s in chapter 9. Myers, however, believes that Yershov's interpretation should be qualified.

A few writers like Grin or Kaverin might be said to have withdrawn into fantasy to escape intolerable reality, but the sturdy lower echelons beavered away with their stories of international intrigue and the struggles between capitalist and Bolshevik over scientific discoveries. Even the famous names like Zamyatin, A. Tolstoy or Bulgakov were anything but uncommitted or escapist. There was of course, plenty of low-grade playful SF in the magazines, but this was written with an eye to profit and went under in 1930 when the large circulation magazines were suppressed.[26]

Whatever the reasons, Mayakovsky's play *The Bed Bug*, Bulgakov's satire of the New Economic Policy, *The Fatal Egg*[27] Boris Pilnyak's sour crack that 'the talent of a writer is inversely proportional to his political awareness and activity' were the last signs of a stream which was to be ruthlessly driven underground. In January 1953 a survey of books in *Literaturnaya Gazeta* could safely say, 'capitalism does not and cannot demand of science fiction the aims that we demand of it. The main function of science fiction is to develop and stimulate scientific creativity in the people through artistic literature.' Between 1930 and 1959 no fictional utopias were written in the land which claimed to be making a reality of utopia. The cold war, and rather more particularly the competitive use of scientific accomplishment which grew out of it, prompted some post-war science fiction writing in the Soviet Union, though for a writer such as Yefremov, whose first stories appeared in 1946, it meant a quick retreat to the safety of palaeontology textbooks until the climate thawed again in the late 1950s. Once the momentum of the post-revolutionary writers had run its initial course, science fiction writing, along with virtually all other creative activities, in effect disappeared until the thaw.

It is perhaps indicative of the Soviet attitude towards science fiction as a means of popularising actual scientific accomplishment that nearly all the leading post-war Russian science fiction writers are primarily practising scientists, or science journalists. It is true that in the West a number of science fiction writers fall into the same category but they by no means comprise even a large minority of those working in this field. The better science-orientated Western science fiction writers tend to be ex-scientists rather than practising scientists. In any anthology of Russian writers at least half will be practising scientists and even if the overall standard is not high the stories of the scientists will not much differ in literary quality from

those of the purely professional writers. Illustrative of the difference from Western SF is a comparison of a collection of stories
edited by Frederik Pohl, *The Expert Dreamers*,[28] with any typical
Russian anthology. In the Western collection, with the exception of
a tale by professional science fiction writer, Asimov, the stories are
all by full-time scientists. They are all almost without exception
poor fiction and surprisingly unimaginative science.

Asimov, himself Russian by birth, is an interesting example of a
Western scientist turned science fiction writer who has continued to
work in both fields. He has over a hundred books to his credit
ranging from the high-level scientific textbooks one would expect
from a successful professor of biochemistry to two-and-a-half-page
science fiction stories of polished brilliance, but he was until recently predominantly a professional science fiction writer. He describes
how he became one in an introduction to *The Rest of the Robots.* 'In
the 1930s I became a science fiction reader, and I quickly grew tired
with this dull, hundred times old tale. As a person interested in
science, I resented the purely Faustian interpretation of science.'[29]

Robert Heinlein is a similar figure. One of the longest surviving
SF writers, he is remarkable in that he can write both a story of
originality and some philosophic and metaphysical interest (such as
Stranger in a Strange Land[30]) and a straightforward, conventional
space-opera (as in *Glory Road*[31]). By training both scientist and
engineer, Heinlein has also made a speciality of writing a great deal
of good science fiction specially for children.[32] It is unusual to make
this distinction in SF between the adult and the child reader and
indeed it is doubtful whether it is particularly valid – some would say
because most science fiction is essentially juvenile in its outlook and
approach, others because it is precisely the demands to be made of
an unfettered imagination which make the adult who has not lost
the childhood capacity for wonder the ideal reader of science
fiction.

Rather less surprising than the conversion of the practising
scientist to the art of science fiction writing is the absence of
romantics – though Robert F. Young, Philip José Farmer and
Theodore Sturgeon are among the few exceptions.[33] Moreover,
until the late 1960s there were very few women writers. Katherine
MacLean, Judith Merril, Zenna Henderson, Marion Zimmer Brad-
ley and, in a more robust vein, Leigh Bracket were rarities in a
man's world. It is almost as if there were no room for emotional
sensitivity in this tough world of primarily intellectual satisfaction.
Until the Second World War the prominent figures in SF were those

who had already established literary reputations elsewhere. Wells, Huxley and Orwell were initially famous for their other work. Those who restricted their writing to SF were deliberately cutting themselves off from the mainstream in which respectability and critical acclaim were to be found. After the war we see the emergence of figures with international reputations, both among the general public and in literary circles, which are solely based on their performance as science fiction writers. Vonnegut and Sturgeon, Pohl and Kornbluth, Asimov and Bradbury in the United States, Arthur Clarke, John Wyndham, John Christopher and J. G. Ballard in Britain.

The audience for the pure science fiction writer prior to the 1950s had been confined to the specialist devotees of the science fiction magazines, a particularly American phenomenon. This had the result of turning such British practitioners as Eric Frank Russell into American style writers by virtue of the fact that ninety five per cent of their output had to be written for the American market. Father of this particular outlet of SF was Hugo Gernsback, who, having started writing science fiction in the guise of items of technological forecasting in electronics journals, was instrumental in founding the early American SF magazines, *Amazing Stories* (1926) and *Science Wonder Stories* (1929). The growth of SF magazines in America was phenomenal. There were five in 1938, thirteen in 1939 and twenty two by 1941. But they were still publications for a specialised 'in' group in America and for the much smaller science fiction audience in Great Britain. In reading these old magazines one notices the chattiness of the editors on the one hand and their solemn self-importance on the other, a characteristic carried forward, it must be admitted, into some contemporary anthologies of science fiction. They were the members of a coterie – a cult even – revelling in an exclusivity which kept out the common herd that did not appreciate science fiction. It was precisely this attitude that was one of the stumbling blocks to the general acceptance of science fiction as an integral and equal part of fictional literature. In America, too, there grew up that most peculiar of institutions, the science fiction fan club, with its solemn meetings and reverential discussions of members' own work or the latest magazine issue. For all that they may sometimes be justly mocked, these dedicated enthusiasts can properly claim a greater share of the credit for the development of science fiction as an independent and self-sustaining genre than can any single creative author.

This sense of fellowship between science fiction writers and readers has never been dissipated and it is a branch of literature which is, I think, uniquely remarkable for the extent of the open references by one author to stories, characters and even the names of others. The song 'The Green Hills of Earth' and the space poet 'The Blind Singer of the Spaceways' are referred to by other writers; Michael Moorcock's hero, Jerry Cornelius, is the hero of stories by at least six other authors, and in *A Saucer of Loneliness* Sturgeon refers directly to *The Quest for Saint Aquin* by Anthony Boucher.[34] Asimov's 'Three Laws of Robotics' have been taken over by virtually every Western writer on the subject, and Robert Conquest, in his poem 'Far Out (Exoskeltonics)' uses a whole list of references to other characters and places from science fiction stories.[35] Again and again authors pay each other compliments by listing fellow writers' names among the 'greats'. In a story called *Flatlander*, Larry Niven, giving a list of the 'greats', writes: 'Dante, Aristotle, Shakespeare, Heinlein, Carter. . . .'[36] But few authors perhaps would go quite as far as Colin Wilson who, in his unfortunate venture into science fiction, looking back over the great philosophers classifies himself as one of them.[37]

After the Second World War, while this attitude of clubbable exclusivity persisted, it became much less significant in the overall picture of science fiction writing. The war had brought many people sharply up against the implications of modern science and they were willing to explore these in a way which had not perhaps occurred to them before. This change in attitude is marked in a number of ways. Before the war little had been written about science fiction in serious vein, except in the prefatory remarks of SF magazine editors. After the war one of the earliest to give it serious treatment was Marjorie Nicolson, *Voyages to the Moon* (USA 1948), followed again in America by Willy Ley's *Lands Beyond* (1952) with Lyon Sprague de Camp and de Camp's own *Science Fiction Handbook* (1952), written with his wife Catherine. In Britain such critical works began to appear at the end of the 1950s and in the early 1960s – Patrick Moore, *Science and Fiction* (1957); Roger Lancelyn Green, *Into Other Worlds* (1957) and Kingsley Amis, *New Maps of Hell* (1961).[38] Writing about SF, like SF itself, had consisted until the 1950s of brief ideas rather than lengthy expositions, introductions to anthologies and essays in magazines, rather than larger works of criticism.

The accolade of critical respectability had been completely

bestowed by 1970. For example, the general fiction review in the *Daily Telegraph* on 25 September 1969 actually led with a review of Michael Crichton's *The Andromeda Strain* without thinking it necessary to apologise or explain. Professor William Thorpe, reviewing Koestler's symposium *Beyond Reductionism*, quoted as his favourite aphorism a sentence from a science fiction magazine (admittedly he got the name of the author wrong).[39] 'The scientific community had come to appreciate its wider literary role and the interaction of science and art.'[40]

In the *New Scientist* of 11 June 1970, there was a review of a broadcast on Radio 3 by Jonathan Miller talking about Dickens which praised Miller as 'a rare bird indeed' because he was 'a critic who appreciates the broadening of literary imagination by scientific ideas and who finds something optimistic in science-shaped fiction'. The article went on to say, 'one wonders if the literary science bashers are perhaps the more virulent because of a sneaking disappointment that science is unable to bespell the world'. In its issue of 23 April 1970, the same journal devoted a full review to a number of science fiction works, including *Slaughterhouse Five* by Kurt Vonnegut,[41] saying in its review, 'science can be a stylistic influence in literature as well as in the visual arts'. It is now clearly no longer considered peculiar that anyone should wish to write or read this particular type of fiction.

Perhaps not surprisingly with the enlarging of the boundaries of the science fiction empire, its original source of strength, the SF magazines, occasionally took something of a knock. There was a noticeable drop in their circulation after the first sputnik was launched, although perhaps Judith Merril was being a little cruel in 1963 when she wrote, 'The special kind of thinking that lies between outright fantasy and scientific hypothesis was focused for a while largely in the SF magazines. Now, some of the best story plots are going into reports by research and development men for the Government, the armed services, etc.'[42] It is reasonable to infer that now that this type of plot motivation is no longer the exclusive preserve of the science fiction magazines these have lost some of their peculiar appeal. That is not to say that a number of them do not still flourish (their are six major ones in the United States and a new launch by Asimov is doing well, but there are none in the United Kingdom), but the glamour of the pioneering days is over and the onward march of the paperback has provided a more usual and lucrative outlet for the SF writer.

One of the consequences of the growing appetite for science fiction after the war was the resurrection of many of the lesser stories of the established science fiction writers – frequently, I imagine, to their considerable embarrassment. Another means of meeting the demand was to stretch out short stories to novel length. Such expedients are partly responsible for the contempt in which the genre has often been held by the more conventional general reader as well as by literary intellectuals. It is strange that people who will pay as much for a transistor as for a valve, for a piece of intricate miniaturisation as for a grandiose object, nevertheless feel themselves thwarted if they are offered between the covers of their book but a single, short perfectly polished story or even a collection of such stories instead of a novel, and if provided with the quantity they complain about the quality. The consequences of this attitude were perfectly exemplified in the attenuation of a nugget of perfection that started out as a short story, 'Flowers for Algernon' by Daniel Keyes.[43] This was turned first into a novel and then into a film in both of which a great deal of superfluous, and rather pompous, romance, sex (presumably for box-office appeal) and philosophy were introduced. In 1979 the story was briefly staged as a musical, so now only pantomime and ice-revue remain. In the short story we experience the remarkable drug-induced emergence of a retarded child into a genius through the eyes of his – quite incidentally female – teacher reading what he writes. Before the boy is treated a trial is run on a mouse which thus heralds each stage of the boy's development. When the mouse ceases to be a supermouse, regresses and perishes, no more needs to be said. In both 'novel' and film a mawkish sexual relationship between pupil and teacher ousts the genuinely moving theme of the short story and the dénouement is ponderously spelt out in full.

Even a writer as deft as Bradbury can succumb to the temptation to make a story too explicit. When he first wrote *Fever Dream*, published in 1948, the boy whose body had been taken over by a fatal disease which lets *him* live is clearly carrying the seeds of destruction of his parents, playmates and the community at large. In the early edition the reader infers this. In a version of this story reproduced in a 1970 collection entitled *Fever Dream* the contagious destructive power is spelt out by the death of ants and other creatures.[44]

James Blish wrote a story called 'Beep' in the collection *Galactic Cluster*.[45] The quality of the tale was lost in superfluous verbiage with no compensating gain when it appeared at double the length as the *Quicunx of Time.*[46] Even his famous *A Case of Conscience* started out as a short story. Changes in Russian stories tend to be for more political reasons. For example, Belaev's pre-conformity story of 1929, *The Man Who Lost His Face*, reappears in 1940 as *The Man Who Found His Face*.

However, deterioration does not always follow expansion. J. G. Ballard wrote a story, 'The Illuminated Man' which was the germ of the later novel *The Crystal World.*[47] Only in this case, instead of losing by the attenuation, Ballard is able in the longer form to go further in his psychological exploration of the characters to let us become involved almost organically in the crystalline petrification of the forest instead of plunging us straight into it. Shock effect is sacrificed for conviction with advantage. There is plenty of scope for academic nicety in examining in detail the changes made by authors between the different publication dates of their stories. On the whole the later versions tend to take subtle implications to which the conditioned science fiction magazine reader was finely attuned and render them clumsily explicit for the benefit of the wider audience.

The very sciences which provided the central germ of the stories tended to change in popularity, if not in importance, and a shift in the fictional preoccupations usually preceded a shift in the amount of public attention, honours and funds devoted to a particular scientific discipline.

Early twentieth-century science fiction was inspired largely by astronomy and to a lesser extent by physics and mathematics. These sciences, together with the preoccupation with gadgets and with a little chemistry thrown in, dominated the scene until about 1948. After the Second World War the biological sciences emerge as major elements in the genre. Having escaped at last from the unpromising side track into which this fiction had long been diverted by the man-made bug-eyed monsters sired, or rather dammed, by Mary Shelley, biology begins to emerge as an SF inspiration with early-twentieth-century writers such as Olaf Stapledon, but it was slow to gain prominence until the Second World War, when plastic surgery in particular made a considerable impact. Two major science fiction stories of the 1950s, Bernard Wolfe's *Limbo 90* and Algis Budrys *Who?* are both entirely based on the science of prosthetics (in Wolfe's case with some cybernetics thrown in).[48] They examine the question 'What is humanity?' and ask how far one can go in physically altering a human being before he ceases to be a human being. By the early 1960s psychology and sociology had become a major source of science fiction stimulus and the mathematical sciences, including economics and cybernetics, were also in greater evidence. The 1970s saw an even greater change, the almost total rejection of scientific reason, which we shall consider in chapter 9. A look at the timetable of science fiction development shows that it has in general terms anticipated by a few years the wider public concern and debate with the matters of which it treats.

The shifts and changes described above are but the side-effects of an otherwise welcome change in status and audience for science fiction. By the 1950s SF had become a firmly established genre which despite being written with certain specialised characteristics had a wide non-specialist following. By virtue both of the size of its audience and of the skill of its practitioners it was firmly established as a particularly sensitive form of literature for reflecting the moods and psychoses of its host society.

Notes

1. But Wilkins at least eschewed magic when he wrote:

> Yet I do seriously, and upon good grounds, affirm it possible to make a flying chariot, in which a man may sit, and give such a motion unto it, as shall convey him through the air . . . . so that notwithstanding all these seeming impossibilities, 'tis likely enough, that there may be means invented of journeying to the moone. And how happy shall they be that are first successful in this attempt!

2. *The True Histories of Lucian, c.* 125 to *c.* 180 AD.

3. In the preface to G. Hay (ed.) *The Disappearing Future* (Panther, 1970).

4. For example in Eric Frank Russell, *A Little Oil From Deep Space* (Panther, 1966), Coco the clown is sent into space as the psychological oil for the abrasive stresses among the crew of a spaceship; it is the social comment which is the item in passing. The story and its scientific theme – the study of behaviour in confined conditions under stress and isolation – are what dominate. We get a passing paragraph referring to penal reform which would in the seventeenth and eighteenth centuries have occupied a tub-thumping three or four pages.

5. Jonathan Swift, *Gulliver's Travels* (1726). Cf. article by Marjorie H. Nicolson and N. B. Mohler 'The scientific background of Swift's Voyage to Laputa and Swift's Flying Island in the Voyage to Laputa' – *Annals of Science,* II, nos 3 and 4 (1957).

6. *New Scientist* (4 Sept 1969).

7. Ibid.

8. Ibid. (4 Sept 1967).

9. Ibid. For more detailed factual discussion of this problem see J. D. Bernal, *The Social Function of Science* (Routledge, 1939); Hilary and Stephen Rose, *Science and Society* (Penguin, 1969); Nigel Calder, *The Great Technopolis* (MacGibbon, 1969).

10. *New Scientist* (4 Sept 1967).

11. But as far back as 1936 this passage could be found in the preface to Karl Mannheim's *Ideology and Utopia* (Kegan Paul, 1936):

If we feel more thoroughly appalled at the threatening loss of our intellectual heritage than was the case in previous cultural crises it is because we have become the victims of more grandiose expectations. For at no time prior to our own were so many men led to indulge in such sublime dreams about the benefits which science could confer upon the human race. This dissolution of the supposedly firm foundations of knowledge and the disillusionment that has followed it have driven some of the 'tender minded' to romantic yearning for the return of an age that is past and for a certainty that is irretrievably lost. Faced by perplexity and bewilderment others have sought to ignore or circumvent the ambiguities, conflicts, and uncertainties of the intellectual world by humour, cynicism, or sheer denial of the facts of life.

12. H. Butterfield *The Origins of Modern Science* (Bell, 1949), pp. 144 *et seq.*

13. *New Scientist* (4 Sept 1969).

14. In the ensuing discussion of Wells and his contemporaries I am greatly indebted to the work of Dr Mark R. Hillegas, *The Future as Nightmare* – H. G. Wells and the Anti-Utopians (New York: Oxford University Press, 1967). Cf. Philmus and Hughes (eds) *H. G. Wells Early Writings in Science and Science Fiction* (University of Calif., 1975).

15. William Wilson, *A Little Earnest Book upon a Great Old Subject* (1851), quoted by Stableford in *Foundation* 10.

16. H. G. Wells, *When the Sleeper Wakes* (1899), *The War of the Worlds* (1898) and *Men Like Gods* (1923).

17. E. M. Forster, 'The Machine Stops' in *The Collected Stories* (first pub. 1928; Penguin 1954).

18. *Journey to the Centre of the Earth* (1864); *From the Earth to the Moon* (1865), *Around the Moon* (1870) and *20,000 Leagues Under the Sea* (1870) are probably the best known, but he wrote literally dozens of others.

19. For example Damon Knight (ed.), *Thirteen French Science Fiction Stories* (Corgi, 1965).

20. *The Spectator* (17 Dec 1936). Quoted in Dr Mark R. Hillegas, *The Future as Nightmare* – H. G. Wells and the Anti-Utopians (New York: Oxford University Press, 1967).

21. E. Zamyatin, *Herbert Wells* (Petrograd: 1922).

22. H. Butterfield, *The Origins of Modern Science* (Bell, 1949) p. 101.

23. Quoted by J. G. Crowther, *New Scientist* (23 April 1970).

24. Lenin, *Works* vol. XVII (1929). Cf. Peter Yershov, *SF and Utopian*

Fantasy in Soviet Literature (New York: 1954). As a general background to political changes in Russia during the period Leonard Schapiro's *The Communist Party of the Soviet Union* (Eyre, 1960) will be found invaluable.

25. In a letter to the author, A. Myers, Aug 1979.

26. Ibid.

27. This work was first published in 1925, so perhaps rather a harbinger, Btk 61.

28. Frederik Pohl, *The Expert Dreamers* (Pan, 1966).

29. Asimov, *The Rest of the Robots* (first pub. 1964; Panther, 1968).

30. Robert Heinlein, *Stranger in a Strange Land* (New English Library, 1970).

31. Robert Heinlein, *Glory Road* (Four Square, 1965).

32. For example, *Time for the Stars* (first pub. 1956; Pan, 1968) and *Red Planet* (first pub. 1949; Pan, 1967).

33. See *The Worlds of Robert F. Young* (Panther, 1968). Short stories by Farmer and Sturgeon in various anthologies. Or Colin Kapp, 'Hunger Over Sweet Waters' in *New Writings in Science Fiction 4* (Corgi, 1965) John Rankine, *Six Cubed Plus One* in *New Writings in Science Fiction 7* (Corgi, 1966).

34. Theodore Sturgeon, *A Saucer of Loneliness* (Galaxy, 1953); Brian Aldiss in 'Man on Bridge' *New Writings in SF*[1] (Corgi, 1964) refers to the Church of St Praz and the Romantic Agony.

35. Robert Conquest 'Far Out (Exoskeltonics)' in *Frontier of Going*, (Panther, 1969).

36. Larry Niven, *Flatlander* in Groff Corklin (ed.), *Seven Trips through Time and Space* (Coronet, 1969).

37. Colin Wilson, *The Mind Parasites* (Science Fiction Book Club, 1968).

38. Willy Ley and Lyon Sprague de Camp, *Lands Beyond* (New York: Rinehart, 1952); Lyon Sprague de Camp and Catherine C. de Camp, *Science Fiction Handbook* (New York: Hermitage, 1953). See Introduction, notes 1–5.

39. 'I have yet to see any problem however complicated, which, when you looked at it the right way, did not become still more complicated.'

40. Professor C. H. Waddington, *Behind Appearance* (Edinburgh: University Press 1969), for a study of the interaction of art and science.

41. Kurt Vonnegut, *Slaughterhouse Five* (Jonathan Cape, 1970).

42. Judith Merril, 'Summation' from *Best of Sci Fi* (Mayflower, 1963).

43. Daniel Keyes 'Flowers for Algernon' in *The Hugo Winners* (Penguin, 1964).

44. Ray Bradbury and Robert Block, *Fever Dream* (Sphere, 1970).

45. James Blish, *Galactic Cluster* (Faber, 1970).

46. James Blish, *The Quicunx of Time* (Faber, 1975).

47. J. G. Ballard 'The Illuminated Man' in *The Venus Hunters* (Panther, 1967); J. G. Ballard, *The Crystal World* (first pub. 1966; Panther 1968).

48. Bernard Wolfe, *Limbo 90* (first pub. 1952; Penguin, 1961: abridged); Algis Budrys, *Who?* (first pub. 1958; Penguin 1964).

3
Literary litmus test

It is nothing new for literature to reflect scientific and social change. The enjoyable bawdiness of Chaucer or Rabelais, the brimstone and hellfire condemnations of sex in much seventeenth- and early-eighteenth-century literature, the total freedom of sexual expression in the mid-twentieth-century novel, only reflect the changing impact of venereal disease from its first appearance in the fifteenth century,[1] which made the consequences of sexual promiscuity as fearful as any inferno, to an age of antibiotics and chemical contraceptives which made safe again sexual enjoyment of Chaucerian abandon – if without Chacerian lightness of heart.

Just as science and technology have displaced religion, politics and philosophy to become the crucial determinants of social behaviour so, as might be expected, the literature which is itself centred on scientific ideas has come more closely than any other to reflect the role of science in society and through it to reveal society's innermost hopes and fears. Or as H. L. Gold, editor of *Galaxy Science Fiction*, put it, 'Few things reveal so sharply as science fiction the wishes, hopes, fears, inner stresses and tensions of an era, or define its limitations with such exactness'.[2] Because SF is concerned with Man's behaviour in unexpected environments it betrays in fact how the originating societies expect, hope or fear Man will behave, reveals by inference the value judgments on which contemporary behaviour in those societies is based.

Amis and Conquest argue in the first of their *Spectrum* series of anthologies,

> It is not, if we may say so, that we do not like and respect conventional fiction, but that we do not find it gives us all we want. There are kinds of ingenuity, kinds of invention, kinds of

question, ways of putting such questions, notions of possibility, effects of irony and wit, of wonder and terror that only science fiction offers and can offer . . . Science fiction, which can presuppose a major change in our environment, is the natural medium [for discussing major social suppositions]. [3]

Thirty years ago a writer might have used an historical novel to point up a contemporary dilemma; now he can isolate the facts he wishes to examine in science fiction. For the Russian writer history has had no analagous function since the Revolution, for turning to that protean jade in a communist society can be a dangerous move. Moreover, in the Soviet Union, scientists enjoy a relatively greater freedom to explore new ideas, within limited fields, than do creative artists or historians. Since the majority of Russian SF writers *are* also scientists, we might expect to find clearer evidence of the ferment shown in a number of recent Russian novels and poems in communist science fiction writing. Yet superficially Russian SF appears depressingly orthodox. However, deeper examination reveals an occasional glimmer of redeeming perversity, which, by the second half of the 1960s had become a positive glare. Science fiction, like any other form of communist creative art, must serve as an instrument of policy. In 1963 *Neues Deutschland*, the East German communist party newspaper, took Horst Müller to task for his story *Destination Ganymede*. In it Man has to abandon a world made uninhabitable by an explosion caused by an impetuous (warmongering, imperialist?) scientist and flee to the planet Ganymede. There the refugees, worthy communists to a man, free the planet's original inhabitants from the dictator under whom they suffer. The paper argues that any story of the distant future must take place in a communist era and therefore such an individual's dictatorship would be impossible; Müller, said *Neues Deutschland*, had described 'Social conditions which would be unthinkable in a communist system, disregarded the basic laws of social development and failed to realise that even science fiction must be scientifically based on Marxism and Leninism'. Since Marxism–Leninism is supposed to be an exact and predictable science, in this kind of writing the science, by its very nature, may limit the scope of the fiction.

Russian communist science fiction, like other literature, is expected to make propaganda points. The most common line is the belligerence of the capitalist world. To convey this impression

Western authors, even the much admired H. G. Wells, are select-
ively quoted and distorted. In *A Visitor from Outer Space* by
Alexander Kazantsev (a story in which incidentally the most notable thing is a footnote on space-shot ballistics twenty-two pages
long, comprising almost half the text) one of the younger scientists
puts forward the suggestion that the spaceship in question came
from Mars to seize earth – and gets the reply:

> I think you're wrong. Wells and other Western writers when they
> imagine the worlds coming together, can only think in terms of
> invasions and wars. To my mind, knowing the state of things as
> regards water on Mars and seeing the vast irrigation works of the
> Martians, we can draw certain conclusions about their social
> system which promotes the carrying out of planned economy on
> the scale of the entire planet.[4]

There is a typical example of misrepresentation of Western SF in
Ivan Yefremov's *The Heart of the Serpent*, in which he makes an
astronaut retell one of the classics of science fiction, Murray Leinster's *The First Contact*.[5]

Far out in space hundreds of light years from their own world two
spaceships meet – the first encounter between man and other
intelligent beings. The crews of both are eager to acquire the
invaluable knowledge they could learn from people from another
world. But both are afraid that they may betray the location of their
own world and so subject it to conquest by a possibly superior race.
To this dilemma the only answer seems to be to fight it out in space,
to keep the secret of the whereabouts of their own world by either
destroying or being destroyed. There the Russian author abandons
the original story, as if it went no further, using it only to make the
point that the Western writer can only think in terms of hostility
between peoples of different planets in contrast in his own tale to
the Russian crew's peaceful approach to a strange craft (an encounter we shall look at again in chapter 7). But the original story
goes on beyond this point. The spaceships make contact, like two
dogs warily sniffing at each other prior to fight or friendship, and
through the sympathy which springs up between the beings in each
crew responsible for contact, a solution eventually emerges. The
dilemma is subtly resolved by the two crews removing everything
which could indicate the spaceships' points of origin, exchanging
vessels and going back to their own worlds in alien craft.

Yefremov criticises Leinster because 'He did not have an inkling of the boundless knowledge implicit in the simplest formulas of the great dialecticians of his time'. Yet from a comparison of these two stories it clearly emerges that it is the Russian who assumes, and had to assume at that time, that his society's present structure of knowledge is in principle perfect and only has to be extended.

One or two Soviet writers have tried to wriggle a little in the strait-jacket imposed by the demands of propaganda and education. The story with a twist in its ending allows them at least to toy with forbidden catastrophes, and is a commonplace technique of SF generally. Alexander Belayev (*Over the Abyss*) describes the destruction of the world at the hands of a lunatic who speeds up its rotation.[6] In fact, the teller of the story is a too curious student who has been hypnotised, as a means of instruction, into believing that this is happening. He is, of course, finally brought out of the trance. Vladimir Savchenko (*Professor Burn's Awakening*) tells the story of the scientist who believes Man is bound to destroy civilisation and so puts himself in an underground deep-freeze programmed to revive him at a time when he can study evolution in progress once more. When he emerges thousands of years later it is indeed in a primitive jungle and he is soon clubbed down by man-apes – thus apparently vindicating his theory. But the jungle is, in fact, an experimental park for studying evolution run by the perfect (and of course communist) society which exists when the scientist de-freezes.[7]

The point in both stories is that the reader does not know the explanation until he has, vicariously, experienced the disaster, and possibly a few improper un-Marxist thoughts – though he will be a naïve Soviet reader indeed who does not know that there is bound to be a let-out in the end.

It is thus from the omissions and the selectivity of Russian writers that we are best able to infer what their real hopes, fears and problems may be. In the case of Yefremov and Kazantsev it is the fear of war – an element which struck me most forcibly in its intensity when working as a journalist in Russia. With Belayev and Savchenko the fear is there, expressed in different form, that there will be no glorious communist future, although they are only able to express such doubts by the twist endings given to their stories. We shall see both these themes implicit in other stories analysed in later chapters.

The same sort of technique can be applied to indicating the fields of knowledge which the Soviet writer would like to have explored, but usually dared not, during the revival of SF in the late 1950s and early 1960s. In *The Boy* by G. Gor, you come across such sentences as *'Except for Herman Ivanovich* the teachers didn't think much of this sort of knowledge ... ', ' ... *some scientists assert* that there exists a so-called psi-field, the physical nature of which is not yet known'.[8] It is phrases like those I have italicised which signpost the approaching heretical remark and at the same time protect the writer from the consequences of having given voice to it.

But any suggestion that the Russian might treat such subjects as ESP seriously meets with an indignant response. Indicative of this was a letter from Vladimir Lvov in the *New Scientist*[9] setting out the strong Russian criticisms of the validity of ESP and parapsychology in reply to an article on that subject, though intelligence sources indicate considerable hush-hush research into this field. It is more rare to find such examples of open heresies as the Strugatskys' story, *Wanderers and Travellers,*[10] which questions the nature of intelligence and speculates on the kind of physiological home in which one may find it. 'We've still got some scientists who, owing to their laziness or poor education, advocate a sort of cheap anthropocentrism.' It might have been difficult for a Russian author until the 1950s to make such a remark and even in this story the criticism of the scientist with this particular outlook is qualified by classical excuses. In due course, Snegov, the Strugatskys and others were to make a break-out from these restrictions.

Pierre Piganiol has admirably expressed the importance of studying any particular nation's scientific policies.

> To analyse a country's science and technical policy is to attempt to understand how a government deals with one of the most evident and least clear phenomena of our times – the inter-action of scientific research and society. The elaboration of a science policy (even its existence) implies the desire to remove at least some of the rigidities inherent in existing structures, groups and programmes in order to tackle more freely and more effectively those projects which best achieve the desired goals of society. It means putting the need *for* research before the needs *of* research
> . . .
>
> The classical distinction between a policy for science – designed to improve the resources and strategy of research – directed

solely towards greater understanding of the universe, and a policy of using knowledge for economic or social ends, is a convenient descriptive device. However, it only imperfectly reflects the real situation where each research activity may be regarded (depending on personal attitudes and the particular moment) either as a general contribution to knowledge or as being directed towards a specific practical goal.[11]

It is in the differing cost–benefit analyses of human activities demonstrated in the science fiction of our three societies that we shall, to some extent, find the values of those societies.

Towards the end of the 1950s academician N. Semenov was arguing,

> the history of the development of science from antiquity to our own day shows clearly that the main social function of science is to improve production, to increase the productivity of labour . . . . This does not mean, however, that science is an appendage of production. Its independent task is to make a profound study of nature, of the inner mechanisms of natural phenomena, and consequently to harness the hidden forces of nature in the interests of man.[12]

Science is now seen much more as a factor influencing the overall development of communist society than merely a direct productive force. This was a point appreciated by Stalin who, believing science to be in fact a branch of Marxism, recognised the importance of bringing it under his own control. The by now famous episode of Lysenkoism in the biological sciences typified this, and such blindness is not entirely absent from modern Soviet attitudes towards science.[13] In 1969 Doctor Adolf Hermann wrote of a Czechoslovakia, just prior to the Russian invasion, in which

> The extent to which research was replaced by dogma is hard to imagine for those who know Marxist theory only from the writings of its classics, and not from its distorted application in Eastern Europe. A classification of scientific theories and results as either 'Marxist' or 'bourgeois' made it impossible for scientists in Eastern Europe to take part in the important advances achieved in the field of genetics, cybernetics, information theory and psychology.[14]

These are tender subjects, too, for the Russian science fiction writer. However, there have been changes in Russian science policy and science fiction in the past two decades. While there has been little diminution either in the absolute confidence in the power of science, or in the belief that it is an essential part of the liberation of man, indeed a prior condition of that liberation, we have seen changes in balance in the arguments between centralisation and an element of free enterprise – if you like between a mechanistic and an organic system. Helgard Weinert in the OECD study referred to above, reports a 'Reordering of priorities within the Soviet Academy of Sciences from an emphasis on the practical solution of economic problems, to primary preoccupation with developing the fundamental sciences.[15] While reconciliation of these points of view has not always been easily attained there has been an undoubted change in Soviet policy since the latter half of the 1960s leading towards an approach permitting more choice. Until recently Russian science has had to be harnessed to immediate problem-solving – economic, agricultural, military and so on. A disproportionately large number of economists and engineers is a consequence of this policy. But there has been an increasing recognition of the need to reconcile political control with operational initiative and even originality, profit and market pricing. This tends to lead to the organic approach in a permanent state of flux which is not always predictable or logical. The mechanistic, social target-orientated Research and Development Programme postulates rational planning and reasoned choice but does not necessarily reflect human behaviour when free. In the Soviet system science is seen as a tool to change society as opposed to the Western view of it as an instrument to serve society – however foolish its demands.

There is in Russia an atmosphere of enthusiasm and public concern about science and technology. Scientists enjoy in society an extremely high status and a great number of material privileges. That they have so seldom used this privileged position to extend the frontiers of freedom, and indeed in the case of psychologists have actively contracted them, has been the subject of SF satire. There is public inspection of plans of scientific research and technical innovation every year. In 1965 for example, 1,600,000 people were said to have taken part in the inspection of these programmes and to have produced a million useful suggestions between them and, of course, the Party plays a role in all this. Or as Weinert somewhat pedantically puts it:

Paradoxically, therefore, Soviet Government leaders and administrators appear to be prepared to rely to a greater extent on the economic calculus and on the desire of enterprises and individuals to maximise their earnings in their planned economy than many Western ministers of science and technology would be prepared to propose even in their own context of a largely private enterprise economy. [16]

The dogmatic insistence on revealed truths, and the planning of science and research by people who had no appreciation of the element of surprise in discovery, tended to obstruct the very process of scientific progress in Russia. This fact has come to be increasingly appreciated and the struggle between the need to retain political control while giving greater intellectual freedom is reflected, as one might expect, in the literature dealing with this area of activity. It has, moreover, led to some diminution in the veneration paid to the scientists and to the method of building up a scientific élite in the Soviet Union. You would not, for example, in Stalin's time have come across such critically intended remarks as 'You see, they take the talented people and put them in secluded surroundings', or 'this was all because of his deep bitterness for the people of this large abandoned district which, thanks to scientific experimentation was in such grievous trouble'. [17] Until the mid-1960s this was probably as near to anti-science as a Russian writer was allowed to go. But, in general, Russia, both in literature and practice, has retained a confidence in the ability of science to solve problems of society which is very different from the uncertainty and soul-searching currently taking place among the Western scientific and lay community.

The situation in the West was described by Dr Philip Handler, President of the US National Academy of Sciences, in a lecture to the Biochemical Society in London in December 1969:

At the very height of scientific success, when the stage has been set for ever more revealing explorations of the nature of life, when the technology bred of science has catalysed stupendous economic growth and gone far to mitigate the brute condition of man, now we are experiencing a violent world reaction. Science is taken to account for the less wise aspects of its use, for the existence of nuclear, chemical and biochemical weapons, for contamination of air, earth, water and food, while its enormous contribution to human welfare seems all too easily to go forgotten. Thoughtful students and their elders, as well as legislators, suddenly allege that science is not relevant and they thrash about for other means to achieve the good life, albeit without notable success.

This outburst revealed a rather surprised indignation by the scientist that the lay community seems to be a little sceptical about the benefits which science claims so abundantly to have bestowed upon it, combined with a genuine concern lest the baby be thrown out with the bath water as a result of hostile popular reaction. Two, both slightly ambivalent, attitudes tend to be revealed by the Western scientific community to the problems posed by the role of science in society. A leading article in *Nature*, having first attacked science fiction, without any grounds or evidence, as 'shallow' goes on to discuss the moral concern of scientists, their duty to consider the use to which their work may be put by those outside the scientific community.[18] The right of the 'outside' thus to dispose of the fruits of science is not, however, seriously disputed by this school. The scientist is expected only to influence the layman. In the same issue a letter from Shapiro, Eron and Beckwith of Harvard Medical School urges 'scientists to work for radical political change' in the United States because of the abuses to which *non*-scientists have put scientific discoveries. These are opposite aspects of the same syndrome, the same sense of guilt, in the scientific community, but the attitudes of the second school would lead, if the writers had their way, to rule by scientists. Moral concern is here perhaps subordinated to injured pride. Scientists such as the authors of the above letter see the solution as action with other people (a kind of popular front to be betrayed in due course?), an acceptance, if necessary, of the temporary slowing of scientific progress in order to give it unfettered scope later. More recent evidence of this self-restraint was shown in 1975 by the voluntary moratorium in the United States on genetic engineering until its safe execution could be guaranteed – a moratorium apparently disregarded despite the Ashby report by ICI in the United Kingdom.

There are those who argue that if the whole business of government and politics were put into the safe and responsible hands of the scientists there would be no conflict of interest between scientific and social goals. I am sure they could remove the conflict of interest but less sure that the ordinary members of society would enjoy this particular form of technocracy. There is a danger, as Paul Johnson pointed out in his article in the *New Scientist*, previously referred to, that the scientists may regard themselves as a new priesthood.[19] Nevertheless there have been very considerable efforts made by scientists themselves to bridge this gap, even to introduce some form of control over their activities from outside their own discipline. In April 1970, Professor John Black was writing about the problems of 'the greater struggle for the social assimilation of science'. He speculated that the uncertainty of society and the attitudes of the young were conditioned by the rapid tempo of transition in modern society, and it is worth noting that science fiction is again and again underlining the need for flexibility and adaptability to ever-changing situations. Indeed James Blish has even claimed that science fiction attempts 'to help to prepare us for these changes'.[20] Again, in April of the previous year, a group of scientists set out to establish The British Society for Social Responsibility in Science, subscribing to the belief that the performance of science is determined 'by the social choices of the community and the personal choices of the scientist.[21]

It is these very problems which are at the heart of a great deal of contemporary science fiction, and the genre, which *Nature* chooses to deride, has been aware of and given serious thought to those dilemmas of the modern scientist to which he himself has only just, apparently, become alert.

It must be admitted that many science fiction stories do fall into the same two over-simplified categories for which some scientists themselves have opted. In the one the assumption is made that all the key people in the world of the future will be scientists and in the other we find the continuation of the old Frankensteinian theory of the mad scientist who must be stopped or controlled. But the great majority of SF stories are not so crude in approach and in fictional form explore a multitude of ways in which the individual, be he scientist or lay citizen, can resolve the dilemma just referred to. Even within a single work the opposing attitudes can be expressed and brought into nicely balanced conflict. In *The Rose* Charles Harness writes:

Science is simply a parasitical, adjectival, and useless occupation devoted to the quantitative restatement of art. Science is functionally sterile; it creates nothing; it says nothing new. The scientist can never be more than a humble camp-follower of the artist. There exists no scientific truism that hasn't been anticipated by creative art.[22]

But then with a nice irony the author later makes one of the characters express the triumph of the new multiple art form of the story in scientific terms. The truth of the matter is that science and art have increasingly influenced each other in a constructive way which displaces today the older belief in their incompatibility.

As might reasonably be expected science fiction has often reflected issues of contemporary interest since Schiaparelli's discovery of Martian 'canals' prompted a number of Martian life stories from the *War of the Worlds* onwards, but it has also frequently detected those underlying developments of which society at large has not yet been fully conscious. Perhaps the most celebrated example of this was a story published in 1944 by Cleeve Cartmill in a science fiction magazine which described not only the principles and use of the atomic bomb one year before it was actually exploded but compelled the reader to consider the moral implications of its use.[23] In this instance the American FBI, while alarmed at the possible implications of the story, could do nothing, not even interrogate him, lest it betray the Allies' intentions to the enemy. There is no evidence to suggest that Cartmill had any access to information which could have led him confidently to predict this particular military development. He had merely, as a science fiction writer, been considering possible developments of military and scientific strategy and their applications and implications. His story was generated in an ethos of large-scale military horror before all but the most limited number of specialists had considered the *practical* possibilities of which he wrote. It is this capacity of science fiction to penetrate beneath the contemporary to the emerging currents of tomorrow which makes it such a significant potentiometer of social change. In a story called *No Life of Their Own* it is argued that children can see fairies and ghosts because they can still see a little bit beyond reality.[24] It is this ability to see a little bit beyond reality which is one of the necessary characteristics of the science fiction writer. In an article entitled 'The Coming of the Unconscious', J. G. Ballard thinks of science fiction as 'a heightened or alternate reality beyond and above those familiar to either our sight or senses'. He goes on to link science fiction with the paintings of Salvador Dali: 'the sensational elements in these paintings are merely a result of their use of the unfamiliar, their revelation of unexpected associations'.[25] So Dali's clock and watches, which in the famous painting have begun to melt and drip, do so because the artist has recognised the invalidity of time as a means of measuring or pin-pointing human activity. Or as Ballard says of the principal character of his story *The Venus Hunters*, 'the real significance of his fantasies, like that of the Ban the Bomb movements, is to be found elsewhere than on the conscious plane as an expression of the immense psychic forces stirring below the surface of rational life . . . .'[26] We shall return later to this more personal explanation for social change.

Delany, whose essay 'About 5175 Words' is well worth reading as a study of science fiction, distinguishes between science fiction and other forms of contemporary fiction:

> Mainstream literature continues to tell us that human behaviour does not change; science fiction that in fact it has changed – for the scientific attitude is an entirely new mode of human behaviour, of which the technological changes I have noted are only side effects. . . . the subjunctive level of SF says that we must make our correction process in accord with what we know of the physically explainable universe. And the physically explainable has a much wider range than the personally observable.[27]

Ray Bradbury, in a story called 'Skeleton,' reveals something of the way the science fiction writer looks at life. 'God Almighty! he thought, why haven't I realised it all these years! All these years I've gone round with a – SKELETON – inside me! How is it we take ourselves for granted? How is it we never question our bodies and our beings?'[28] This story goes on to look at the skeleton within a man's body as if it were an alien being that had taken it over. The principal character begins to believe that his skeleton is eating him up but no one else will accept this view. The way Bradbury tells the story the reader accepts the hypothesis as medically possible. The story in question has one of the more horrific endings I have encountered. Hearing a cry of desperation, the man's wife runs into the room and treads on a slimy little jellyfish which calls her by name. It is these pseudo experiences and allegories which attempt to force the reader to examine in an entirely different way assumptions which he has taken for granted.

Nor is this challenge to think radically limited to society's leaders, politicians and philosophers. Science fiction is a fiction of responsibility precisely because it makes the ordinary man consider problems which are usually the serious concern of only a few. It enables us to discuss subjects rationally which if discussed in terms of straightforward human problems and relationships would involve too much emotion for an objective analysis to be made. It is perhaps also something of an attempt to impose order on the bizarre and fantastic chaos of our nightmares.

One of the principal differences between the scientific exposition in Western and Russian science fiction is that whereas Russian science fiction is based on contemporary scientific and technical knowledge[29] the Western story may in fact be the exposition of hypothetical scientific situation or the explanation of a scientific assumption essential to the unfolding of the plot but which needs at some stage to be justified to the reader. In the last twenty years the writers in this area have come to recognise that they are writing for a breed of sceptics rather than for people who have picked up a book because they were willing to have their disbelief suspended. It is in this process of justification to the sceptic that one can detect the preoccupations which we are concerned to analyse.

Notes

1. There is a very interesting article in *Science Journal* (Sept 1970), tracing the actual path of the disease, imported not as commonly supposed from the Americas but from Central Asia to this country.

2. Quoted in Kingsley Amis, *New Maps of Hell* (first pub. 1961; New English Library, 1969).

3. Kingsley Amis and Robert Conquest (eds.), *Spectrum* (first pub. 1961; Pan, 1964).

4. Alexander Kazantsev, *A Visitor from Outer Space* (Btk 383, 1958).

5. Ivan Yefremov, *The Heart of the Serpent* (Btk 367, Yunost 1959); Murray Leinster, *The First Contact* (first pub. Astounding, 1945) and in *The Leinster Omnibus* (Sidgwick and Jackson, 1968).

6. Alexander Belayev, *Over the Abyss* (Btk 49, 1928).

7. Vladimir Savchenko, *Professor Burn's Awakening* (Tekhnika Molodyozhi, no. 11, Btk 471, 1956).

8. G. Gor, *The Boy* (Btk 326, 1966).

9. *New Scientist* (27 Mar 1969).

10. Boris and Arcady Strugatsky, *Wanderers and Travellers* (Btk 553, 1963).

11. OECD Report, *An Introduction to Science Policy in the U.S.S.R.* (OECD, 1969).

12. Ibid.

13. Cf. Z. A. Medvedev, *The Rise and Fall of T. D. Lysenko* (Columbia University Press, 1969).

14. *New Scientist* (9 Jan 1969).

15. OECD report, *An Introduction to Science Policy in the U.S.S.R.*

16. Ibid.

17. Sever Gansovsky, *A Day of Wrath* (Btk 311, 1965).

18. *Nature*, CCXXIV (17 Dec 1969).

19. *New Scientist* (4 Sept 1967).

20. James Blish, 'Future Recall', an essay in *The Disappearing Future* (Panther, 1970).

21. This organisation has since shown itself to be a highly political body more concerned to propagate an anti-capitalist point of view than to safeguard scientific discovery and technique from abuse whencesoever it comes.

22. Charles Harness, *The Rose* (first pub. 1953, Panther, 1969).

23. For a detailed account of this see Blish, 'Future Recall'.

24. Clifford Simak, 'No Life of Their Own', in *All the Traps of Earth* (Four Square, 1964).

25. J. G. Ballard, 'The Coming of the Unconscious', in *The Overloaded Man* (Panther, 1967).

26. Ibid.

27. R. Delany, 'About 5175 Words', in *The Disappearing Future* (Panther, 1970).

28. Ray Bradbury, 'Skeleton', in *The October Country* (first pub. 1956; Four Square, 1963).

29. However the Strugatskys wrote a story involving matter transference and in Snegov's *Men Like Gods* spaceships do travel faster than light, but these are exceptions.

4
Disaster, survival and salvation

Despite the ever increasing conformity of the nations of the world to a single anaemic pattern, the preoccupations which Britain, America and Russia revealed in their science fiction were, until the late 1960s, very different. We shall examine the ensuing brief period of convergence in chapter 9 but we shall here concentrate on the larger period of divergence.

Surprisingly enough on a small island in the nuclear age, it is not destruction in nuclear war which worries the British writer, nor is it that enslavement by commercial interests which haunts his American counterpart. He is not interested purely in physical survival, but in whether Man can survive as a civilised being in a society recognisably descended from the one we know today. John Christopher's *The Death of Grass* is the classic example of the simplest form of this preoccupation. [1]

John Custance and his family listen with only the mildest interest to the news that a virus which attacks rice is devastating China and other parts of Asia. The virus is checked, only to break out again in more virulent and apparently unstoppable forms which attack all grasses, leaving the ground brown and bare behind them. The disease spreads all over the world. The crowded British Isles are facing catastrophic starvation. Only the Government knows the full extent of the crisis and it is preparing a drastic solution for the big cities which is described in this dialogue between Custance and his friend:

'Atom bombs for the small cities, hydrogen bombs for places like Liverpool, Birmingham, Glasgow, Leeds and two or three of them for London. It doesn't matter about wasting them – they won't be needed in the foreseeable future.'

'I can't believe that. No one could do that. They will never get people to man the planes.'

'We are in a new era. Or a very old one. Wide loyalties are civilised luxuries. Loyalties are going to be narrow from now on and the narrower the fiercer. If it were the only way of saving Olivia and Steve I'd man one of those planes myself.'

'No!'

'When I spoke about murdering bastards, I spoke with admiration as well as disgust. From now on, I propose to be one where necessary, and I very much hope you are prepared to do the same.'

John and his friend gradually acquire some of that ruthlessness in fighting their way, with their families, out of London towards a Scottish farm in a naturally defended valley owned by John's brother. They take with them Pirie, a sharpshooting gunsmith, who is already utterly ruthless. Civilised behaviour is swiftly torn away in a welter of robbery, rape and murder as the little band fights to survive, a fight which drives John near to despair.

His old self, his civilised self, challenged him to an accounting. When it sank below a certain level, was life itself worth the having any longer? They had lived in a world of morality whose lineage could be traced back nearly four thousand years. In a day, it had been swept from under them.

The chaos grows worse and they realise that they are too few to win through. John refuses to allow a feeble defenceless group to join them but plans to join up with any other suitable armed party. His group falls in with one slightly larger, but the swift and ruthless gunning down of the rival leader by the sharpshooting killer, Pirie, puts the second band under John's command also.

Where Wells used a time machine to reach a point in past history, in *The Death of Grass* Christopher makes his whole society move backwards through time.

For himself, John saw, it signified a new role, of enhanced power. The leadership of his own small party, accidental at first, into which he had grown, was of a different order from this acceptance of loyalty from another man's followers. The pattern of feudal chieftain was forming, and he was surprised by the degree of his own acquiescence – and even pleasure – in it.

When the band reaches the valley farm, John's brother is powerless to admit them against the wishes of those who have already joined him. The band fights its way in, again with the aid of Pirie's sporting rifle and shooting skill, and in the battle both Pirie and John's brother are killed before the invading refugees and their families take over the valley. The conclusion is one of only guarded optimism. The question of whether physical survival in these circumstances must entail a lapse into barbarism is unanswered. The story ends with this conversation between John and his wife:

'Everything's going to be all right. The children can grow up here in peace, even if the world is in ruins. Davy will farm the valley land.'

'He'll do more than farm it, won't he? He will own it. It's a nice bit of land. Not as much as Cain left Enoch, though.'

'You mustn't talk like that. And it wasn't you who killed him – it was Pirie.'

'Wasn't it? I don't know. We'll blame Pirie, shall we? And Pirie is gone, washed away with the river, so the land flows with milk and honey again, and with innocence. Is that all right?'

'John! It *was* Pirie.'

'Pirie gave me his gun. He must have known, then, that he was finished. And when I saw that he had gone under, I thought of throwing it after him – that was the gun which brought us here to the valley, killing its way across England. I could have got to the shore more easily without it, and I was deadly tired, even so I hung on to it.'

'You can still throw it away. You don't have to keep it.'

'No. Pirie was right. You don't throw away a good weapon. It will be Davy's when he is old enough.'

'No! He won't need it. It will be peace then.'

'Enoch was a man of peace. He lived in the city which his father built for him. But he kept his father's dagger in his belt.'

The story in *Death of Grass* springs from the action of the virus at the beginning. Yet apart from occasional reminders that this was the agent of change the interest is entirely concentrated on the consequential human behaviour. In John Wyndham's stories, the catalyst is more frequently with us and he takes the analysis of survival a stage further. Where Christopher examined the dilemma of choice between survival and barbarism, Wyndham's is between evolution and extinction. He explores a variety of answers on this theme and it is interesting to follow his development from Man surviving the monster in *The Kraken Awakes* and the 'alien' monster from the vegetable kingdom in *The Day of the Triffids*, to the alternative solutions of his two late 1950s books with a pessimistic outcome in Man's destruction of an alien, superior and quasi-human intelligence in *The Midwich Cuckoos* and the triumphant emergence of *homo superior* in the earlier story *The Chrysalids*.[2] It is worth looking at these last two stories in greater detail, particularly as his work on the two themes overlapped.

The inhabitants of the small village of Midwich in rural England are rendered mysteriously unconscious for twenty four hours and the village is isolated by a barrier which knocks out any one who crosses it during that time. Unknown to the villagers this has also happened in a few other parts of the world. Later it transpires that all the women of child-bearing age in the village are pregnant, and as the significance of this fact slowly dawns on them, all are horrified by the thought of the monsters to which they might give birth. But the children, born within a week of each other, are all perfectly normal except for their bright golden eyes. Yet these are the Cuckoos of the title. Soon they begin to reveal remarkable powers of influencing the adults of the village. When only a few weeks old they can prevent their parents taking them away from the village, and one mother who accidentally pricks her baby finds she is compulsively jabbing herself with a safety pin. Gradually it is realised that the children of each sex are, as it were, a single collective personality, with enormous and growing mental powers. At the age of nine, they already physically resemble children of sixteen. They have the will and the ability to supplant mankind. Both they and their host community believe that the choice lies between survival at the expense of the other or extinction. With their powers over men's will the Cuckoos can protect themselves from conventional attack. The primitive people among whom other colonies of Cuckoos arrived destroyed them at birth. The Russians, when they realised the danger they posed, obliterated the entire community in which the Cuckoos lived with an atom bomb. The English are at an impasse, for ruthless destruction of the children, let alone a whole village, would not be tolerated, yet to let them grow up spells the end of the human race. The dilemma is resolved by the one man who appreciates that this is not a matter for weighing crime by conventional social definitions but of primitive survival. It so happens that the children trust him alone of the local 'humans', so when he goes to show them some films he blows them up and himself with them.

Wyndham clearly approves of the human self-sacrifice and the sacrifice of the aliens, however mentally superior, in the interests of human evolutionary *status quo*, but we have again moved from the problems of simple physical survival to those of the price to be paid. It is the mutual nature of the desire for survival which makes this such a sophisticated study of the survival instinct and what it entails. (Notably the *Midwich Cuckoos* made a far better film than *The Day of the Triffids*; the latter was exciting as a book, hilarious as a Percy Thrower nightmare on film.)

In *The Chrysalids*, a good novel by any standards, a different situation arises. Post-nuclear-holocaust society is a simple agricultural one, of Calvanistic strictness. Deviants with physical deformities are destroyed at birth and the process is rationalised by the belief that they are religiously speaking 'an abomination'. (On the fringe of the normal community are the badlands where some deformed creatures survive and from which they rather ineffectually harry the settlements.) Into this primitively puritanical society a new kind of deviant is born. These few children also have telepathic powers, as later did the Cuckoos, but have to keep them secret if they are to be allowed to survive. When they are adolescents their secret is discovered and despite flight to the savage but strangely sympathetic badlands they only escape destruction at the hands of their families through the intervention of other telepaths with a highly developed technology. These have sensed the young people's danger and left their complex and wonderful city, peopled only by telepaths, to make the rescue and draw them into the fold of *homo superior*. Wyndham has arrived, as it were, at the almost religious, mystical conclusion that the survival of the spirit of Man can only be brought about by the disappearance of *homo sapiens*. It is a crucifixion which he welcomes. It is a pity, good as *The Midwich Cuckoos* is, that he should have moved away from this theme to revert to the more traditional response to encounter with aliens. In the last ten years of his life he wrote little of real significance, though in *Chocky* he did revert to his Chrysalids theme of telepathic communication, this time between an earth boy and an extra-terrestrial child. [3]

The other principal theme of British science fiction is the enervating effect of any survival which depends on imposed conformity. Stories dealing with this theme often begin with some alien, and usually benevolent, force ending the conflict between the world's nations and banishing injustice and oppression. Arthur Clarke's *Childhood's End* is probably the best and best known of this kind – with plenty of contemporary political bite. [4] The peace factor in this instance is the presence over all the world's cities of huge spaceships belonging to the 'guardians'. These order South Africa to end racial strife, are not heeded and take action which gives a typically neat SF twist to the story.

> All that happened was that as the sun passed the meridian at Cape Town – it went out. There remained visible merely a pale, purple ghost, giving no heat or light. Somehow, out in space, the light of the sun had been polarised by two crossed fields so that no radiation could pass. The area affected was five hundred kilometres across, and perfectly circular.
>
> The demonstration lasted thirty minutes. It was sufficient: the next day the Government of South Africa announced that full civil rights would be restored to the white minority.

'Splendid' is the automatic response of the well-conditioned radical reader of either right or left; but is it?

Peace and order soothe the world under the patronage of the invisible guardians, and with the disappearance of strife men cease to make scientific progress or to create original works of art. Nor in this story does Man survive in the usual sense, for children with enormous visionary powers are born to later generations, the old people die out and the children are absorbed into the universal 'Over-mind'. This is perhaps not as gratifying a solution as the one achieved through suffering and struggle but it is a vanity-satisfying survival of a kind, and one of the most common features of British science fiction is an invigorating conceit. Some of the stories are more simple cases where the odd man out, the eccentric professor or telepath, or even the man who was asleep when 'it' happened, defeat the alien powers – a theme we shall see more extensively treated in American SF. One way or another from Wells onwards, Man somehow always gets the better of the 'superior intelligence' either by chance or through some particularly human quirk of behaviour. The innate and irrepressible assumption in British SF and to a lesser extent in Western SF as a whole is not that Man *has* no superior, indeed in chapter 7 we shall encounter many such, but that it does not matter because he will survive anyway. If you can't beat them, you join them or ignore them. But writers like Wyndham and Christopher embarrassingly insist on asking, 'Survive as what?'

If the science fiction writers are a reliable guide, then, Britain's principal fears are that Man may cease to survive as a civilised being, or that the demands for conformity made by highly complex or totalitarian societies will leave no room for individualism and eccentricity. The theme of the violation of free will in various ways occurs repeatedly. The hope, amounting almost to belief, is that Man is such a gifted creature that he will, in fact, survive all external threats to create a peaceful but still stimulating society. The genesis of such science fiction stories was aptly described many years ago by Wells's Time Traveller to his incredulous audience. 'No. I cannot expect you to believe it. Take it as a lie or a prophecy. Say I dreamed it in the workshop. Consider I have been speculating upon the destinies of our race, until I have hatched this fiction.'[5]

If a moral must be drawn from British science fiction, it was made by Arthur Clarke in 1963 (the year in which he received the Kalinga prize for popularising science) describing the role of the science fiction writer. 'By mapping out possible futures, as well as a good many impossible ones, the science fiction writer can do a great service to the community. He encourages in his readers flexibility of mind, readiness to accept and even welcome change – in one word, adaptability.'[6] An excellent illustration of this preoccupation with adaptability can be found in American writer Raymond Jones's *Noise Level*, which should be a warning against too rigid a classification on national lines. Here the thesis is that just as we filter out and select sounds from a general background of total noise, so we select from the general background of total knowledge and thought. But in childhood we are encouraged and conditioned to set the standards of our filtering-out apparatus too severely. In *Noise Level* a psychologist gathers together a group of scientists and by means of an elaborate hoax convinces them that a young man has invented and flown with an anti-gravity machine, but that the man and the machine have been totally destroyed. Although all of them have been led to believe in the past that such a machine would be impossible they are persuaded that it is urgent, in the interest of national security, that this young man's work should be reproduced. The hoax breaks down the scientists' mental barriers, questions their preconceptions and challenges their notion of the impossible. As a result an anti-gravity machine *is* invented.

Although the manipulation of Man is more often an American

than a British theme, a particular form of it, manipulation by the state, does feature in modern British SF which has carried on the earlier traditions of Huxley and Orwell. Winston's situation in *1984* typifies the direct attack on state manipulation.

> Behind Winston's back the voice from the telescreen was still babbling away about the pig-iron and the overfulfilment of the Ninth Three-Year Plan. The telescreen received and transmitted simultaneously. Any sound that Winston made, above the level of a very low whisper, would be picked up by it; moreover, so long as he remained within the field of vision which the metal plaque commanded, he could be seen as well as heard. There was of course no way of knowing whether you were being watched at any given moment. How often, or on what system, the Thought Police plugged in on any individual wire was guesswork. It was even conceivable that they watched everybody all the time. But at any rate they could plug in your wire whenever they wanted to. You had to live – did live, from habit that became instinct – in the assumption that every sound you made was overheard, and, except in darkness, every moment scrutinized.[8]

Here the futuristic scientific device, the telescreen, is unimportant. Technical devices are only the instruments for enabling the author to make social and political criticisms. The society he attacks is not the consequence of technical developments, but a projection and magnification of certain political characteristics of contemporary totalitarian society transformed to the author's own nightmare. Thus one of the basic requirements of good science fiction is fulfilled; that the futuristic story should be a plausible continuation, however exaggerated, of some quality or pattern of behaviour which can already be discerned, however faintly, in our own society. Whether political science or sociology can qualify as the scientific ingredient is more open to debate.

The influence of Orwell, and of *1984* in particular, has been much greater than the older, more subtle theme of Huxley's *Brave New World*, the dictatorship of misplaced benevolence, not only on the modern British science fiction writer, but on such Americans as David Karp. In his story, *One*,[9] the hero, a professor living in a placid and apparently well-ordered society, reveals a tiny hint of the great heresy – individualism. The heresy is found to be deeply ingrained, so using every trick of psychology and physiology the authorities disintegrate his personality, eradicate every memory of his former life, and rebuild him as a mere clerk. Here is how the destruction of personality takes place. The professor, drugged and exhausted, lies naked in a large bare concrete room and the insidious voice echoes in his ear,

> 'You are a citizen of the State,' the far-off mechanical voice of the tape said flatly. 'As a citizen of the State there are certain obligations you assume. All citizens of the State assume the same obligations. If they did not, there could be no State. If there were no State, there would be chaos. The strong would rob the weak, murder the helpless, rape the women, degrade the children. Man is an animal and like an animal he has no morals, no character. Without the State he reverts to the nature of the animal. The State is the only check man knows. The tiny strength of one man is multiplied a million times in the form of the State. The State, then, is stronger than any man. It protects each man from his own animal nature. This is the function of a State. This is the reason men have States and governments. For the safety of every citizen the State is necessary. In order that you or any citizen may live in safety, in happiness, free from attack, from plunder, from out-rage, you must uphold the State. You are helpless without the State. The State is your protector, your father, your mother, your family. You are helpless without the State.' The voice went on and on, but Lark [the interrogator] had long since ceased to listen to it.

In fact, although the professor has been changed into an entirely new person, in the old body shell, he still shows evidence of unrepentant individualism, and the State, by destroying him, has to admit its defeat.

It is, I think, possible to distinguish between the fears of British writers of the breakdown of society and the disintegration of the individual personality and those of the Americans of the annihilation of society or the manipulation of the personality.

Basically the American SF writer is interested in brainwashing,[10] in the loss of individual free will. In its crudest form this is represented by straightforward indoctrination, as in Robert Young's *A Little Red Schoolhouse*, a horrific satirical story of educational brainwashing on Huxley lines.[11] Typical of this theme of manipulation of the personality through totalitarian persecution is Wyman

Guin's *Beyond Bedlam*.[12] In this story schizophrenia is the normal state of mind, with everyone living turn and turn about with their other personality. The hero is the man who tries to have a single integrated personality, and not to change at the designated shift time. He is, of course, eventually destroyed.

Frank Herbert is another American writer fascinated by the conflicting challenges thrown up by the necessity to accelerate the process of physical and, more importantly, moral evolution if we are to escape man-made disaster and the risks of manipulation and the loss of free will implicit in such acceleration. This is the argument in *Hellstrom's Hive*.[13] In *The Santaroga Barrier*, one of his most readable novels, he explores the dilemma still more thoroughly.[14] His hero, Dasein (The One?), investigates an isolated community which seems too good to be true. His entrée comes from the fact that his fiancée is one of the rather special people that make up this community. The values of the community are again highly commendable, particularly against the background of the declining standards of the rest of America wrapped in 'Virgilian autumn . . . the dusk of civilisation'.

The moving force behind the community is Dasein's potential father-in-law, Doctor Piaget (significantly named?). As he puts it:

Contending is too soft a word, Dasein. There's power struggle going on over control of the human consciousness. We are a cell of health surrounded by plague. It's not men's minds that are at stake, but their consciousness, their awareness. This isn't a struggle over what's to be judged valuable in our universe. Outside, they value whatever can be measured, counted or tabulated. Here, we go by different standards.

Or as another of the locals says 'Outside, they don't really try to understand the universe. Oh, they say they do, but that's not really what they're up to. You can tell by what they do. They're trying to conquer the universe.' As far as the community was concerned, 'The trouble was that they couldn't be culturally neutral. The world out there would keep trying to make people – all people – be everywhere alike.'

Dasein resists the idea. 'He felt a jealous possessiveness about this self. No smallest part of it was cheap enough to discard.' And when near fatal accidents keep befalling him and sometimes killing others he is scathing:

'Societies don't believe they can die,' Piaget said. 'It must follow that a society, as such, does not worship at all. If it cannot die, it'll never face a final judgment.'

'And if it'll never face judgment,' Dasein said, 'it can do things as a society that it'd be too much for an individual to stomach.'

'Perhaps,' Piaget muttered. 'Perhaps.'

But eventually Dasein is tricked into dependence on the drug-impregnated food which is the community's means both of isolating it from the outside world and of enhancing its members' powers with such extras as telepathy. He begins to adopt the community view:

Dasein cleared his throat. Here was the core of Santaroga's indictment against the outside. How did you use people? With dignity? Or did you tap their most basic functions for your own purposes? The outside began to appear more and more as a place of irritating emptiness and contrived blandishments.

The irony is that Herbert does not, I think, imply that it is wrong to use people in any way, even for their own good. The very addiction that Pohl and Kornbluth indict in *The Space Merchants*[15] as the means by which commercial corporations manipulate ordinary people is in *The Santaroga Barrier* the means of escape from a materialist society. The skill in Herbert's story is that he creates sharper contradictions in his readers' minds than is possible in *The Space Merchants*, where we adopt the hero's rebellious point of view from the outset. Herbert allows his reader to applaud the ends while instinctively rejecting the means which are forced upon the hero. Whether Herbert himself shares that rejection I am less certain.

Many of the American analyses of the extent of the freedom of human will are less ambiguous. And this is particularly true where collective manipulation is the theme of the story. In *Methusala's Children*, Robert Heinlein writes: 'mass psychology is not simply a summation of individual psychologies;...it is the social mass action rule, the mob hysteria law, known and used by military, political and religious leaders, by advertising men and prophets and propagandists, by rabble rousers and actors and gang leaders. . . .'[16] This manipulation of the mass mind is one of the principal concerns of American science fiction. It is interesting to speculate whether the frequency with which collective personalities occur in Western and in particular American science fiction is in a subtle way an attempt to reconcile the existence of an integrated, nearly uniform, multiplicity of physical entities with the longing for some sort of particular identifiable ego or totally distinctive personality.

The Little People in Heinlein's story, a parallel with the Irish leprechauns which somehow just avoids being ridiculous, exemplify this preservation of the individual within the collective. Again, Theodore Sturgeon clearly has contemporary American society in mind when he writes:

> Given a culture of sybaritics, with an endless choice of mechanical titillations, and you have a people of unbreakable and hidebound formality, a people with few but massive taboos, a shockable, narrow, prissy people obeying the rules – even the rules of their calculated depravity – and protecting their treasured, specialised pruderies.[17]

This collective conformist personality and its manipulation take a variety of forms. Politically it is expressed in a horror of the average man:

> Man's political viewpoints have been in thrall to the conception that the best should govern . . . . but hitherto no political system has ventured away from the implicit and unexamined assumption first embodied in the philosopher state of Plato's Republic.... The young democracy to the West, which introduced the concept of the right of man to jurisprudence, now gives a feverish world the doctrine of the lowest denominator in government.[18]

Null-P, from which the foregoing quotation is taken, is a story about the absolutely average man, a study of the American obsession with normality which satirises the too-much admired and all too typical all-American male. In 'Franchise' Asimov has written a nice political satire on the art of psephology and in particular those dreadful election-night programmes with their computers and swingometers.[19] In this story the computers choose the totally average voter and he is the *only* person eventually allowed to vote and decide the election. In contrast it is rare to find that touch of patriotism used by Asimov in *The Stars Like Dust* when the constitution of the new, free galaxy which emerges at the end of this futuristic story is in fact that of the United States.[20]

Frank Herbert, again, makes a humorous and skilful anaylsis of the need for the establishment to be opposed in contemporary American society. In 'The Tactful Saboteur', a study of immunity and privilege, he describes the role of professional saboteurs of the constitution whose job it is to try to undermine, in a whole variety of ways and with complete immunity from retribution, the leading men of the day.[21] The saboteurs are, as it were, the future's counterparts of a paid opposition, or of the Court Jester, the fool licensed to tell the truth. But to the American, perhaps, political manipulation by money, murder and the media is such an everyday and obvious matter as scarcely any longer to be a subject amenable to open political satire.

Much more devastating are the many penetrating analyses of the way in which the affluent society conditions contemporary Americans. No one has been more consistently devoted to this theme than Frederik Pohl who, together with C. M. Kornbluth, wrote one of the best known of all science fiction novels, *The Space Merchants*. The essential ingredients in almost all these commercial manipulation stories seem to be an overcrowded world – overcrowded either by people or consumer goods – and the dominance of the giant corporation. In the case of *The Space Merchants* it is the advertising agencies which are struggling to condition the people in their consuming habits and in so doing engage in an armed warfare which would have done credit to a feudal baron. Democracy is seen as a mockery. The President has become a puppet and, for the benefit of the so-called state watchdogs of society, when meetings of top executives are held to discuss the next nefarious piece of psychological sales-fare a pre-recorded tape is played back into the monitoring devices. The advertising executive who finally steps out of line is sent to work as a penal labourer on Chicken Little, a monstrous artificial growing source of food tended by deviants of all kinds. The hero is sent to Chicken Little almost by accident, but while there questions even more the society which condemns men to such a life in the sacred name of consumption. Although virtue does triumph in the end the story concludes on a far from optimistic note and it is hard for even the most cheerful reader to feel that there will be any improvement in the situation. Pohl, again with Kornbluth, treats the same theme in *Gladiator at Law*,[22] set in a densely packed slum district with a proletariat manipulated in the same way as in *The Space Merchants*. Here the underground movement is represented by children who are both vicious and independent in a way which is at the same time frightening and encouraging.

Pohl writing on his own treats the theme more humorously but no less effectively in a number of other stories, of which the best known, and an outstanding example of science fiction satire, is *The Midas Plague*.[23] This time the story deals with the theme of compulsive consumption. It is a citizen's duty to consume designated and vast quantities of material goods produced by robots whose output appears to increase exponentially. The whole idea of credit, on which contemporary American consumer society is based, is reversed, and if a citizen returns any item insufficiently used he is assigned additional consuming points which have to be accounted for next time round. All the things which the American advertising industry conditions the citizens of that country to think of as supremely desirable are rendered the subject of agonised conscience-searching and self-inflicted misery if not consumed in the prescribed wasteful quantities.

The hero, Morrie Fry, is an incurably bad 'consumer' who can never get through his quota, so he solves his problem by setting his own household robots to consume and wear out the goods produced by the industrial robots. Contrary to his fears, far from being punished when he is eventually found out, he is much praised and promoted for having solved the consumption problem in this way. Such a story is a more biting criticism of a political economy based on expanding consumption in an expanding market at all costs than any Marxist stricture could be, and Pohl can reasonably claim to have anticipated Dr Mansholt by twenty years.

Pohl wrote a sequel to this tale, *The Man Who Ate the World*, which looks a little further and more hopefully into the future.[24] It contains references to Morrie Fry and his liberation of the world from compulsive consumption as if to a religious prophet. On this occasion the hero of the story has to cure a compulsive eater who is a throw-back to the previous age. In this story we see the compulsion to consume in terms of the psychoanalysis of an individual's insecurity. *The Midas Plague* has had many imitators,[25] but none have I think so successfully pilloried American society with the missiles of its own making as the original.

Although many American writers have concerned themselves with this theme there are two whose work is of an even higher literary standard than Pohl's. In *Cat's Cradle*, bizarre, zany, expertly written and full of pungent aphorisms and observations of life in general, Kurt Vonnegut snipes at a whole range of social targets, but in *Player Piano* he mounts a sustained attack on a particular aspect of consumer society, that of the self-justifying corporation.[26] One of the prime objects of this satire is that particularly American phenomenon, the corporation man's outlook, which he describes as 'the ability to be moved emotionally, almost like a lover, by the omni-present and omniscient spook, the corporate personality'. Vonnegut traces the root of the current sense of alienation from society in America to the Second World War when 'maybe the actual jobs weren't taken from the people, but the sense of participation, the sense of importance was'. He is much more concerned with this aspect of automation than the more conventional fears of such writers as Asimov. *Player Piano* is unusual, too, in being an attack on the concept of meritocracy. Vonnegut recognises that with all the other 'ocracies' one can make some sort of self-justifying excuse for not being at the top of the heap. With a meritocracy that becomes impossible. He also very percipiently demonstrates that the advent of the all-doing machine takes away the ordinary person's vital feeling of being needed.

> Everybody used to have some personal skill or willingness to work or something he could trade for what he wanted. Now that the machines have taken over, it's quite somebody who has anything to offer. All most people can do is hope to be given something.
>   The rest of us, for what we perceive as good, plain reasons, have changed our minds about the divine right of machines, efficiency and organisation, just as men of another age changed their minds about the divine right of kings and about the divine rights of many other things.

We shall take a further look at this story in the chapter on cybernetics, but in this context we must note in particular the delightful satire on that calculated regression to the inhumanities of a tribalised childhood, the corporation outing. Had I not in the course of business visits to the United States actually encountered companies spending thousands of dollars and valuable man-hours on planning and indulging in these orgies of self-abasing togetherness, I would have found it hard to believe anything so horrible in its inanity as the island gathering which our hero, as a senior executive and leader of one of the 'teams', is compelled to attend.

The same theme of the ghastliness of the body corporate and the giant industrial corporation often preoccupies another of America's most able science fiction writers, Alfred Bester. He writes in *The Demolished Man*:

> . . . a Monarch jumper picked him up and carried him in one graceful hop to the giant tower that housed the hundreds of floors and thousands of employees of Monarch's New York office. Monarch Tower was the central nervous system of an incredibly vast corporation, a pyramid of transportation, communication, heavy industry, manufacture, sales, distribution, research, exploration, importation. Monarch Utility and Resources, Inc. bought and sold, traded and gave, made and destroyed. . . .[27]

This is a perfectly legitimate starting point for an SF story, as such situations already exist in the United States. He then takes some of the fears of that society and extrapolates from them. For example, the peeping Tom into the mind, as illustrated in this story, seems to be a standard American dread; the threat to mental privacy being the ultimate challenge to ego in a world where more and more threats to physical privacy have had to be compromised with. This story is most unusually presented typographically and in terms of lay-out, and instead, as is so often the case in SF, of being merely a gimmick this device helps to create the feeling of a mental conversation. Bester returns to his theme in *Tiger, Tiger* and pillories the great corporation syndrome again, this time having made the basic assumption that teleportation is possible.[28] It does not matter whether it is or not, for the assumption permits society to be studied from an illuminatingly oblique angle.

These stories were all the product of science fiction writing in the mid-1950s and although they made perhaps little impact at the time they thus anticipated by a decade the flourishing of the consumer movement and its active and political criticism of commercial manipulation and exploitation. It is scarcely surprising that these stories were nearly all republished in paperback versions in the second half of the 1960s with great success.

A significant sub-theme of the stories of commercial manipulation is that of over-population and loss of privacy, and this features as the central theme of a number of other American science fiction writers. In 'The Dead Past' Isaac Asimov demonstrates the fear of the destruction of privacy.[29] Harry Harrison's *Make Room, Make*

Room examines the phobia of overcrowding again.[30] It may seem surprising that this is an American rather than a British theme,[31] but it is perhaps linked with the general hatred of urban communities and their representation of all that is corrupt and disturbing in American society. The Rousseauesque cry of 'Back to the country' is frequently raised by the science fiction writer.

The consequences of overcrowding can vary from the horrors of noise, from which relief can only be obtained by surgical operation to make one deaf,[32] to the disposable babies of Walter Miller's *Conditionally Human.*[33] Cynically Miller describes the problem thus:

> The populace thoughtlessly responded by pouring forth a flood of babies and doddering old codgers to clutter the earth and make things tougher again by eating and not producing; but again science increased the individual's chance to survive and augmented his motives for doing so – and again the populace responded with fecundity and long white beards, making more trouble for science again. So it had continued until it became obvious that progress wasn't headed toward the good life but toward more lives to continue the same old meagre life as always. What could be done? Impede science? Unthinkable? Chuck the old codgers into the sea? Advance the retirement age to 90 and work them to death? The old codgers still had the suffrage, and plenty of time to go to the polls. The unborn, however, were not permitted to vote.

 So Man abuses his knowledge of chemistry and biology to create the artificial disposable baby, the neutroid, in order to solve this population problem. The hero's profession is destroying neutroids and it is his rebellion against this by making and then helping a neutroid to survive that provides the conflict of the story. Although the writer expresses the usual fears of genetic tampering, in this, as in so many of the other population explosion stories, no practical solution to the problem is suggested, despite the revulsion of the principal characters towards the horrific 'final' solutions which are the main themes of the stories themselves.

American science fiction has a number of other interesting sub-themes. That of the teenage take-over features in Robert Thom's *Wild in the Streets.*[34] The story is based on the fact that already some fifty-five per cent of Americans are under twenty-five. 'America was at last set free to pursue the worship of youth to a logical conclusion. Adolescence was all, rightness was nothing, and there were few who seemed displeased.' This theme is taken up by a number of other American authors, though by none I think so well as by the British writer John Christopher in *Pendulum* in which the teenagers take over with horrifying and bloodthirsty results before themselves being largely destroyed by a fanatical puritan backlash by the older generation.[35]

As one might expect, personal violence plays an important role in American science fiction. We have already seen that some science fiction is just the Western translated to some other location. In stories of this kind freedom of will is frequently seen as freedom to destroy and be destroyed. The classic belief of right-wing Americans was expressed by one of the characters in Robert Heinlein's *Revolt in 2100* when he said, 'The police of a state should never be stronger or better armed than the citizenry. An armed citizenry, willing to fight, is the foundation of civil freedom.'[36] But this neo-Western story is in fact a very effective send-up of the American ideal of gun-toting free men and a sharp criticism of the violence with which modern American society tries to work out its frustrations and solve its problems.

Such acceptance of the relative cheapness of human life is perhaps to some extent dependent on a belief in a life hereafter. The theme of immortality in its different ways is common to the science fiction of all three countries with which we are concerned. British writers, as we have seen, are concerned that the race itself should survive, or at least its spirit. Later we shall come to study the approach of at least one British writer to the problem of personal salvation. The theme of Mankind's perpetuation and survival is taken up on the other side of the Atlantic. The common expression of it in a number of stories has been best captured in *Starburst* by Alfred Bester, in which we have the fairly typical story of a space pilot who returns to his planet to find the race has died but, inadvertently, repeoples it by the bacterial decomposition of his own body – Adam, as it were, without an Eve.[37]

The immortality of parasitism and mind transference is also fairly common, but perhaps the most significant of the variations on the theme of immortality in American science fiction is that it is seen as a problem of tedium. Such immortals as there may be as a result of future advances in surgery and medicine are constantly plagued with the fear of boredom and the desperate search for physical, intellectual and emotional titillation.[38] It seems that the fear of boredom and a highly materialistic society go together. It is interesting to note in Russian science fiction that while any concept of immortality has to be pooh-poohed as wishful escapist thinking, again and again we come across the theme of longevity. While superficially the Russian writer may be content to look forward to the collective immortality of the human race in a glorious socialist millennium, in practice he seems to be substituting for the immortality of religion, length of years in this life. A commonplace of his utopias is the man or woman of 170 years, just as in the Soviet Union itself a remarkable amount of scientific research is devoted to solving the biological problems of ageing and death.

This obsession with longevity is one of the few fears that it is possible at first glance to identify in Russian science fiction. We need, of course, to take some note of what Russian writers do *not* write about. There is a notable absence, for example, of stories of oppression of the individual by the state. But even to those finely attuned to the subtle nuances of Russian newspeak, this type of literary Kremlinology can be riskily misleading. It is, however, perhaps inevitable that we should try to look for the obvious omissions when Russian authors are describing the problems and difficulties of imaginary futures. We have already noted that the apparent fear of war and the many references to 'dangerous experiments to create murderous atomic weapons' in Russian science fiction. Their protests are almost too strident. 'In the writings of those who sought to defend the old society, proclaiming the inevitability of war and the external existence of capitalism, I also see the heart of a poisonous snake.'[39]

The handicap to Russian SF of the first two post-war decades is that the writer is apparently afraid of nothing. There are no potentially victorious horrors, only a few obstacles on the road to the inevitable triumph of Soviet science, Soviet man and the communist society of the universe. There is seldom any doubt in the reader's mind about the outcome of the adventure, even on the rare occasions when he can be persuaded to care. This lack of uncertainty makes very dull reading, for, as Kingsley Amis pointed out in a BBC Radio interview with the author, the very essence of this type of writing is the capacity for surprise. If the outcome is in Marxist terms inevitable the surprise element is gone. The occasional nostalgic glance at the days before the millennium – the glance whose 'incorrectness' is always quickly pointed out – does little to dispel the dullness.

However, if we sub-edit these stories to remove the propaganda element, to ignore the admonitions of 'incorrect' thinking and to discard those little twists like hypnotism and dreams with which the unorthodox is made respectable, we can perhaps arrive at some indication of the real preoccupations of the Russian writer.

Take, for example, *The Maxwell Equation* by Anatoly Dneprov.[40] This story could not unfairly be interpreted to defy the purely materialist interpretation of life. It is a study of the physical techniques used in brainwashing and of the hero's ability to withstand those techniques. The story, incidentally, contains a number of good adventure touches, such as when the hero uses a hard graphite pencil as a resistance to alter the output of a machine stimulating mental reactions at various frequencies. The author can only explain his hero's inner source of strength in resisting the brainwashing by calling it 'this supreme psychic authority'. He goes on to say, 'I find your arguments revolting. There's a normal tempo in human life and it is criminal to try to accelerate it.' The story ends with a propaganda plug whose implication is that the inhuman methods described are employed by the West German Defence Ministry. Once that concluding paragraph has been excised it is not too fanciful to read into it a fearful censure of the methods employed in the Soviet Union itself and which have come only relatively recently to be criticised in public.

In so far as the Russian writer sees any necessity for salvation it seems to lie in collective effort, that very collective effort which the American writer struggles so hard to resist and avoid. It is rare to find a Western writer (the most notable exception is probably Howard Fast, himself a Marxist) trying seriously to examine the potential for good, as well as for evil, of collective thinking. The Russian writer, who appears to take team work and collective effort for granted, by the naming and selection of his principal characters – villains Germanic, heroes Slav – reveals perhaps that even in a collective consciousness some are more equal than others!

Salvation for the British writer lies in a different direction. There is the survival by reversion to feudalism of which John Christopher is the principal analyst.[41] Much of Christopher's talent lies in the ease with which he establishes the ordinary relationships, particularly between the sexes, of the conventional novel before slowly exposing his characters to natural disaster. Thus their survival becomes a matter of real importance to the reader – this is unusual in science fiction. Conventionally one launches straight into the idea which is the crux of the story. Among British writers, there seems to be a hankering for feudal society, perhaps because of its simplicity, which by-passes the complex technological problems which are not under our ordinary control as a declining – declined? – economic power.

The study by Christopher, Wyndham and other British writers of the survival group in a post-cataclysmic situation is a study in the fundamental nature of human society. These studies are not utopian, or even dystopian, so much as analytical and scientific. Some of these British survival stories are no more than just a stringing together of a succession of improvisations, but the great majority of them recount at various levels of seriousness and penetration this reversion to a feudal pattern of society. The argument seems to be, in British science fiction at least, that this would be the natural devolutionary process, the purged feudal society having by implication the potential to advance in due course to a higher level of civilisation than that from which it tumbled. The science fiction writer seems to be postulating the corollary of Dr Magnus Pyke's suggestion that 'It is of the nature of scientific technology to detribalise our society',[42] by saying that when technology and science are destroyed or rendered impotent society reverts to tribal or feudal form.

Christopher has a great knack of using sexual indignity, particularly rape in the presence of the male lover or husband, to bring home the full horror of the situations he creates. The stripping of *all* the illusions is the sort of uncompromising reality which shows how clearly Christopher has grasped the fundamentals of survival. In a parallel way Ballard is doing the same with his stripping of personal illusions to achieve spiritual survival. Christopher's final message generally carries a glimmer of hope of some kind of material survival while Ballard – although like many other British science fiction writers he is obsessed with survival after the cataclysm or during it, rather than concerned with averting it – becomes increasingly preoccupied with spiritual rather than physical survival.

In Ballard's *The Wind from Nowhere* winds of more than cyclonic force are rapidly destroying all life on the face of the earth. In this situation the hero and the group of people he is with encounter a madman who has been building a tower upwards against the ever rising wind.

I alone have built upward, have dared to challenge the wind, asserting man's courage and determination to master nature. If I

were to claim political power – which, most absolutely, I will not –
I would do so simply on the basis of my own moral superiority.
Only I, in the face of the greatest holocaust ever to strike the
earth, have had the moral courage to attempt to outstare nature.
That is my sole reason for building this tower. Here on the surface
of the globe I meet nature on her own terms, in the arena of her
choice. If I fail, man has no right to assert his innate superiority
over the unreason of the natural world.[43]

In due course it seems that Ballard comes to precisely the conclusion that Man does *not* have that right.

In *The Wind from Nowhere* the principal characters are eventually saved quite by chance, for the wind starts dropping after the
megolamaniac has himself been destroyed. But thereafter Ballard
uses no such easy let-outs. In *The Drowned World* first published in
the same year (1962),[44] the disastrous situation is that of the world
gradually heating up. Kerans, the principal character, after a certain
amount of indolence and indecision finds himself heading south into
the sun and still greater heat in a kind of self-immolation, or process
of emotional suttee, on what Ballard has chosen to call a neuronic
odyssey. In this story Ballard asked why there exists in Man this
compulsion to self-destruction – without fully providing an answer.
Kerans is clearly going to become no salamander nor is there much
sign of any form of spiritual salvation. However, by the time that
The Drought came to be published,[45] Ballard had progressed a great
deal further. Now he almost delights in disaster, this time from the
disappearance of water. Again there is a study of the identity of Man
with his environment and his capacity to identify even with a totally
changed environment, and again we have the steady spread of a
natural disaster. This time the 'S' idea behind the 'F' is that

> covering the offshore waters of the world's oceans, to a distance
> of about a thousand miles from the coast, is a thin but resilient
> mono-molecular film formed from a complex of saturated long-
> chain polymers, generated within the sea from the vast quantities
> of industrial waste discharged into the ocean basins during the
> previous fifty years.

At this stage in his development Ballard still feels, as he did in *The
Wind from Nowhere* and *The Drowned World* that he needs to
explain scientifically the changes which are the springboard for his

psychoanalytical novels. His repeated theme is that we need exceptional catastrophic events and changes in our environment to bring
us face to face with the reality which has been obscured by the
preoccupations of so-called civilised life. It is a secular version of the
scriptural injunction to lose your life in order to save it. His
subconscious theme seems to be that of survival by adaptation
rather than by resistance and this, I think, is the central obsession of
the British SF writer (I must confess that my own first SF novel was
called *The Survivors*[46]), the paradox of the challenge of joyfully
accepting the inevitable in order to change both it and ourselves

> 'You know, I sometimes think we ought to accept the challenge
> and set off north, right into the centre of the drought.'
>   In time, the sand drifting across the dunes would reunite them
> on its own terms but for the present each of them formed a
> self-contained and discrete world of his own.
>   On the beach, time was not absent but immobilised, what was
> new in their lives and relationships they could form only from the
> residues of the past, from the failures and omissions that persisted
> into the present like the wreckage and scrap metal from which
> they built their cabins.

But even at the end of *The Drought* it starts to rain. Not until *The
Crystal World*[47] and *The Disaster Area*[48] does Ballard reach his
final, uncompromising solution where he seems to suggest that
conscious self-destruction, or at least a willingness to allow the self
to be destroyed and absorbed by the outside forces operating on it,
is almost the only true form of survival. We shall look in chapter 10
at how he further developed this nihilist approach in his later work.
    The way in which British writers concentrate on the survival of
the individual or the small group through or after a disaster suggests
surely an underlying recognition, at whatever level of consciousness, that Britain is no longer in a position to determine whether or
not such disasters shall take place, or whether or not Britain shall
survive as a recognisable entity. Long before the politicians were
prepared to admit it, the science fiction writers had recognised that
Britain had become a third-class power. No such humility is to be
found in the forms of salvation suggested by the American science
fiction writer. Here while it is often the odd-ball and the drop-out,
the eccentric individualist, who is the saviour figure and bringer of
salvation, it is salvation not for a group of survivors but for society at

large. And salvation is quite as comprehensive and material a thing as it is seen to be in Russian science fiction although it tends to be little more than survival of some outward threat of annihilation.

The path to salvation for the American science fiction writer weaves uncertainly between freedom and Fascism. Whereas to the British science fiction writer survival has been achieved through the deviant group – telepaths as in *The Chrysalids* or in John Brunner's *Telepathist*[49] or some other form of mutant – in American science fiction it is the non-conforming individual who is the saviour figure. Indeed, the hero is frequently a social misfit or at least someone indulging at some critical moment in the story in normally socially unacceptable behaviour. Eric Frank Russell (although British by birth, in most respects classifiable as an American science fiction writer) is one of the principal exponents of this theme, as for example in *Dreadful Sanctuary*.[50]

That most American of writers, Clifford Simak, whose heroes possess all the small-town virtues and limitations of the Mid-West, harps on the theme that only the man who values and will fight to preserve his own individuality, however eccentric, will have this stubborn courage and self-confidence necessary to resist the subjugation of the race. The heroes of 'Idiot's Crusade', 'The Big Front Yard' and *All Flesh Is Grass*, for example, are all abnormal, even subnormal, misfits with supranormal powers.[51] Again Frederik Pohl in *Drunkard's Walk*[52] looks at the theme of the taking-over of our free will by outside hostile forces overcome in due course by the intervention of a hero who was drunk at the time of the takeover. In *The Sleeping Planet*[53] by William Birkett, narcotic dust is unleashed by alien spaceships and only ten people – all odd men out in the sense that they are cripples of various kinds and are therefore, largely fortuitously, immune – are not affected and are thus able to save the planet.

This role of the independent individual is frequently set out as the antithesis of the collective if benevolent force of an alien power trying to impose peaceful conformity on mankind in a way which Arthur Clarke ultimately found acceptable in *Childhood's End* but which to the American is anathema. The American writer would rather endorse Clarke's interim attitude. 'They were not the future, he realised with sharp clarity. No super potent force was the future; a kennelman could breed dogs only to his own specifications, he could not give the species the chance of free growth that could go on and on.'[54] The American fear of compulsory conformity in what is apparently such a diverse and supposedly free society is the hall-mark of its SF. One might expect to see signs of this anxiety within the strait-jacket of the Russian social and political structure, but not, surely, in America. Yet this is a justifiable fear in that it is a clear recognition by the American science fiction writer that economic, social and cultural forces, such as are at work within the United States today, are quite as debilitating and conducive to conformity as the political pressures applied in the Soviet Union. The practical reaction to these forces of the consumers, conservationists and even drop-outs in recent times may in fact be partially due to the anticipation of the need to react by America's SF writers.

But it is precisely this emphasis on the critical role of the independent individual that has made some American science fiction the home of right-wing political philosophy and satire, and it is arguable that much of this kind of writing is essentially a *Herrenvolk* or Fascist literature. This philosophy is certainy reflected in many of the stories of Kornbluth. His thesis, set out in *The Little Black Bag*,[55] is that we are gradually breeding ourselves into idiocy and that this fact is disguised by the increasing sophistication of our technology, putting devices at the disposal of morons which make them appear to be more intelligent and capable than their less technically-equipped predecessors. The mutant, the non-conformist, becomes less valuable in the evolutionary process the more he conforms to the acceptable conventional patterns of his day. B. F. Skinner has expressed the dilemma in *Walden Two*: 'the option for the few not to conform depends on a multitude of conformists'.[56] Or again in the *Thin Edge* by Jonathan Blake Mackenzie: 'they were better beliefs than the obviously stupid belief that every human being had as much right to respect and dignity as every other, that a man had a right to be respected, that he deserved it. Out there they thought that a man had a right only to what he earned.'[57]

Robert Heinlein is another usually sensitive writer who is occasionally sympathetic to the superman approach. For example, in *Revolt in 2100* he studies élitism through genetic selection.[58] This is a repeated SF theme but like the pragmatist he is Heinlein tests it out by seeing whether the creations can survive or not. His theme, related to that of the odd-man-out saviour theme of other SF stories, is that generally the scientifically-reached conclusion is not the one that leads to survival. Survival is generally dependent on some blind chance characteristic of the hero. But this casual vision of some future racial superiority may be one of the dangers of SF in the Western sense. Whereas Marxist science fiction almost inevitably has to assume that man in his present form is virtually perfect and that the working out of historical inevitability and economic forces will lead to the eventual perfect society, so the Western writer, while wishing to defend as satisfactory the main concepts of contemporary society as he sees them, yet has to do his engineering, biologically and organically, on the human beings themselves. This conflicts sharply with the antipathy for that type of manipulation which is at the same time shown to be a very Western fear. In *Revolt in 2100* Heinlein gives the arguments of the genetic engineers a very good run indeed and criticises their wilder opponents: 'Romantic writers of the first days of genetics dreamed of many fantastic possibilities – test-tube babies, monsters formed by artificial mutation, fatherless babies, babies assembled piece by bit from a hundred different parents. . . .' To be fair, however nicely balanced the pros and cons are, the scales generally come down on the side of the individual who while engineering the salvation of his society still rejects the idea that either he or his fellows may be supermen. But the anxiety is clearly there. Can American society preserve the freedom to which it continually pays lip-service without lapsing on the one hand into chaos or on the other into meritocratic injustice? Indeed, just what kind of society does the science fiction of these three countries suggest that they will find desirable?

Notes

1. John Christopher, *The Death of Grass* (first pub. 1956; Penguin, 1970). Thirteen years later in *Weed Science*, xvii 1 (20 Feb 1969) 113, Professor Holms, in his list of the world's worst weeds, lists eight grasses which occur in virtually every known agriculture area in the world.

2. John Wyndham, *The Kraken Awakes* (first pub. Joseph, 1953);
The Day of the Triffids (first pub. 1951; Penguin, 1970);
The Midwich Cuckoos (first pub. Joseph 1957);
The Chrysalids (first pub. 1955; Penguin, 1969).

3. John Wyndham, *Chocky* (first pub. 1968; Penguin, 1972). The Christopher/Wyndham tradition has many other British adherents. John Blackburn, *Scent of New Mown Hay* (first pub. 1958; New English Library, 1968), George R. Stewart, *Earth Abides* (Corgi, 1956) and John Lymington, *The Screaming Face* (Corgi, 1965) are but three of the more skilful examples.

4. Arthur Clarke, *Childhood's End* (first pub. 1954; Pan, 1956).

5. H. G. Wells, *The Time Machine* (London: 1895).

6. Arthur Clarke, Speech on receiving the 1963 Kalinga prize in Ceylon (27 Sept 1962). Clarke thus sides with Blish rather than Stableford (intro. n.18).

7. Raymond Jones, 'Noise Level', *Best SF* 5 (first pub. 1952; Faber 1963).

8. George Orwell, *1984* (first pub. 1949; Penguin, 1969).

9. David Karp, *One* (Gollancz, 1967).

10. For a good British example, see L. P. Davies, *Twilight Journey* (SF Book Club and Herbert Jenkins, 1968), a study of brainwashing by the implanting of electrodes.

11. Robert Young, 'A Little Red Schoolhouse', in *The Worlds of Robert F. Young* (first pub. 1956; Panther, 1968).

12. Wyman Guin, *Beyond Bedlam* (Galaxy, 1951).

13. Frank Herbert, *Hellstrom's Hive* (New English Library, 1974).

14. Frank Herbert, *The Santaroga Barrier* (New English Library, 1972).

15. Frederik Pohl and C. M. Kornbluth, *The Space Merchants* (first pub. 1953; Penguin, 1965).

16. Robert Heinlein, *Methusala's Children* (Pan, 1966), published in shortened version in 1941.

17. Theodore Sturgeon, 'The World Well Lost', in *A Pluribus Unicorn*, (first pub. 1953; Panther, 1961).

18. William Tenn, *Null-P*, in Worlds Beyond (1951).

19. Isaac Asimov, 'Franchise', in *Earth is Room Enough* (first pub. 1957; Panther, 1967).

20. Isaac Asimov, *The Stars Like Dust* (Panther, 1958).

21. Frank Herbert, 'The Tactful Saboteur', in *Seven Trips Through Time and Space* (Coronet, 1969). A theme he continues in *Whipping Star* (first pub. 1970; New English Library 1972) and *The Dosadi Experiment* (Putnam, 1977).

22. Frederik Pohl and C. M. Kornbluth, *Gladiator at Law* (first pub. 1955; Pan, 1966).

23. Frederik Pohl, *The Midas Plague* (Galaxy, 1951).

24. Frederik Pohl, *The Man Who Ate the World* (first pub. 1959 in *Science Fiction Showcase*; Mayflower, 1968).

25. E.g. Thomas M. Disch, 'The Affluence of Edwin Lollard' in *New Writings in SF 10* (Corgi, 1967).

26. Kurt Vonnegut, *Cat's Cradle* (first pub. 1963; Penguin, 1965). *Player Piano* (first pub. 1952; Panther, 1969).

27. Alfred Bester, *The Demolished Man* (first pub. 1953; Penguin, 1966).

28. Alfred Bester, *Tiger, Tiger* (first pub. 1955; Penguin, 1967).

29. Isaac Asimov, 'The Dead Past', in *Earth is Room Enough* (first pub. 1956; Panther, 1967).

30. Harry Harrison, *Make Room, Make Room* (Penguin, 1967).

31. For a dramatic British treatment of this theme, see J. G. Ballard, 'Billenium', in *The Terminal Beach* (Penguin, 1966).

32. Keith Roberts, 'Therapy 2000', in *New Writings in SF 15* (Corgi, 1969).

33. Walter Miller, *Conditionally Human* (Panther, 1966).

34. Robert Thom, *Wild in the Streets* (Sphere, 1968).

35. John Christopher, *Pendulum* (Hodder, 1969).

36. Robert Heinlein, *Revolt in 2100* (first pub. 1939; Digit, 1953).

37. Alfred Bester, *Starburst* (first pub. 1958; Sphere, 1968).

38. William Spencer, 'The Horizontal Man', in *New Writings in SF 6* (Corgi, 1966); or Gerald W. Page, 'Spacemen Live Forever', in *New Writings in SF 8* (Corgi, 1966); Thomas Disch, 'Now is for Ever', in *Under Compulsion* (Panther, 1970); Joseph Green, *The Loafers of Refuge* (Pan, 1967) or Michael Moorcock's trilogy, *Dancers at the End of Time* (Avon, 1977).

39. Ivan Yefremov, 'The Heart of the Serpent', in *Yunost* (Btk 367, 1959).

40. Anatoly Dneprov, *The Maxwell Equation* (first pub. 1960; Btk 348).

41. John Christopher, *The Death of Grass* (first pub. 1956; Penguin, 1970) or *A Wrinkle in the Skin* (first pub. 1965; Hodder, 1968).

42. *New Scientist* (29 May 1969).

43. J. G. Ballard, *The Wind from Nowhere* (first pub. 1962; Penguin, 1967).

44. J. G. Ballard, *The Drowned World* (first pub. 1962; Penguin, 1965).

45. J. G. Ballard, *The Drought* (first pub. 1965; Penguin, 1968).

46. J. C. Griffiths, *The Survivors* (Collins, 1964).

47. J. G. Ballard, *The Crystal World* (first pub. 1966; Panther, 1968).

48. J. G. Ballard, *The Disaster Area* (first pub. 1967; Panther 1969).

49. John Brunner, *Telepathist* (Penguin, 1968).

50. Eric Frank Russell, *Dreadful Sanctuary* (first pub. 1953; Four Square, 1967).

51. Clifford Simak, 'Idiot's Crusade', *Galaxy* (April 1954); 'The Big Front Yard' in *The Hugo Winners* (Penguin, 1964); *All Flesh is Grass* (New York: Doubleday, 1965).

52. Frederik Pohl, *Drunkard's Walk* (first pub. 1960; Penguin, 1966).

53. William Birkett, *The Sleeping Planet* (New York: Doubleday, 1965).

54. Clarke, *Childhood's End* (Pan, 1965).

55. C. M. Kornbluth, *The Little Black Bag* (Astounding, July 1950).

56. B. F. Skinner, *Walden Two* (1948).

57. Jonathan Blake Mackenzie, 'Thin Edge', in *Analog 3* (first pub. 1963; Panther, 1968).

58. Robert Heinlein, *Revolt in 2100*, see Ch. 1, n. 1, above.

5

Utopia and dystopia[1]

Utopias were the creation of an age of arbitrary authority and frequent, albeit creative, disorder, in which the security and prosperity of the majority could be imperilled at any moment by the wilful behaviour of a determined and powerful individual or minority. These were the wishful systems devised, by men of goodwill, for the constraint of the turbulent individual by means of institutions and laws. Their objective was order, their by-products were general prosperity and peace, and their foundation was a strict hierarchy in which each person not only knew and kept his proper station but enjoyed it. They were written from the point of view at the top of the ladder by men who expected, probably quite rightly, that that is where they would find themselves should their ideas – their good place 'nowhere' as Sir Thomas More's word may be translated – ever be realised in practice. No one in the West writes of classical utopias today.

Dystopia, in the sense of a bad place anywhere, is by contrast the obsession, at one time or another, of the great majority of Western science fiction writers. The optimistic hope of order has been replaced by the pessimistic dread of conformity, the fear of the disruptive minority by that of the acquiescent majority. As Berdiaeff observed, 'Utopias are realisable . . . and towards Utopias we are moving. But it is possible that a new age is already beginning in which cultured and intelligent people will dream of ways to avoid ideal states and to get back to a society that is less "perfect" and more free.'[2] Thus it is not entirely surprising that paranoid dictators have based their tyrannies on their own Utopian concepts and the ruthless suppression of any Utopian ideal in conflict with them. Norman Cohn[3] has equated such Nazi and Marxist–Leninist fantasy (pseudo-scientific) with the millennial fantasies (pseudo-religious) of the Middle Ages – both leading theoretically to a utopian state after violent conflict with 'evil' as defined by the paranoid Messianic figure and unthinkingly embraced by his enthusiast followers. The horrifying wholesale acts of inhumanity of totalitarian regimes in their tragic absurdity

> are not the product of ordinary human fallibility or ignorance, but of a chronically impaired sense of reality. Such monstrous pogroms and persecutions are illustrations in fact of the compelling nature of that type of vision, at once rigorously self-consistent and fatally distorting, which is so characteristic of paranoia.

Karl Mannheim tackled the same theme in the early 1930s under the terrible shadow of just such a lunatic development. Not surprisingly, he was more concerned as a sociologist with the collective response to such possibilities than with the individual embodiment of them – the individual was for him after all but the manifestation of the collective impulse. 'In the Utopian mentality, the collective unconscious, guided by wishful representation and the will to action, hides certain aspects of reality. It turns its back on everything which would shake its belief or paralyse its desire to change things.' He defined that mentality most succinctly: 'A state of mind is Utopian when it is incongruous with the state of reality within which it occurs.' In the Russia of Stalin no state of mind was permitted that was incongruous with the Dictator's idea of reality so no utopias were allowed to be postulated by SF writers during his rule. Only after the thaw in 1959 could Yefremov utopianise, albeit very cautiously, against a background of recognition that reality might not be perfect. Lamartine's rather more optimistic description was to call utopias 'premature truths' and Mannheim does not deny this more hopeful interpretation of utopianism.

> Wishful thinking has always figured in human affairs. When the imagination finds no satisfaction in existing reality, it seeks refuge in wishfully constructed places and periods. Myths, fairy tales, other-worldly promises of religion, humanistic fantasies, travel romances, have been continually changing expressions of that which was lacking in actual life. They were more nearly complementary colours in the picture of the reality existing at the time than utopias working in opposition to the status quo and disintegrating it.

Outstanding research in cultural history has shown that the forms of human yearnings can be stated in terms of general principles, and that in certain historical periods wish-fulfilment takes place through projection into time while, in others, it proceeds through projection into space. In accord with this differentiation, it would be possible to call spatial wishes utopias, and temporal wishes chiliasms.

Mannheim's definition of the distinction between ideology and utopia remains, after forty years, the seminal work in this field of study.[4] Utopias then may, by inference, indicate the unrealistic hopes of the societies whose writers produce them, but utopias are now scarcely ever written of by Western writers – that particular form of unreality seems to have taken up a permanent home in the manifestos of the political parties. Yet dystopias abound. Can we, by the same process of inference, conclude that the fears they express are equally unrealistic? Or are they in fact a defiantly nihilistic form of realism? Do the utopian and dystopian versions of our three groups of writers coincide?

The Soviet writer had no misgivings until the late 1960s and prior to that he did indeed attempt to describe the utopian ideal which ought to be the logical outcome of his Marxism. But what is the nature of the future society he sees? Let me construct such a utopia from the works of various Russian authors, and in particular from two novels[5] by one of their best known SF writers, Ivan Yefremov:

Seventy eight light years separated them from the good and beautiful earth which mankind had made a haven of happy life, of inspired creative labour. In the classless society which Man had created for himself the laws of development must not be violated. Single-handed responsibility had long since been abandoned, decisions were taken collectively. We plot the vector of friendship as though that, and even love, were scientific relationships. The dream of some Western utopias of liberation from the necessity to work is rejected. The only alternative to technological perfection is the perfection of Man himself and that is only achieved by common labour. Knowledge and creative labour have freed earth from hunger, over-population, disease, and so on. Children are, of course, brought up separately from their parents for one of mankind's greatest victories is the conquest of the blind instinct of maternity, the realisation that only the collective upbringing of children by people trained and selected for the job can produce a man of our society. One step forward and nine-tenths backward – backward while the next shift in the relay is learning.

At one end of the Russian spectrum we have people aged 170 looking forward to being 300, with longevity the substitute for immortality, and at the other a child whose favourite occupation is the grinding of optical lenses and a man who is thought virtuous because he is a tireless fossil hunter. We have a census to compute sorrow and happiness which are 'investigated' by agents. Destroyer battalions ruthlessly deal with sharks, bacteria, poisonous reptiles and any individuals who do not conform. You are described as a bull if you enter into conspiracies and organise rebellions, but your main fault would be ignoring the inviolable laws of economics.

The struggle against the personal, against the I that is man's most dangerous enemy, is essential for the good of society and for the maximum expansion of his own intellect. Only people of the distant past could speak in that way about immortal fame. They did not know the joy and fullness of real life, they did not feel they were particles of mankind engaged in collective creative activity, they were afraid of inevitable death and clung to the faintest hope of immortality.

The worst feature of these utopias is the banality and astonishing bad taste of their leisure activities: 'The flat surface of the island, level with the water, was surrounded by rows of shells in mother of pearl plastic big enough to squeeze in three or four people from the sun and wind and isolate them from their neighbours.' How they hanker for the most vulgar manifestations of capitalist society!

But to be fair to the Russian science fiction writer his utopian stories do also contain a great number of pertinent and just criticisms of the more corrupting aspects of Western life and an occasional nostalgic glance to the painful freedoms of pre-millennial times:

For the first time in his life he realised that the people of ancient times whose life seemed so hard to his contemporaries had also known the meaning of happiness, hope and creative activity, at times, perhaps, even to a greater extent than was the case in the Great Circle Era.

Or again:

> I had thought that the mysterious and unfathomed existed only in
> the cosmos – that it didn't apply to earth any more. It certainly
> doesn't to people – there's nothing enigmatic or unpredictable
> about us. Do you regret it? Sometimes I should like to meet
> someone like the people who lived in the distant past. Someone
> who has to hide his dreams and his feelings from a hostile
> environment, to steel his resolve in secret and to build up his will
> till nothing can shake it.

But in the end, in deference to orthodoxy, every Russian science
fiction writer of utopias has to admit 'science is a struggle for the
happiness of Man and it demands its victims in the same way as any
other struggle'.

The utopia depicted above would conform very closely to a
definition of hell for most citizens of the Western world. But equally
the hells of their own depicting come in for some justifiable criticism
from Russian commentators.

> The most striking feature of the prophecies of the American and
> English fantasy writers is that they are not based on any concept
> of the progressive development of society, but involve regression,
> decline, degeneracy, backwardness and the destruction of man-
> kind. Modern Western science fiction writes of an anti-Utopia,
> and it is significant that bourgeois critics and writers themselves
> use this term in speaking of social science fiction. . . . The charac-
> teristic aspect of contemporary science fiction by Anglo-
> American bourgeois writers is the projection into the future of
> present state relations, social problems, and events and conflicts
> inherent in modern capitalism. These writers transfer imperialist
> contradictions to imaginary space worlds, supposing they will be
> dominated by the old master–servant relations, by colonialism,
> and by the wolfish laws of plunder and profit.[6]

What the Russian critics are legitimately saying, I think, is that
the Western science fiction writer is adept at extrapolating his fears
into the future but seems to have lost the capacity to do the same for
his hopes, or to imagine completely new social situations. In the
work of the Strugatskys, which we shall study in detail in chapter 9,
and to a lesser extent in that of other Russians writing in the late

1960s, we shall see that they are willing to dissent from these conventional visions. This dissent is expressed not only by making fun of boring orthodoxy – in *Snail on the Slope*⁷ there is a glorious send-up of Yefremovian pleasures – but in the creation of non-specific dystopias, dystopias which are more than just polemical attacks on the capitalist ethos. What the great majority of writers on both sides of the Iron Curtain seem to have failed to take account of is that the environmental changes which they envisage are likely to affect the attitudes and behaviour of the individuals within those new postulated environments. That is to say that it is not logical within the terms and the definition of science fiction we have adopted to translate your fictional society far into the future without, at the same time, translating your characters' state of mind from the present day to that same hypothetical future. It is probably a realisation of this difficulty that prompts so many Western science fiction writers of dystopias to locate their hells around the turn of our present century. For its analysis of this contradiction and a critique of both utopian and dystopian science fiction writing a letter to *The Guardian*, from Philip O'Connor, is worth fairly extensive quotation:

Utopias are concerned with individuals, and science fiction with amenities.

The improvements of the latter do not necessarily apply to the former; however, there is a connection which, to the best of my knowledge, escapes almost all writers of science fiction (a notable exception is John Wyndham): the connection which is absent is between people and amenities. Even at the most elementary level of conception a more technically advanced environment will change individuals.

But that is not the chief fault to be detected in science fiction. What is grotesquely missing is any conception of a change that is absolutely inevitable if we are to survive, let alone 'improve' – and that is the whole field of social relations – the economic system.

Can we really imagine a world endlessly littered with the mental horrors of advertising, of the catastrophic unpredictability of 'the market', of the antiquated ethics which sees life as an *internecine* struggle for survival, with ethical progress as a kind of impossible obstacle race through it? If we can, we write our obituaries.

Neither side of the 'curtain' seems to have speculated much upon the enormous changes in the individual co-operation must bring about. They certainly will be more radical than the early Communist picture of 'comradeship', which defines the adventurous overcoming of competitive individualism. What will change, in ways difficult as yet to imagine, is the very 'feel' and character of the self. The contemporary 'I' is as much a product of our social system as cars are of factories.

What the self will be like when it ceased to resemble a tank trundling down a High Street cannot be conjectured here. It will certainly not be the complex of compensations we know today; having no need to 'sell' its talents, it will the more be identified with them, to their enhancement.

Why have Utopias ceased to be written?

The true cause of the death of Utopias was the anti-Communist campaign initiated 49 years ago.

Until then it had been the dream of all men, and one sustained by Christianity, to live at peace, co-operatively. Communism was the self-acclaimed scientific application of this dream; the reality – especially the 'reality' filtered through a hostile press – made us throw out the baby with the bathwater.

What we truly need is Utopian science fiction which includes the fascinating changes from competitive to co-operative individualism and depicts them materially equipped for the civilisation of which they constitute the basis.[8]

To see why it has proved impossible to write the kind of utopias O'Connor would like we would have to backtrack a little. While a number of commentators have claimed that E. M. Forster's *The Machine Stops*[9] was the first dystopia, he undoubtedly has a number of forerunners. Indeed, the story we have accepted as the first to meet our own science fiction definition, Part III of *Gulliver's Travels*, is itself part of a quartet of just such dystopias. Then, depending on how one interprets Butler's intentions, *Erewhon* is to the modern reader certainly dystopian in outlook. One is, I think, doing Butler an injustice if one does not believe that he clearly recognised that the social and scientific means by which Man was increasingly bringing the society of his day under his control carried in themselves the seeds of almost unlimited misery. But both Swift and Butler were isolated individuals whose almost excessive prescience had made them pessimists. Despite the failure of the French

Revolution and a century later of the Paris Commune it was not until the early decades of the twentieth century, when we were able to see on the one hand the horrors of applied utopianism in the Soviet Union and on the other the failure of almost unimaginable advances in science to ameliorate the lot of Man, that the flood of dystopias was unloosed and the optimists shamed into silence. Credit for the first modern dystopia should perhaps most properly be given to the writer who found himself in the very midst of one of those processes of disillusion. Zamyatin welcomed the Revolution in Russia when it came but found himself by 1922 writing in *We* a savage attack on the consequences of that revolution.[10] Where Forster later made fun of the pompous imaginings of H. G. Wells, Zamyatin was clearly putting into fictional form criticisms of a reality which he had experienced at first hand. From here on the dystopias divide into two branches: those of unalloyed pessimism, going on through Huxley to Orwell and Karp, in which the valiant efforts of the hero to behave in an individualistic and human fashion are crushed or thwarted, and those in which the hero succeeds in thwarting in turn the attempts of aliens or dictatorial humans to impose their conformity on mankind. In both we deal mainly in terms of disaster endured or averted, but seldom in terms of some better alternative, or even of hope that such an alternative might exist.

Dystopias, and in particular the many American manifestations of them, reveal two quite distinct major fears: naturally, fear of what it would be like to live in such a society, but also fear of the means by which such a society might be brought about.

This second category raises again in different guise the whole argument of determinism. Are the processes of social or genetic engineering – the two most popular forms of obtaining dystopia – once started, irreversible by any process of human will? Can Huxley's or Miller's heroes, by tampering with the chemical 'system', restore the divine perversity of individualist Man? Can the heroes of Pohl or Karp by rebelling against the social machine force it to change, or at least to change gear? The answer in such stories is nearly always a tentative 'Yes', but it is noticeable that the heroic action is no more than preventative or ameliorative, it is no longer the age-old moral choice of the Garden of Eden but only of thwarting the devil we do know in the none too certain hope that the one we don't will be better. In the long Russian tradition of stoic pessimism it is largely left to Soviet authors, and in particular to the

Strugatskys, to suggest that even certain knowledge that such efforts are doomed to failure does not absolve us from the responsibility of resisting if an inner moral imperative tells us to do so.

Utopia, in so far as it is ever imagined at all in Western SF as opposed to the elfin utopias of fantasy, also falls into one of two categories. In one, utopia is imposed by outside alien forces, animate (as in the case of *Childhood's End*[11]) or inanimate (as in Wells's *In The Days of the Comet*[12]) and leads to a 'higher' form of life and a society no longer recognisable as human. 'Never again as far ahead as imagination could roam, would the human race be divided against itself,' writes Clarke, and both he and Wells reveal an unconscious recognition that the elimination of intra-human conflict creates a need for external alien aggression as the sole alternative to stagnation. In the other category writers escape into the past, a past usually medieval, mystico-religious – but Islamic rather than Christian – and full of trials of individual qualities of courage, wisdom, and so on. In this category come such voluminous romances as *Dune*,[13] effective short novels like Budrys's *The Iron Thorn*,[14] or such highly imaginative exercises as *Canticle for Liebowitz*,[15] Miller's renowned study of the Roman Church of the future. These desert societies – such stories are nearly always set in a desert – not only foster the primitive virtues but are primitive in scale, the monsters and the tribulations may be gigantic, but the men who combat them are always few, known to each other in love or hatred, but known and numerable.

It has taken a woman writer, Ursula LeGuin,[16] to create quasi-utopias, deliberately less than perfect, mystical, even slightly medieval in flavour, yet coherent in their logic and completely believable in their characterisation. LeGuin is an optimist who believes that reason and feeling, the classical and the romantic, can be brought into balance, or at least that it is still worth trying. That the great bulk of her work should have been written at a time when most other writers were retreating to nihilistic pessimism is further indication of the individuality of her talent.

The attitude of those Western SF writers who arrive at dystopia by way of social engineering is often ambivalent. The argument put forward by a number of them, for example Skinner in *Walden Two*,[17] in which the techniques of behavioural engineering form the foundation of a utopian community, is that since human behaviour is governed by various outside environmental factors it would be as well to ensure that the behaviour is – in the writer's opinion – 'desirable' by shaping those factors quite deliberately. Or as

Vonnegut has rather more colourfully put it: 'There is no reason why good cannot triumph as often as evil. The triumph of anything is a matter of organisation. If there are such things as angels, I hope that they are organised along the lines of the Mafia.'[18] Wells had argued much earlier 'that the creation of utopias – and their exhaustive criticism – is the proper and distinctive method of sociology'.[19]

With some justification, the great majority of Western SF writers share the fear, expressed forty years ago by Stapledon, that the sociologist's dream may prove to be everyone else's nightmare. These sociologists envisage 'progress towards some kind of utopia, in which beings like themselves live in unmitigated bliss amongst circumstances perfectly suited to a *fixed* [my italics] human nature'.[20] This school of writers does not dispute the power of the forces concerned, only the likelihood that man will put such forces to any good use. I would find this depressing were it not for that other school of salvationists who seem confident of the capacity of the human spirit to survive any form of conditioning. They may well be encouraged in their view by the confident end-product of social engineering predicted by Soviet writers, and recoil from what their Russian counterparts, superficially at least, appear to welcome.

A number of the Western writers of the social engineering school are, in fact, indulging in a great degree of wishful thinking. 'It was something that the scientists of earth, no doubt, could use to make possible the engineering of the social sciences as logically and as efficiently as the common brand of math had been used to build the gadgets of the earth.'[21] This seems to be an obsessive American fear, not a Soviet one; yet, presumably, in the Soviet Union it may be taken for granted that social engineering will become an exact science. Or again:

> Martian civilisation had developed in a quite different direction from that of Earth. It had developed no important knowledge of the physical sciences, no technology. But it had developed social sciences to the point where there had not been a single crime, let alone a war, on Mars for 50,000 years.[22]

This, of course is SF at its most escapist. This piece of wishful thinking, with its implied blame for our misfortunes on the physical sciences and technology, is a fairly common theme, as is the hankering for sociology and psychology to become exact sciences – a hankering doubtless shared by the sociologists and psychologists themselves.

A fairly typical piece of such wishful thinking occurs repeatedly with regard to the easy assimilation of knowledge. This is usually brought about either by injection or by the use of tape recordings under hypnosis and other subliminal techniques – all of which have been experimented with in practice. The more exacting writers, such as Asimov in 'Profession',[23] criticise this type of approach to the uses and applications of science. The chief character, in a world where callings have to be very strictly adhered to and training is by the tape method, says, 'tapes are actually bad. They teach too much; they're too painless. A man who learns that way doesn't know how to learn any other way. He's frozen into whatever position he's been taped.' In other words, he does not learn how to learn.

It is possible that Asimov in his *Foundation* trilogy[24] has written an almost utopian story which might find favour with the orthodox communist, although that is certainly not its intent. I am not sure to what extent this trilogy is in fact science fiction. It is true that many of the situations are brought about on the basis of certain technical and scientific assumptions of an original nature. But they are in many ways incidental to the story which is an analogous study of the growth, weakness, fall and reconstruction of an empire which might just as well have been an earthly empire as a galactic one. The third volume is very much concerned with that major American SF theme, the role of the odd man out, in this case the 'Mule', in either preserving or threatening the integrity of society. It is interesting to speculate how closely the vision of the future described in Asimov's trilogy would be acceptable to a communist world. There are certainly parallels to be found between 'the plan' and the science of psychohistory in Asimov's Empire, and Marxist theories on the role of socio-economic forces. However, the theme of the work is given in the third volume when the First Speaker says, 'It is the first lesson you must unlearn. The Seldon plan is neither complete nor correct. Instead, it is merely the best that could be done at the time.'[25] This would presumably be too much for the communist reader to stomach.

The same pattern of fear of the abuse of a technology is evident amongst the genetic engineering school of Western science fiction. The possibility of genetic manipulation to achieve behavioural characteristics has been inescapably demonstrated by contemporary science and while some writers may react by total rejection, as in Frank Herbert's *The Eyes of Heisenberg*,[26] an almost unintelligibly scientific story whose theme is 'nature doesn't like being meddled with', the question which concerns the great majority of writers is what characteristics shall we choose to produce? The Western fear is that dictatorially-inclined men will create through genetic interference a race of obedient slaves; the Russian writer assumes that obedience to the collective and naturally Marxist–Leninist will is not only inevitable and desirable but pleasurable. Only in a writer like Fast, a Western Marxist, or Wyndham and others of the British school, do we see any attempt to reconcile these two views; to suggest the pleasure that the individual may derive by identifying with, or even by being part of, the collective will whilst retaining perhaps some individual characteristics. In a story such as *Babel 17*,[27] in which very different beings are called upon to furnish different attributes of a spacecraft, we see that the distinctiveness is what is essential to the effectiveness of the collective mind. But on the whole the western world, which until recently has largely rejected the mystical, religious concept of beatitude in absorption into a higher being, also rejects any such surrender of personal identity to political or social entities. This is shown in a number of repeated utopian themes, race, legitimised murder, the urban–rural antithesis and its sub-divisions, the hostile animate city, the conflict between man and motorcar, games-playing and, above all, art.

Future utopias and dystopias alike are almost invariably dominated by people of Caucasian stock. Although the occasional Negro or Indian may be given a role it is seldom the major role in the story and even where in Clarke's *Childhood's End* South Africa is ruled by the blacks, it is clearly an exceptional part of the world. As one might expect, American SF reflects the obsession with race in the United States. SF, moreover, provides a convenient way in which contemporary racial matters can be discussed and commented on without raising too much emotional heat. The technique of trans-position to relationships between alien beings and mankind in general is most commonly used. But even with this proviso few authors face up to the realities of the situation as honestly as Asimov. He recognises, for example, in *Pebble in the Sky*[28] that racial prejudice may be such a deep-rooted emotion that only the strictest and most disciplined exercise of the control of reason can keep it from expressing itself. This is probably the best we can hope for, eradication being beyond the bounds of human nature. The principal alien character says,

> I lived my life in an atmosphere of anti-terrestrialism in the formative years, so I can't help what flaws and follies lie at the

roots of my subconscious. And look on the surface and tell me if, in my adult years, I have not fought bigotry in myself. Not in others; that would be easy. But in myself, and as hard as I could.

Again, in the *Currents of Space*, both a thriller and a piece of speculative sociology, he spotlights the role of the Uncle Toms.

Those who worked directly for the squires were only too glad to identify themselves with the rulers and make up for their real inferiority by a tighter adherence to the rules of segregation, a harsh and haughty attitude toward their fellows. They were the 'other men' for whom the other Fleurinians reserved their particular hate, unalloyed by the carefully taught awe they felt for the squire.[29]

Heinlein, a writer of such versatility that one is able within a few pages to suspect him of the most rabid right-wing élitism and of fervent socialism, tackles this theme among a number of other sacred cows in *Farnham's Freehold*.[30] This has an ironic inversion of the conventional catastrophe pattern – the gateway to this utopian escapism is a nuclear cataclysm. Only, as so often with Heinlein, utopia is not arrived at without a great deal of pain and struggle and in particular of self-examination by the characters as their roles within the group are readjusted. For example, the Negro servant – a conventional SF cliché this – emerges as one of the top people in the new community. Soon, however, utopia becomes dystopia.

Heinlein clearly believes, like most American SF writers, that conflict, even suffering, is essential for human progress. But writing for an American audience he seems to feel unable to take his black inversion theory to its logical conclusion and leave that as the outcome. The white *status quo* has somehow to be restored – if only by reversing the time jump which produced the inversion in the first place. In psychological terms Heinlein expressed this belief in the importance of distinctive individuality most tellingly in *Beyond this Horizon* (1942).[31] In it a psychiatrist cannot cure one character's lack of happiness: 'he will start with the assumption there is something wrong with you. He can't find it so he's stuck. It doesn't occur to him that there might be nothing wrong with you and that might be what was wrong.'

To be fair, Heinlein does insist that his readers examine his propositions critically and nowhere more so than when he is studying various communal groups. In *Orphans of the Sky*[32] for example, a group of people in a huge, apparently stationary spaceship, is used as a complex parable of Man on his moving planet. He likes in such tales to suggest to the reader that just as the obvious is not in fact the true in the case of the occupants of the spaceship, so our own apparently obvious explanations of the behaviour of the world and its place in the universe may equally not be true and we should be sceptical of them.

It is Heinlein, too, in his best space-opera mood in *Revolt in 2100*[33] who writes most effectively on our next theme – legitimised murder. The theme finds favour, too, with Poul Anderson in 'License'[34] and in Robert Sheckley's *The Tenth Victim*.[35] The premise of all these American stories is that the only way in which Man's destructive killer instincts can be kept within bounds and thus avert the destruction of the entire human race in nuclear wars is by permitting him, within certain carefully prescribed limits, to kill. Those limits may, for example, include the right of a motorist to kill a pedestrian or of a pedestrian to shoot a motorist in certain circumstances. This is the theme of *The Sellers of the Dream* in which is used the splendid phrase, 'to arrest him for pedestrianship'.[36]

American writers as might be expected are genuinely concerned with the dominance of the motor car and nowhere has this been better satirised than in 'Romance in a 21st Century Used Car Lot'.[37] In this story, to be seen without one's car about one – the whole of the writing treats the car as if it were part of one's personal clothing – is a case of indecent exposure. The romance of the story is the young man persuading his 'correctly brought up' girl eventually to join him in a virtually pariah community where people are content to wear ordinary clothes and where the notice over the gate says 'the wearing of mechanical figleaves prohibited'. The motor car as a permanent extension of the personality is, of course, a logical extrapolation from the current obsessive attachment of most people to their motor cars. Surprisingly, not many writers have taken this theme further to see that the basic fallacy of life in the United States – and perhaps in a rather different way in the Soviet Union also – is that productivity equals civilisation.

There is something of this perhaps in the many stories dealing with that archetypal product of modern technology, the great city. The theme of urban–rural conflict starts in early science fiction and is never dropped. The idea of the animate city, intent on the destruction of the individual, occurs repeatedly and is even present as a sub-theme in such stories as Bradbury's *Fahrenheit 451*.[38] The city is endless, squalid, crowded; it symbolises in a hundred ways the restrictions imposed by modern life on the soul of Man in contrast to that (non-existent) Rousseauesque ideal, the pure country spirit. It is interesting to note that in the description of the banal joys of the Russian utopia's mother of pearl plastic beach huts, we find the phrase, 'and isolate them from their neighbours'. In my own experience, the Russian is in this instance a man of the Western not the Eastern world in that the still considerable crowding of Soviet living conditions is one of his greatest sources of stress. Russians long for individual privacy as much as their Western cousins.

It is, I think, in the leisure time of the utopias and dystopias, much more than in their social, political, industrial and economic organisations, that we find the most revealing characteristics of the distinctive hopes and fears of Russian and Western SF writers.

We have seen in both this and the preceding chapter the importance ascribed by Western SF writers, and more particularly Americans, to the role of the odd man out. It reveals a basic fear of the elimination of variety and individuality, of divine discontent. 'They need people who've made lunacy a profession.' And what could be more closely akin to the lunatic than the artistic? In *Manscarer*,[39] from which the above quotation is taken, Keith Roberts, while not very successfully trying to describe future art forms, does claim that the role of the artist in society is to be the outcast, the questioner, the challenger and that as soon as he accepts patronage and help, becomes a *paid* leader of the opposition, he has emasculated himself.

It is probably because of their common radical tinge that so many SF stories are concerned with jazz.[40] Both are essentially protestant media but as Kingsley Amis suggests in *New Maps of Hell:*[41] 'Both of these fields, again, have thrown up a large number of interesting and competent figures without producing anybody of first-rate importance.' Yet it may reasonably be argued that their modest talents have had, collectively, considerable influence on the social conduct of the human race.

Moreover, SF is, like much modern painting and sculpture, not concerned with actuality in the sense of imitative realism but with a symbolic truth, not with minor variations from the normal but with bizarre and major differences. Michael Moorcock's trilogy, *Dancers at the End of Time*, takes the search for art forms by the immortal to its logical, or rather imaginatively illogical, conclusion.[42] Even

Russian writers, however unintentionally, make this link between SF themes and modern symbolic art. In *The Astronaut*,[43] for example, Valentina Zhuravlyeva describes the painting of certain planetary scenes in such a way as to show them to be of a modern style which would have been severely criticised and quite unacceptable had any Soviet artist of the time actually tried to paint them thus. Usually, however the greatest praise in a Russian SF story is reserved for the interpretive not the creative artist.

One method of trying to convey both the credibility and desirability of future utopias is to show them to be universally culturally advanced, to depict higher art forms to which poor contemporary Man cannot aspire. The general majority of such attempts try to blend music with some form of colour production; for example, in the *Telepathist*[44] the effect is obtained by thinking the music/colours into a machine. The music/art concepts of Alan Nourse in 'The Link'[45] or of Asimov in *The Stars Like Dust*[46] are very similar to those in Yefremov's stories referred to above and show one of the few genuine areas of common ground between 1950s Soviet and Western SF. However, very few such attempts to describe the art forms of the future are successful. After all, if a writer could today successfully describe such a new art form, presumably either he or someone else would quickly set about practising it.

The few successful attempts to suggest future art forms of a more exciting nature than those we currently enjoy all achieve their objective by avoiding this particular dilemma. Harness in *The Rose*[47] succeeds because although art is the central theme of the story the basic arts, like the crucial dance, are fairly conventional. It is the attitude of the artists which transforms them. Or again, Henry Kutner in *Vintage Season*[48] by making sociology an art for time travel connoisseurs succeeds in challenging our established conceptions of art. There are one or two fairly original new art forms, as in 'Prima Bella Donna' in which Ballard in his first story describes how 'Cora Flora Flowers Sing'. Or rather make music. 'It was a difficult bloom, with a normal full range of 24 octaves, but like all the tetracot K3 plus 25C5AO chorotropes, unless it got a lot of exercise it tended to relapse into neurotic minor key transpositions which were the devil to break. . . .'[49] Intellectually – but not artistically – convincing.

On the dystopian side the neglect of the arts is one of the consequences of imposed conformity or is used to satirise contemporary vulgarity as in Vonnegut's *The Sirens of Titan*.[50]

Constance's father had done a similar thing when he found he could not buy Leonardo's Mona Lisa at any price. The old man had punished Mona Lisa by having her used in an advertising campaign for suppositories. It was the free enterprise way of handling beauty that threatened to get the upper hand.

But if in general all SF writers fail, as might be expected, to convince us of the artistic bliss which awaits us in utopia, in their dystopias they fully confirm the worst fears of those who detest organised games.

The games in science fiction, like the arts, are created primarily for the spectators, not for the participants. They are either a means of amusing or rousing the masses or a test of skill between men and races in which the majority can only share vicariously. Occasionally the violence on the field is cynically allowed directly to involve the partisan groups of the watching crowd, as in Norman Spinrad's story about combat football,[51] which extrapolates the behaviour of a typical contemporary football crowd to its logical formalised conclusion. The hero, playing to save the human race at whatever cost to himself, is often found in SF and would have been immediately recognisable to the Victorians, just as the gladiators of so much space opera would have been to the Romans. The theme of the representative human playing for his race has been admirably treated in the British children's television SF serial *Dr Who* or in such novels as *The Game Players of Titan*[52] – a story in which there is an ironic piece of social comment in that wife-swapping is the only hope of conception for a largely sterile human race. In such a typical story (but one which incidentally is better written than most of its kind) we are not just being asked to share the excitement of beating the aliens, literally, at their own game, we are being driven yet again to study the question of human adaptability. I think it is precisely because games-playing is in real life an important human tool for adapting to new and changing environments – rather than as is often suggested as a controlled or sublimated form of aggression – that it features so often in science fiction.

In *Irrational Numbers* a new writer to SF, G. A. Effinger,[53] spins a number of ingenious tales round Man's irrational compulsion to play games. Indeed he suggests that politics, industry and war are themselves games which we play as much from a desire to lose as to win, that in fact we enjoy disaster and defeat – a theme which, though he is American, should particularly appeal to the British.

Barry Malzberg's *Tactics of Conquest*[54] exploits this conception to pinpoint the human dilemma in choosing a morally acceptable course of action when such is not clearly discernible. The hero thinks he has been chosen to represent good against evil in a galactic chess match – but then he *might* be playing for evil. How does he know? Can he win? Should he win? Will a draw resolve the problem? This story is typical of those which ask us to consider the possibility that mankind is itself but the plaything of some superior race or intelligence.

In dystopia, then, man is always the victim of something – often of himself. He is faced with the choice of oppression or boredom. He is at the mercy of manipulators of all possible kinds and species, and subject to every kind of apparently irresistible influence – terrestrial and extra-terrestrial. Yet he emerges, pitiful but unbowed and unchanged, with the human spirit, however tatty, almost always triumphant. He continues to hope and dream his utopias, for, as Mannheim has said:

> the complete disappearance of the Utopian element from human thought and action would mean that human nature and human development would take on a totally new character. The disappearance of Utopia brings about a static state of affairs in which man himself becomes no more than a thing. We would be faced then with the greatest paradox imaginable, namely, that man, who has achieved the highest degree of rational mastery of existence, left without any ideals, becomes a mere creature of impulses. Thus, after a long tortuous, but heroic development, just at the highest stage of awareness, when history is ceasing to be blind fate, and is becoming more and more man's own creation, with the relinquishment of utopias, man would lose his will to shape history and therewith his ability to understand it.[55]

The writers of the utopias of earlier days were telling Man how to build heaven; today they are content to teach him how to survive in hell.

Notes

1. I am indebted for the title of this chapter to Rupert Sheldrake of King's College, Cambridge, whose two papers 'Retreat from Utopia' and 'A

Variety of Futures', printed in *Theoria to Theory*, I (Oct 1966) and I (Jan 1967), are both stimulating studies on the theme of this chapter. Though Auberon Waugh may pour pedantic scorn on the solecism 'dystopia' (*Books and Bookmen*, July 1979) it provides a convenient shorthand means of expressing a genuine dichotomy, so I shall use it. Similarly, though More simply wished to imply the non-existence of his theoretical society the association of the term 'utopia' with ideal, and by inference good societies, justifies the term to identify proposedly beneficial social structures. Indispensable to any study of the theme of this chapter is Karl Mannheim, *Ideology and Utopia* (Kegan Paul, 1936), esp. pp. 184–9.

2. Berdiaeff, *The End of Our Time* (London: 1933) p. 188.

3. Norman Cohn, *The Pursuit of the Millennium* (Secker, 1957).

4. Karl Mannheim, *Ideology and Utopia* (Kegan Paul, 1936) p. 36 *et seq.*:

The concept 'ideology' reflects the one discovery which emerged from political conflict, namely, that ruling groups can in their thinking become so intensively interest-bound to a situation that they are simply no longer able to see certain facts which would undermine their sense of domination. There is implicit in the word 'ideology' the insight that in certain situations the collective unconscious of certain groups obscures the real condition of society both to itself and to others and thereby stabilizes it.

The concept of *utopian* thinking reflects the opposite discovery of the political struggle, namely that certain oppressed groups are intellectually so strongly interested in the destruction and transformation of a given condition of society that they unwittingly see only those elements in the situation which tend to negate it.

5. Ivan Yefremov, *The Heart of the Serpent* (Btk 367, 1959) and, *The Andromeda Nebula* (Btk 365, 1957).

6. An article in *Kommunist* by E. Brandis and V. Dmitrevsky, translated in *The Magazine of Fantasy and Science Fiction* (October 1965).

7. Arcady and Boris Strugatsky, *Snail on the Slope* (Leningrad: Btk 501, 1966). Translation by A. Myers due at the time of writing to be published by Bantam.

8. Letter to *The Guardian*, November 1966, Philip O'Connor. Courtesy Philip O'Connor.

9. E. M. Forster, *The Machine Stops* in *The Collected Stories* (first pub. 1928; Penguin 1954).

10. Yevgeny Zamyatin, *We* (first pub. 1922; trans. Mirra Ginsberg, Bantam, 1972).

11. Arthur Clarke, *Childhood's End* (first pub. 1954; Pan, 1956).

12. H. G. Wells, *In the Days of the Comet* (Macmillan, 1906).

13. Frank Herbert, *Dune* (first pub. 1965; New English Library, 1968); *Dune Messiah* (Gollancz, 1971).

14. Algis Budry's *The Iron Thorn* (Gollancz, 1969), expanded from a shorter version which appeared in *If* magazine in 1966.

15. W. M. Miller, *Canticle for Liebowitz* (first pub. 1960; Corgi, 1970).

16. Ursula LeGuin, *The Left Hand of Darkness* (Macdonald, 1969); *The Lathe of Heaven* (Gollancz, 1972) and *The Dispossessed* (New York; Harper & Row, 1974).

17. See ch. 4, n. 56.

18. Kurt Vonnegut, *The Sirens of Titan* (first pub. 1950; Hodder, 1967).

19. Quoted in Mark Hillegas, *The Future as Nightmare* (Oxford University Press, 1967).

20. Olaf Stapledon, *First and Last Men* (first pub. 1930; Penguin, 1963).

21. Clifford Simak, *Way Station* (first pub. 1963; Pan, 1966).

22. Frederick Brown, 'Earthmen Bearing Gifts', in *Seventh Galaxy Reader* (Pan, 1967). This passage bears a very close relation to the account of Martian life in A. Bogdanov's *Red Star* (1908). Lenin was highly critical of Bogdanov's work. He gave up writing SF in 1926 to concentrate on his scientific research.

23. Isaac Asimov, 'Profession', in *Nine Tomorrows* (first pub. 1957; Pan, 1967).

24. This Isaac Asimov trilogy (first pub. 1951; Panther, 1960) consists of *Foundation*, *Foundation and Empire* and *Second Foundation*. It would be interesting to know if it influenced Snegov in his space trilogy *Men Like Gods*, which we shall look at in ch. 9.

25. Asimov, *Second Foundation*.

26. Frank Herbert, *The Eyes of Heisenberg* (first pub. 1966; Sphere, 1968), though Herbert's work develops to take a far more sophisticated view of genetic engineering, cf. ch. 7.

27. Samuel R. Delany, *Babel 17* (Sphere, 1969).

28. Isaac Asimov, *Pebble in the Sky* (first pub. 1933; Bantam Pathfinder, 1964).

29. Isaac Asimov, *The Currents of Space* (first pub. 1955; Panther, 1967).

30. Robert Heinlein, *Farnham's Freehold* (first pub. 1964; Corgi, 1967).

31. Robert Heinlein, *Beyond This Horizon* (first pub. 1942; Panther, 1967).

32. Robert Heinlein, *Orphans of the Sky* (first pub. in two parts, 1941; Mayflower, 1965).

33. Robert Heinlein, *Revolt in 2100* (first pub. 1939; Digit, 1953).

34. Poul Anderson, 'License', *F and SF* (April 1957).

35. Robert Sheckley, *The Tenth Victim* (Mayflower/Dell, 1966).

36. John Jacques, *The Sellers of the Dream* (Galaxy, 1963).

37. Robert F. Young, 'Romance in a 21st Century Used Car Lot', in *The Worlds of Robert F. Young* (first pub. 1960; Panther, 1968).

38. Ray Bradbury, *Fahrenheit 451* (first pub. 1954; Corgi, 1967).

39. Keith Roberts 'Manscarer', in *New Writings in SF* 7 (Corgi, 1966).

40. Holley Cantine, 'Double Double Toil and Trouble', in *Best from S and SF*, Series 10 (Mercury Press, 1959); John Brunner, 'The Man Who Played the Blues', in *Science Fantasy*, 17 (Feb 1956); Douglas R. Mason,

'There Was This Fella', in *New Writings in SF 10* (Corgi, 1967); Theodore Sturgeon, 'Die, Maestro, Die!', in *E Pluribus Unicorn* (Panther, 1961).

41. Kingsley Amis, *New Maps of Hell* (first pub. 1961; New English Library, 1969).

42. Michael Moorcock's trilogy, *Dancers at the End of Time: The Alien Heat, The Hollow Land, The End of All Songs* (Avon, 1977).

43. Valentina Zhuravlyeva, *The Astronaut* (Btk 532, 1960).

44. John Brunner, *Telepathist* (Penguin, 1968).

45. Alan Nourse, 'The Link' in *The Counterfeit Man* (Corgi, 1965).

46. Isaac Asimov, *The Stars Like Dust* (first pub. 1952; Panther, 1965).

47. Charles L. Harness, *The Rose* (first pub. 1953; Panther, 1969).

48. Henry Kutner, 'Vintage Season', in *Spectrum IV* (first pub. Astounding, 1946; Pan, 1967).

49. J. G. Ballard, 'Prima Bella Donna', in *The Four Dimensional Nightmare* (first pub. 1963; Penguin, 1965).

50. Kurt Vonnegut, *The Sirens of Titan* (first pub. 1950; Hodder, 1967).

51. Norman Spinrad, 'The National Pastime', in *No Direction Home* (first pub. 1969–74; Fontana, 1977).

52. Philip Dick, *The Game Players of Titan* (first pub. 1963; Sphere, 1969).

53. George Alex Effinger, *Irrational Numbers* (Fontana, 1977).

54. Barry Malzberg, *Tactics of Conquest* (New York: Pyramid, 1974).

55. Karl Mannheim, *Ideology and Utopia* (Kegan Paul, 1936).

6
The cybernetic society

We have so far looked at Man, through SF, rather subjectively, asking what does he feel, fear, think? In the next two chapters we shall see how, in two quite separate species of story, the SF writer tries to look at him objectively. In this chapter, principally about robots, and the next about aliens and other worlds, we shall be studying an approach which is not what at first it seems, for the stories are fundamentally concerned not with their ostensible strange themes but with the question, 'What makes us human? What is distinctive – whether admirable or not – about Man?'

Probably long before primitive man banged his thumb with the first flint axe he had a love-hate relationship with his tools. Perhaps curiosity-fear relationship would describe it better, the Luddite and the lover of the simple life in conflict with the sophisticate and the incurable gadgeteer. The essential inventiveness of Man is a recurring SF theme. Sometimes it is shown in his ingenuity in escaping from impossible situations. Colin Kapp's *Lambda I*[1] and 'Hunger over Sweet Waters'[2] are splendid examples of this, and even the Russians have in *The Maxwell Equation*[3] a story where the hero uses a graphite pencil to alter the resistance of a brainwashing machine. Sometimes Man's inventiveness is demonstrated in his determination to re-invent the basics, like the wheel or the aeroplane, in the face of inhibitions or prohibitions arising from his ancestors' disastrous experiences with these devices. Man is an insatiable experimenter, always asking, 'What happens if?' It is reasonable, therefore, that this curiosity should so often be expressed in SF, the 'let us suppose' fiction.

Vonnegut in his devastating satire on machine-mad Man, *Player Piano*,[4] writes: 'Bud's mentality was one that had been remarked upon as being peculiarly American since the Nation had been born –

the restless, erratic insight and imagination of the gadgeteer' – but finds in the end that 'we have to reject the divine right of machines', to which this approach can lead. The more human the machine the more intense and ambivalent the attitude towards it, until with robots and cybernetics we are no longer studying the machine but Man, or rather the machine's effect on Man. We are asking whether the relationship is symbiotic or parasitic.

The idea of mechanical slaves is an old one. We find them even in Book XVIII of the *Iliad*:[5] 'These are made of gold exactly like living girls; they have sense in their heads, they can speak and use their muscles, they can spin and weave and do their work. . . .' Another instance is the Chinese Emperor's mechanical nightingale. Perhaps the first robot story proper was *Moxon's Master* by Ambrose Bierce (1893).[6] It raises the question of where the borderline lies between instinct – that is, conditioned patterns of behaviour – and thinking. The chess-playing robot, of which Moxon's is the forerunner, is a recurrent theme in SF since chess is a purely rational and therefore computer-susceptible game. But twenty years earlier (1872) Butler had begun that half-rational campaign of hostility to the decision-making, self-correcting machine against which Harvey Matusow now leads the crusade with such delightful eccentricity with his anti-computer society or in his book *The Beast of Business*.[7] Butler was seeing into the future with remarkable clarity when he wrote:

Do not let me be misunderstood as living in fear of any actually existing machine; there is probably no known machine which is more than a prototype of future mechanical life. The present machines are to the future as the early Saurians to man. I would repeat that I fear none of the existing machines; what I fear is the extraordinary rapidity with which they are becoming something very different to what they are at present. No class of beings have in any time past made so rapid a movement forward. Should not that movement be jealously watched and checked while we can still check it? And is it not necessary for this end to destroy the more advanced of the machines which are in use at present, though it is admitted that they are in themselves harmless? We cannot calculate on any corresponding advance in man's intellectual or physical powers which shall be set off against the far greater development which seems in store for the machines. Some people may say that man's moral influence will suffice to rule them; but I cannot think it will ever be safe to repose much trust in the moral sense of any machine.[8]

Neither Bierce nor Butler called their 'thinking' devices robots, of course, for the word, from the Czech for 'a worker', was coined by Joseph Capek and made famous by his brother Karel in the play *R.U.R.*, Rossum's Universal Robots, in 1921.[9] While *R.U.R.* is basically satirical it is also simply funny because Capek reveals the robot, the brain no longer under natural control, as the clown of science. But it has become in the last decade a clown of whom the children of the twentieth century are increasingly frightened. Yet surprisingly, until the late 1960s, it was a fear very little discussed outside the pages of SF. As late as 1969 Rex Malik, a professional writer on computer affairs, could claim:

> While serious speculation still holds an honoured place in science, it is disturbing that there should be so little speculation about the possible effects of the widespread introduction of advanced computer technology. Discussion – such as it is – still progresses in terms of the threat of the computer to overall employment, its threat to privacy and the problems of leisure, and in none of these is it carried out at any great depth.[10]

Malik also recognises that the development of computers and cybernetics in general challenges the fundamental concept of both left and right of the desirability in itself of work or employment.

Man has tried to come to terms with robots and computers either by proving them subject to rules and systems to show how unlike humans they are – a school of which Asimov is the chief if not the most consistent exponent – or by anthropomorphising them. The process of anthropomorphism in the past fifty years has been of three kinds: the straight transference of human characteristics to robots and other machines (we shall study separately in the next chapter the concept of the animate or possessed machine); the invention of the positronic brain by which the thinking process becomes organic and electro-chemical but the functions remain electronic or mechanical; and finally the android, the literally organic but manufactured and programmed 'human' robot. Clones, properly neither androids nor aliens, will be looked at in the next chapter.

The conventional conception of the robot is of a caricature of the human form, clumsy movements, brassy voice and flashing eyes, and although no such creature exists outside the fun-fair we do, of course, have robots, programmed devices, in our lives already, from the simple alarm clock to the automatic car-assembly plant. These carry out planned activities on Man's behalf or in his place. Although such devices are frequently executing functions too tedious, complex, dangerous or fast for Man to do, the fear of replacement of Man, and particularly of the less skilled Man, by the machine is one of our most obsessive. The final extrapolation of this fear is the total replacement of the human race by such 'thinking' devices. Another fear that robots and computers seem to provoke is that they will reveal human fallibility – although hostility is usually directed at one remove at the machine's apparent (but programmed!) mistakes. They also reveal that Man, claiming to be the most rational of creatures, is too swayed by his emotions to be completely logical. While this may be claimed as a human virtue by many writers, some stories raise the unpalatable possibility that the human emotions in question may be as automatic as the built-in pseudo-emotions of the robots.

A great many robot stories, therefore, are concerned with the question of the difference between Man and machine. H. Beam Pipe in the 'Ministry of Disturbance' writes of the conventional robot:

> The robot was nothing but steel and plastic and magnetised tape and photomicro positronic circuits, whereas a man ... was nothing but tissues and cells and colloids and electroneuronic circuits. There was a difference; anybody knew that. The trouble was that he had never met anybody – which included physicists, biologists, psychologists, psionicists, philosophers and theologians – who could define the difference in satisfactorily exact terms.[11]

The SF writer himself falls victim to this confusion or, in the case of writers such as Bester and Asimov, deliberately exploits it. Bester's computer Mose, for example, 'behaves' as if human because eventually it must be demonstrated that it is not.

> Mose's eyes blinked in hard meditation; his stomach rumbled softly; his memories began to hiss and stutter. Powell and the others waited with mounting suspense. Abruptly, Mose hiccupped. A soft bell began to ping-ping-ping-ping-ping-ping – and Mose's type began to flail the virgin tape under it.[12]

Similarly robots are made to look and move like men so that we have to think about the difference. This similarity can be used almost cruelly in such a story as 'Robot Dozen', a delightful series of thirteen letters about the hiring of a house robot.[13] In the early letters the similarity between the house robot and the rather stiff householder is gradually established. In the last letter the robot mortician resigns because of the realistic scream given by the faulty 'robot' when pushed into the incinerator. On a fairly lighthearted level this story contains the implication that if robots can be like men then perhaps men are like robots. This postulates a deterministic view which most Western readers find repugnant. There is the suggestion that the emotions can be, as it were, intellectually, rationally simulated in cause, response and manifestation and that a well-programmed robot and an under-emotional man may seem to be almost the same thing. The same approach can be used provocatively in a story like 'Jay Score',[14] which only reveals in the last line that the principal character is a robot. Until then the reader has assumed that the 'hero', with whom he sympathises and whose abilities he recognises, is human. He can hardly withdraw his approbation at the last line and is forced to infer that equal tolerance should be shown to humans who differ from him.

It is this misleading confusion, due to Man's wish to endow the robot with human characteristics, that Harry Harrison begs us to renounce in *War with the Robots*.[15] He writes in his preface that he does not want the anthropomorphic robot, he does not want as the logical outcome of this trend to see his cybernetic gadgets, record players, electric alarm clock, radios, blankets, and so on, being replaced by devices that look like humans but perform the same function as the earlier device of different appearance. Asimov rationalises this anthropomorphising tendency by claiming in *Caves of Steel*[16] that robots are made in human form so often 'because the human form is the most successful generalised form in all nature'. – although the same author cautions us in 'Catch That Rabbit'[17] that human disorders apply to robots only as romantic analogies. Daniel Gallouey in *Homey Atmosphere*[18] underlines the dangers in investing the machine with human qualities. In this story it is done deliberately and the machines take over from the humans.

To defeat the argument that no amount of electronic circuitry could ever begin to match the complexity of the human mind, the robot writers invented the positronic brain. This mass of spongy tissue, possessing all the billions of synapses of the natural human brain but artificially created, enabled writers to go beyond the simple elements of binary logic to more typically human patterns of behaviour. These, nevertheless, were generally exclusive of imagination and emotion, save by analogy. Dr Kit Pedlar, a writer of television SF, has called his second generation robot the biomim or biological mimic but argues, for some peculiar reason, that it cannot possess memory – what else is a computer's store of data? This thesis is, in any case, difficult to accept when we are considering biochemical (organic) as opposed to electronic (binary) replication of memory. Indeed Dr Ian Aleksander of the University of Kent[19] graphically describes future neuronic computers acting in a way similar to the human brain and memory – that is with the capacity to call simultaneously on a great number of stored items of information and correlate them instead of processing single items sequentially as in the conventional computer. Even so, as Asimov says in *The Caves of Steel,*[20] 'There's no way we can raise a positronic brain one inch above the level of perfect materialism.' In this Western story such a remark is intended as criticism of the limitations of the robot; to an orthodox Russian, however, it might seem to be a proper goal for which to strive.

But if the printed circuit can be replaced by artificial brain tissues so can the mechanical limbs be replaced by those of flesh; or conversely those of flesh by mechanical ones. What David Fishlock[21] has called the uneasy symbiosis between man and his synthetic organs – cardiac pacemakers, kidney machines, and so on – is a common theme of SF. How far can we take prosthetics, for example, and still call the owner of the artificial limbs human? We have already referred to Wolfe's long novel *Limbo 90.*[22] This book links cybernetics and prosthetics. It examines the question of what happens when we voluntarily surrender a great many of our physical functions to be machine-controlled. It runs quite closely parallel to substantial research during the last decade in the United States on the control of behaviour and motor responses by the implanting of electrodes in certain sectors of the animal – and indeed human – brain which can be activated by radio transmissions to induce passivity, aggression, and so on. Here we have information, data or stimuli applied artificially by outside forces instead of taken in voluntarily and haphazardly through the senses. Perhaps what such writers are struggling to say is that it is the ability to choose even part of our input, however foolishly, which makes us human; not a distinction acceptable to the behaviourists.

A story such as 'Flight of a Plastic Bee'[23] asks the simple question, 'How much of a human being could you replace and leave a human being?' One way to answer is to retreat to the fundamentalist position that our diseases and infirmities are an essential part of our humanity rather than a fall from it. This is the argument of the old man in 'The Diehard'[24] who, with all his infirmities, in a world of perfect but partially artificial specimens of Man can claim, 'I am the last man on earth'. Certainly the possibility of a surgical evolution, by means of organic prosthetics, away from humanity as we know it today cannot be ignored. It may be treated as a form of grotesque hell, as in Cordwainer Smith's 'A Planet Named Shayol'[25] in which criminal or diseased creatures are conditioned to survive on a dreadful penal planet and are used to grow a multiplicity of limbs for use as spare parts for human surgery. Or the approach may be inverted to become more detached: 'He wondered faintly if he were still robot – or was he something else? Could a machine evolve, he wondered, as man himself evolved? And if a machine evolved, whatever would it be? Not man, of course, for it never could be that, but could it be machine?'[26] This is a theme treated in non-fictional form by Professor D. F. Lawden[27] and by H. Putnam in *Robots: Machines or Artificially Created Life?*

> Given the ever accelerating rate of both technological and social change it is entirely possible that robots will one day exist, and argue 'we *are* alive; we *are* conscious!' In that event what are today only philosophical prejudices of a traditional anthropocentric and mentalistic kind would all too likely develop into conservative political attitudes. But fortunately, we today have the advantages of being able to discuss this problem disinterestedly, and a little more chance, therefore, of arriving at the correct answer.[28]

It should again be noted that SF, in studying the nature of Man by asking questions about robots, was concerned with this dilemma long before Professor Barnard's first successful heart transplant compelled members of the general public to ask themselves the same questions.

The positronic brain and the prosthetic limb are, in a sense, deliberately used by the SF writer to make the distinction between Man and machine more difficult. By eliminating superficial differences he hopes to compel the reader to concentrate more on the essential ones – or the lack of them. The Tralfamadorinians, for example, in Vonnegut's novel *Slaughterhouse Five*[29] say 'that every creature and plant in the universe is a machine. It amuses them that so many earthlings are offended by the idea of being machines.' He returns to his idea in a much more pessimistic vein in *Breakfast of Champions*.[30]

The logical development of the positronics and prosthetics is the biological machine, the android. The android is virtually human but for the fact that it has been created, not conceived and born of woman, and cannot reproduce its kind (a limitation not, incidentally, imposed on the ordinary electro-mechanical robot which can literally – if not sexually – reproduce itself). The android's degree of obedience to human will varies from story to story.

How then do you tell an android from a man? One of the best and most tellingly ironic SF stories I know, 'And Miles To Go Before I Sleep',[31] suggests perhaps that we cannot. A spaceman returning home after twenty years knows he will die before he lands but has promised his parents to return, so he creates an android to replace himself. This is so perfect that his parents, who have been longing for his return, are bound to be deceived. The twist in the last paragraph of the story, however, shows that meanwhile back on earth his parents, who had promised to be alive when he returned, have died and in turn been replaced by two other androids so that the returning spaceman shall not be disappointed. In the last sentence the three androids are described walking off unwittingly together.

We have come a long way from the clumsy tin can to a 'creature' indistinguishable from Man except by his creator or by the quirks his creator has put into the programme of his thought patterns. A number of stories deal with rights for androids, their feelings, thoughts and ambitions – they become virtually analogous to a slave race seeking emancipation. Even love between Man and android is not only possible but acceptable; its tragedy – I have never been able to understand the logic of this conventional SF stipulation other than as taboo – that it is a love than can have no progeny. We have so far anthropomorphised the machine that we have forgotten its mechanical origins; the god from the machine has become the god in the machine – even god the machine, intervening in our lives to determine our fate.

The other pattern of approach has been not to emancipate our technical slaves but to enchain them with rules. The past-master of this approach is that guru of fictional robotics, Isaac Asimov. His 'Three Laws of Robotics' formulated in 1941 have become the inescapable premise for robot stories by virtually all other SF writers. It is as if every nineteenth-century novelist had been content, without question, to accept the social judgements of Dickens as the basis for his own stories. A whole sub-genre has grown round Asimov's three simple sentences.

1. – A robot may not injure a human being, or, through inaction, allow a human being to come to harm.

2. – A robot must obey the orders given it by human beings except where such orders would conflict with the first law.

3. – A robot must protect its own existence as long as protection does not conflict with the first or second law.

Asimov's own reaction to this flattering universal emulation was to say, 'In a way this bothers me, for I am accustomed to thinking of myself as a scientist, and to be remembered for the non-existent basis of a non-existent science is embarrassing.'[32] But he then suggests that perhaps the three laws would in fact become necessary if the science of robotics ever reached the levels it does in his stories.

I believe, however, that there is a critical omission in the three laws of robotics, the absence of the word 'wittingly'. If robots lack volition and only have precognitive response then any technical failure, due to whatever cause, could lead to a robot *un*wittingly harming the human. The positronic brain is an ingenious attempt to resolve this paradox. This brain was described by Asimov as early as 1940 as 'the miles of relays and photocells [which] had given way to the spongy globe of plantinumiridium about the size of the human brain.'[33] Asimov says in an early robot story, 'The conflict between the various rules is ironed out by the different positronic potentials in the brain.'[34] But he is not usually so unsubtle. Much of Asimov's appeal in the robot stories lies in the ingenuity with which he continually gets round his own three laws in a perfectly logical fashion. The laws are in fact never broken, they only appear to be and the challenge to the reader in this form of SF detective novel is to anticipate the true explanation of the apparent contradictions. As Asimov himself admitted, 'There was just enough ambiguity in the three laws to provide the conflicts and uncertainties required for new stories and, to my great relief, it seemed always to be possible to think up a new angle out of the 61 words of the three laws.'

A good example of this technique is to be found in 'Satisfaction Guaranteed'.[35] Here the household robot by pretending to be its human mistress's lover solves her competitive social problems and is in fact obeying the first law of robotics of not allowing harm to come to a human being. But when the woman falls in love with the robot the situation is complicated in a way which forcefully poses the question, 'What is harm?' And in particular, to what extent can illusory beliefs be said to be harmful? This theme is pursued in 'Liar',[36] in which we have another gloss put on the first law of robotics. What weight should a robot attribute to emotional harm to a human being? What if this conflicts with the necessity for the robot to be logical and to give truthful answers? 'I confronted him with the insoluble dilemma, and he broke down,'[37] says the 'roboticist' and this approach becomes a cliché in the end. But Asimov is at pains at all times to point out that the robot behaves logically and that it is the humans who are irrational and illogical – sometimes revealingly so.

One of the best 'paradox' stories is James Blish's *Polar Station*.[38] An egocentric criminal character arrives at a one-man polar station and is sceptical of its engineer's claims both that the station is completely run by the computer and that the computer is infallible. Keen to display how clever and correct he is he puts in a logical paradox question to the computer which applies more and more of its capacity to trying to solve the insoluble problem with the result that it abandons its care of the station and the two men perish. The underlying message of this story is that rational behaviour is not necessarily intelligent behaviour, that perfectly logical – or rather literal – behaviour can be exasperating and inefficient. The compulsive 'logicality' of the computer is the solution to the paradox in 'The Sixth Palace',[39] which asks whether robots can cheat or behave in other than a perfectly logical fashion. A priceless treasure is guarded by a robot which destroys even those who appear to answer its questions correctly. So the protagonist confounds it by total and utter illogicality, as it were by an almost surrealist, existentialist approach to logic. Question, 'What is the excretory unit of the vertebrate kidney called?' Answer, 'The frog in the pond utters an azure cry.' Having circumvented the robot by refusing to deal in logic the adventurer, preoccupied with the treasure in his hand, greedily lapses into rationality in replying to the parting question as to why he wants wealth, and is destroyed.

It must not be supposed that Asimov also does not sometimes cheat his own rules. In 'All the Troubles of the World'[40] he is guilty of anthropomorphising his machines and writing a story about a computer with a death wish, and in 'Galley Slave'[41] he reneges on his anti-Frankenstein credo (cf. chapter 2). In 'Run Around'[42] he cheats a little by saying that Rule 3 has been specially strengthened because of the expense of the robot and Rule 2 was weakened by the fact that the command was given casually and without emphasis, and that the two factors at some stage had resulted in the disobedience of the robot. Again, in 'Little Lost Robot'[43] the first law has been modified to leave out the words 'through inaction allow a human being to come to harm'. This presents a new paradox.

> If a modified robot were to drop a heavy weight upon a human being, he would not be breaking the first law, if he did so with the knowledge that his strength and reaction speed would be sufficient to snatch the weight away before it struck the man. However, once the weight left his fingers, he would be no longer the active medium. Only the blind force of gravity would be that. The robot could then change his mind and merely by inaction, allow the weight to strike. The modified first law allows that.

So the new robots start to reason themselves.

> It occurred to me [says a robot] that if I died on my way to him I wouldn't be able to save him anyway. The weight would crush him and then I would be dead for no purpose and perhaps some day some other master might come to harm who wouldn't have, if I had only stayed alive . . . it was impossible to save the master. He might be considered dead. In that case it is inconceivable that I destroy myself for nothing – without orders.[44]

One of the repeated fallacies in robot stories, by both Asimov and others, is that a logical conflict will make a robot 'mad'. There is thus a strong element of anthropomorphising even in Asimov's stories. But presumably if two courses are weighed against each other one will be found to conform, however marginally, to the three laws more than the other. Once the robot has reached that conclusion it will act, unaffected by a mere matter of finite degree – however small. If the two conflicting elements are exactly balanced then inaction will result, not madness.

'Reason'[45] is another delightful Asimov parody of the obtuse and purely rational being. A space station robot refuses to believe that the men who operate the station and are clearly inferior to him could have created him on the basis of 'the self-evident proposition that no being can create another being superior to itself'. There is, therefore, no reason to obey the men or even permit them to survive. You can argue your way *ad nauseam* in an essay but it is an SF story like this which brings such contemporary fears and dilemmas to life for most people.

The argument that a robot is logical but not reasonable is used frequently to imply that it is inferior to a human. The robot cannot falsify his answers, says Asimov:

> that is the difference between a robot and a man. A human brain, or any mammalian brain, cannot be completely analysed by any mathematical discipline now known. No response can therefore be counted upon as a certainty. The robot brain is completely analysable, or it could not be constructed. We know exactly what the response to a given stimulus must be. No robot can truly falsify answers. The thing you call falsification just doesn't exist in the robot's mental horizon.[46]

Perhaps in reading such stories as Asimov's, people are seeking reassurance on the fallibility of machines and need to be reminded that the failings of the machines sometimes have to be made up for by the ingenuity of Man.

The false hope is held out that the complex and unfathomable must be superior to the less complex and logically determinable, a hope more naïvely but more entertainingly expressed in Murray Leinster's *Exploration Team*[47] in which a man uses bears to explore a strange and dangerous planet. The official exploration team explores with robots. The man with the bears provides a factor which the robot-based team cannot and thus succeeds where it fails. While the Middle Ages exhorted us to control our inferior animal selves to promote the exercise of pure reason, the twentieth century pleads that it is only our animal natures that make us superior to those creatures of pure reason, the robots and the computers.

In *The Caves of Steel*[48] and *The Naked Sun*[49] Asimov develops a useful method of separating human nature into its component elements of logic and instinct so that their conflict and co-operation can be better understood. In both novels a human detective and a robot detective work together to solve mysteries which involve a mixture of robot, human and alien characters. The strengths of the human detective are his intuition, instinct and even emotions, those of the robot logic and deduction. Optimistically, Asimov's stories suggest that the relationship is a symbiotic one.

Why then are we so afraid of our technical Frankenstein monsters? Why do we usually endow the robot, the computer, the machine, if not with hostile intent, then with the role of instrument to execute some vague, hostile intent towards mankind? In 'The Jokester'[50] a researcher is using a huge computer to analyse all the jokes ever made to try to determine their origins. The twist in the concluding paragraph is that all jokes have been put into our minds by an alien source as part of a psychological experiment. Now we know this, the experiment is invalidated, there will be no more jokes and we shall never laugh again. In this, fairly typical, story the computer has done nothing but reveal to the protagonists a situation which already existed, as a microscope might reveal for the first time the aetiology of one of Man's diseases. We do not blame the microscope because it has enlarged one of our senses, yet we often blame the computer because it has enlarged the scope of our reasoning. The computer shocks us because it reveals in nanoseconds of calculation those devastating conclusions to which the human mind used to adapt itself more gradually by years of reasoning; Athena springing fully armed from the head of Zeus is rather more startling than a seven pound baby girl taking twenty years to grow up into a member of Women's Lib.

Nor do the devices of the cybernetic society merely show up our deficiencies, they also focus attention on our faults. Such stories as 'Computers Mate'[51] by John Racham make us ask whether men are afraid of machines not because of the harm the machines might do to them or the mistakes the machines might make but because of the harm and mistakes that machines show men to have made.

There is, I believe, a parallel in the way we look at insects and reptiles and our attitude to our self-regulating machines. Usually, through our entomologists at least, we understand the physiology and behaviour of insects but because we cannot tame or domesticate them, nor understand them, nor recognise common behaviour patterns, we fear them in a way we do not generically fear animals, however ferocious. Often you may hear someone exclaim that they are paralysed with fright by spiders or snakes, never that they are petrified by panthers – though doubtless they would be if confronted by an individual member of the species. Our fear and hostility towards computers, for example, is always against computers – that is, what we think they stand for – rather than against a particular computer – that is, what it is. In the obedient yet so powerful computer we see, perhaps, a reflected fear that our own apparent free will, like that of the insect, is illusory.

Professor Donald McKay has tried to explain away the apparently illusory nature of human free will by what he calls a cerebral state uncertainty principle.

> Ever since Heisenberg's uncertainty principle shattered the deterministic image of physics nearly half a century ago there is something of a tug of war between those who hold it as restoring the scientific respectability of free will and others who argue that it made no practical difference to the physical determinateness of brain function. I hope to show that even if the workings of our brains were as mechanical as planetary motion, our freedom in choosing would be no illusion, but a matter of fact.[52]

He coins the phrase 'logical indeterminacy' to show that, as in the physical parallel, the exact locus where belief and knowledge can both simultaneously be determined does not exist. The resolution of this paradox is a frequent theme in this sub-genre of SF. In many stories[53] the machine acts like an omnipotent deity in laying down the inescapable patterns of our lives. ' "But are you telling me . . . that mankind *has* lost its own say in its future?" "It never had any, really. It was always at the mercy of economic and sociological forces it did not understand. . . ." ' This is a point of view with which many Russian authors would presumably not disagree, nor dislike.

The robot plays a slightly different role in Russain SF. Our Russians will argue that the highest form of matter is 'brain tissue'. They go along the android path as far as admitting that 'living matter may be produced synthetically as recognised by our philosophy'.[54] In *Six Matches*[55] the Strugatskys are 'convinced that the potentialities of the brain are inexhaustible. All that is needed is training in activation.' But in 'Marxist' human beings the concept of brain function is rather mechanistic, so much so that it is not suprising that in *The Conflict*[56] by Ilya Varshavsky one character says, 'Don't you know that the law has made thinking robots man's equal?' These attitudes might tempt the Western reader to dismiss the Russian robot story as a vehicle for mechanical orthodox communist humans but closer examination shows that this is precisely what they are not. The build-up of a story in which robots resemble Marxist orthodox humans as closely as possible is sometimes a literary device to enable the writer to hide an heretical attitude behind the fact that his characters are *not* humans. While it is not permissible, even conceivable, that 'correct' socialist man should err it *is* allowable for a no less socialist machine to go wrong. In *Spontaneous Reflex*,[57] the Strugatskys' story of a self-programming robot with a passion for experiment, or Ilya Var-shavsky's *Robby*,[58] the principal cybernetic protagonists indulge in a great deal of un-Marxist thinking and behaviour. The robots in *Snail on the Slope*[59] go even further in parading, with nice deftness, attitudes which would be hard even for the Strugatskys to give to human protagonists. We have already warned against Kremlinolog-ical comma-spotting but it is tempting to suggest that the apparently orthodox Russian writers may, by analogy, be suggesting dissent and experiment – although the chances are that in most cases the suggestions are subconscious rather than deliberate.

What the better writers from both countries – there are few British robot writers, John Brunner, Steve Gallagher and Arthur Clarke[60] being occasional exceptions – make us do is challenge both the mechanistic conception of human behaviour and the an-thropomorphic approach to our inventions, our brain children. Two stories by Asimov epitomise a sane and balanced approach by their insistence that Man must look into himself for the motivating force behind his use of machines, and not to the machines. In 'The Feeling of Power',[61] a superb story of a future world where everyone has a pocket computer even for every-day calculations, a mere technician rediscovers the ability to calculate sums in his head and on bits of paper. The top brass of this society decide to use this wonderful 'new discovery' for purposes of death and destruction ('piloted missiles'!). In despair at the use to which his discovery has been put, little technician Aub commits suicide. The story is not only a nice ironic inversion but focuses on the important contemporary dilem-ma of scientists as to the use to which their discoveries may be put. Less successfully he repeats this approach in 'Some Day',[62] with the rediscovery of reading and writing as a way of passing secret messages instead of using computers. The point dramatically brought home in the few short paragraphs of both stories is that we already have devices, the three Rs even, quite as potentially deadly as any robot or computer. You may use your ploughshare for tilling the soil or for cracking open Abel's skull.

The rapid growth of cybernetics in the past decade has resulted in a false re-allocation of responsibilities. Because the computers and robots have become essential *tools* for dealing with an increasingly technically complicated society, they have sometimes become *substitutes* for dealing with the problems of that society. As Colin Wilson says, 'The more the mind produces labour saving machines, the more it blinds itself to its own possibilities, the more it tends to regard itself as a passive "reasoning machine".'[63]

Joel de Rosnay, in October 1970, gave a lecture which painted a vivid picture of how computers might be used to turn complex human societies into self-regulating systems capable of maintaining continuous ecological balance with the environment and of making 'real time' adjustment to changes coming both from without and from within. But such systems still require programming for moral priority. The paradox with which the human race is faced is that the more sophisticated the aids to decision-making the more reluctant we seem to be to make real decisions. What the SF writers discussed in this chapter are trying to do is ensure that we cannot plead ignorance of the need for decisions on these moral priorities, and to nudge us in the direction which they think to be correct.

Notes

1. Colin Kapp, *Lambda I* (Penguin, 1965).

2. Colin Kapp, 'Hunger Over Sweet Waters', in *New Writings in Science Fiction 4* (Corgi, 1965).

3. Anatoly Dneprov, *The Maxwell Equation* (NF 348, 1960).

4. Kurt Vonnegut, *Player Piano* (first pub. 1952; Panther, 1969).

5. Homer, *The Iliad*, Book XVIII (W. H. D. Rouse translation).

6. Ambrose Bierce, *Moxon's Master* (London, 1893).

7. Harvey Matusow, *The Beast of Business* (Wolfe Publishing, 1968).

8. Samuel Butler, *Erewhon* (London: 1872). In a TV programme in 1968 Louis Mumford suggested that 'the machines we have now appeared long ago in our dreams, long before they were technologically possible' – and in our nightmares too it would seem.

9. Karel Capek, *R.U.R.* (Prague, 1921).

10. Rex Malik, *New Scientist* (28 Aug 1969). For a general introduction to this field I found *An Approach to Cybernetics* by Gordon Pask useful (Hutchinson/Radius, 1968).

11. H. Beam Pipe, 'Ministry of Disturbance', in *Seven Trips Through Time and Space* (first pub. 1958; Coronet, 1969).

12. Alfred Bester, *The Demolished Man* (first pub. 1953; Penguin, 1966).

13. G. L. Lack, 'Robot Dozen', in *New Writings in Science Fiction 10* (Corgi, 1967).

14. Eric Frank Russell, 'Jay Score', in *Men Martians and Machines* (first pub. 1955; Panther, 1965).

15. Harry Harrison, *War with the Robots* (Science Book Club/Dennis Dobson, 1968).

16. Isaac Asimov, *The Caves of Steel* (first pub. 1954; Panther, 1964).

17. Isaac Asimov, 'Catch that Rabbit' (1944) in *I Robot* (Panther, 1968).

18. Daniel Gallouey, *Homey Atmosphere* (Galaxy, 1961).

19. *New Scientist* (4 September, 1969).

20. Isaac Asimov, *The Caves of Steel* (first pub. UK, 1954; Panther, 1964).

21. David Fishlock, *Man Modified: An Exploration of the Man Machine Relationship* (Cape, 1969).

22. Bernard Wolfe, *Limbo 90* (first pub. 1952; Penguin, 1961: abridged).

23. John Rankine, 'Flight of a Plastic Bee', in *New Writings in Science Fiction 13* (Corgi, 1968).

24. Alfred Bester, 'The Diehard', in *Starburst* (first pub. 1958; Sphere, 1968).

25. Cordwainer Smith, 'A Planet Named Shayol', from *Spectrum IV* (first pub. 1961; Pan, 1967).

26. Clifford Simak, *All the Traps of Earth* (first pub. 1955; Four Square, 1964).

27. *New Scientist* (4 September 1969).

28. H. Putnam, *Robots: Machines or Artificially Created Life?* (Harper & Row, 1966). See p. 63 *et seq.*

29. Kurt Vonnegut, *Slaughterhouse Five* (first pub. 1969; Panther, 1972).

30. Kurt Vonnegut, *Breakfast of Champions* (Panther, 1974). See ch. 10.

31. William Nolan, 'And Miles To Go Before I Sleep', in *Impact 20* (Corgi, 1966).

32. Isaac Asimov, Preface to *The Rest of the Robots* (first pub. 1951; Panther, 1968).

33. Quoted in Isaac Asimov, *I Robot* (Panther, 1968), containing stories dating back to 1940.

34. Isaac Asimov, 'Run Around' (1942), in *I Robot* (Panther, 1968).

35. Isaac Asimov, 'Satisfaction Guaranteed' (1951), in *The Rest of the Robots* (Panther, 1968).

36. Isaac Asimov, 'Liar' (1941), in *I Robot* (Panther, 1968).

37. Ibid.

38. James Blish, *Polar Station*

39. Robert Silverberg, 'The Sixth Palace', in *Needle in a Time Stack* (first pub. 1955; Sphere, 1967).

40. Isaac Asimov, 'All the Troubles of the World' (1959), in *Nine Tomorrows* (Pan, 1966).

41. Isaac Asimov, 'Galley Slave' (1957), in *The Rest of the Robots* (Panther, 1968).

42. Isaac Asimov, 'Run Around' (1942), in *I Robot* (Panther, 1968).

43. Isaac Asimov, 'Little Lost Robot' (1947), in *I Robot* (Panther, 1968).

44. Ibid.

45. Isaac Asimov, 'Reason' (1941), in *I Robot* (Panther, 1968).

46. Isaac Asimov, *The Caves of Steel* (first pub. 1954; Panther, 1964).

47. Murray Leinster, *Exploration Team* (Astounding, 1956).

48. Isaac Asimov, *The Caves of Steel* (first pub. 1954; Panther, 1958).

49. Isaac Asimov, *The Naked Sun* (first pub. 1957; Panther, 1960). Detectives are surprisingly rare in this related genre. Lloyd Biggle Jnr, *All the Colours of Darkness* (Penguin, 1966), is an enjoyable case.

50. Isaac Asimov, 'The Jokester', in *Earth is Room Enough* (first pub. 1956; Panther, 1960).

51. John Racham, 'Computers Mate', *New Writings in Science Fiction 8* (Corgi, 1966).

52. *New Scientist* (2 July, 1970).

53. Isaac Asimov, 'The Evitable Conflict' (1950), in *I Robot* (Panther, 1968).

54. Valentina Zhurarlyeva, 'Stone from the Stars', in *Tekhnika Molodyozhi*, no. 9 (1959).

55. Arcady and Boris Strugatsky, *Six Matches* (Btk 490, 1960).

56. Ilya Varshavsky, *The Conflict* (Btk 289, 1964). Translated in: *The Best Soviet SF* (Science Fiction Book Club/McGibbon & Kee, 1966). Cf. Anatoly Dneprov, *Siema* (Btk 348, 1960; New York: Collier, 1966).

57. Boris and Arcady Strugatsky, 'Spontaneous Reflex' *Znanie Sila* No. 8 – virtually the only pre-1976 work of theirs not listed in Britikov's bibliography of *Russian/Soviet Science Fiction* (Leningrad: Institute of Foreign Literature, 1970) which even acknowledges the 'Baikal' half of *Snail on the Slope* (Btk 501).

58. Ilya Varshavsky, *Robby* (Btk 289, 1964).

59. Arcady and Boris Strugatsky, *Snail on the Slope* (Leningrad: Btk 501, 1966). Translation by A. Myers due at the time of writing to be published by Bantam.

60. E.g. Steve Gallagher, *The Last Rose of Summer* (Corgi, 1978), first written for radio.

61. Isaac Asimov, 'The Feeling of Power' (1957), in *Nine Tomorrows* (Pan, 1966).

62. Isaac Asimov, 'Some Day', in *Earth is Room Enough* (first pub. 1956; Panther, 1960).

63. Colin Wilson, *The Mind Parasites* (Science Fiction Book Club, 1968).

7
Aliens and other worlds

If robot and computer SF are means of interpreting mathematics, electronics and cybernetics to the layman and of forcing him to consider the essence of Man's reasoning process, then aliens are the bridge for biologists, sociologists and psychologists seeking to focus attention on the way Man feels and behaves.

The bug-eyed monster, affectionately abbreviated to BEM among SF fans, has been with us since stories were first told: Perseus and the Gorgon, Theseus and the Minotaur and a multitude of other embodiments of the horrific side of nature. But even if all these creatures did not behave in accordance with the natural laws which governed the animal kingdom of Man's world – they might fly or breathe fire or even turn their victims to stone – they were in general less intelligent than their human opponents, even if sometimes more cunning. The early monsters of SF were no less akin to the nightmares of our ancestral subconscious than those of classical mythology. Take the Martians of Wells's *War of the Worlds*:

> A big greyish, rounded bulk, the size perhaps of a bear, was rising slowly and painfully out of the cylinder. As it bulged up and caught the light it glistened like wet leather. Two large dark coloured eyes were regarding me steadfastly. It was rounded and had, one might say, a face. There was a mouth under the eyes, the lipless brim of which quivered and panted and dropped saliva. The body heaved and pulsated convulsively. A lank tentacular appendage gripped the edge of the cylinder, another swayed in the air.[1]

Today this would probably make the reader chuckle rather than recoil, although the simple BEM developed very little indeed from that Martian invader in 1898. The Martians strode about in their huge tripod robots devastating the land with their heat-rays and gas and it all seems a little primitive to us now, but as Wells said: 'The most extraordinary thing to my mind, of all the strange and wonderful things that happened upon that Friday, was the dove-tailing of the commonplace habits of our social order with the first beginnings of the series of events that was to topple that social order headlong.'[2]

So while Wells was establishing one role for the SF monster – the threat to Man's physical survival – he also clearly anticipated the catalytic role to be played by the aliens of later SF. The BEM tradition remains strong in the SF magazines and together with the grotesque and lurid magazine covers did much to establish in the mind of the general reader the idea that SF was faintly porno-sadistic rubbish. There are some good, enjoyable SF adventures featuring BEMs, but the main line of development has been away from the alien as a problem in human survival and towards the alien as a problem in communications, psychology and even sociology. C. S. Lewis played a significant part in breaking the traditional BEM concept in his trilogy.[3] The hero of *Out of the Silent Planet*, for instance, dreads his encounter with the life forms of Mars – quite unnecessarily.

> His universe was peopled with horrors such as ancient and medieval mythology could hardly rival. No insect-like vermiculate or crustacean abominable, no twitching feelers, rasping wings, slimy coils, curling tentacles, no monstrous union of super-human intelligence and insatiable cruelty seemed to him anything but likely on an alien world.[4]

Lewis repeatedly tries to break his readers of the mental conditioning which makes them assume that superhuman intelligence must go hand in hand with monstrosity of form and ruthlessness of will. He tries, by using a cosmic scale, to put Man in what he thinks is Man's proper place, and deploys all sorts of tricks to do so.

> They were much shorter than any animal he had yet seen on Malacandra, and he gathered that they were bi-peds, though the lower limbs were so thick and sausage-like that he hesitated to call them legs. The bodies were a little narrower at the top than at the bottom so as to be very slightly pear-shaped, and the heads were neither round like those of Hrossa nor long like those of the

Sorns, but almost square. They stumped along on narrow, heavy-looking feet which they seemed to press into the ground with unnecessary violence. And now their faces were becoming visible as masses of lumped and puckered flesh of variegated colour fringed in some bristly, dark substance . . . Suddenly, with an indescribable change of feeling, he realised that he was looking at men.[5]

Or, as one of the new SF writers put it: 'We venture out into space, at least in our minds, expecting to find wonderful monsters, monstrous wonders, instead we encounter distortions of ourselves.'[6]

A number of writers besides Lewis have effectively employed the trick of revealing a character's racial identity only at the last moment. 'The Last Martian'[7] by Frederic Brown is the story of a drunk in a bar who says he is a Martian. The twist in the last paragraph shows that he is and fortunately for him so were the people he was talking to! Here the technique of the 180 degree turnabout is used for dramatic effect rather than to make a point.

'In the Bag'[8] is another inversion story with the alien only revealing in the punch line that he is not in fact a man. The narrator describes himself going back to a laundry to complain about having been given the wrong clothes – those he received had five arms, one-leg trousers, and so on. The laundryman tells him what appears in human terms to be a tall story that these are the garments of a small group of refugees – who happen to be these peculiar shapes – from the tyrant of a distant planet; that they are here trying to plot the overthrow of the tyrant in secret and that unfortunately they'll have to kill this particular customer since he knows. The pay-off line is when the customer shoots the laundryman first because he is in fact one of the tyrant's own agents. The reader has already identified himself with the apparently human hero in his difficult situation and cannot decently abandon 'him' when he turns out to be an alien.

A not dissimilar technique is employed to criticise more overtly the aggressivenesss of Man to other species and in particular his tendency to shoot first and ask questions afterwards. Howard Fast is particularly adept at examining the blind and sudden irrationality of human fears. In 'The Large Ant'[9] the hero sees a giant ant at the bottom of his bed, instinctively lashes out with a golf club and kills it. It is later demonstrated to him it was in fact a highly intelligent creature, with a little built-in case of tools, and almost certainly a visitor from another world. All the other giant ants have been similarly killed in panic and the reader is left with an uncomfortable certainty as to what this intelligent species must think of Man and its likely reactions to him. We are meant to feel in the same way as the hero of Heinlein's satire *Revolt in 2100*[10] gun-toting, violent America: 'He turned away at once, feeling a little sick. It was the first non-human animal he had ever killed.' Sometimes the table are turned by the right-wing writers whose stories are intended to demonstrate that the only good alien is a dead alien. In one such story[11], the general, almost a caricature of the military establishment, urges the destruction of the alien craft just landed. The political leaders are horrified – we must make friendly contact. The alien craft proceeds to spread havoc and the politicians beg the general to take over. In time? We never know. But this type of story is the exception. The majority, in the last twenty years at least, follow the reasoning of Lewis's Malacandra story. Here Lewis is trying to reverse the process of anthropomorphism so common in SF stories, both of robots and alien worlds, by showing us monsters who turn out to be men, in the hope that we shall be able to look for the humanity in what appear to be monsters, indeed to realise that they may possess a greater degree of divine humanity than Man himself. This is a theme echoed by Clifford Simak in *Way Station*:[12] '... not humanity in the common and accepted sense of being a member of the human race of earth, but in the sense that certain rules of conduct must underlie all racial concepts even as the thing called humanity in its narrow sense underlay the human concept.'

If Lewis uses superior aliens to bring home the deficiencies of Man it must be admitted that most SF writers are still concerned to show Man's general, as opposed to specifically intellectual, moral or technical superiority, or at least his equality with supposedly superior aliens. But as Simak says, 'He had been trained in the human way of thinking and, even after all these years, that way of thought persisted. Persisted to a point where any way of thought that conflicted with it must automatically seem wrong.'[13] This attitude is adopted by several of the most distinguished SF writers. Bradbury, in 'The Strawberry Window',[14] writes: 'There's nothing better than Man with a capital M in my books. I'm prejudiced, of course, because I'm one of the breed. But if there's any way to get hold of that immortality men are always talking about, this is the way – spread out – seed the universe.' Or again Lloyd Biggle, Jnr, in *The Fury Out of Time*:

There is no lovelier planet in the galaxy, the Overseer said. To me it is always a majestic sight – an old, old world, its resources exhausted, its people ridiculously backward, yet scudding about in this obscure corner of space quite as nonchantly as if the Universe pivoted upon it. In an oblique sense the Universe does, you know. Earth is undeniably the birthplace of Man.[15]

This is typical both of SF's self-deprecatory intellectual recognition of the insignifance of our world and its place in the Universe and the simultaneous subconscious and psychological assertion that Man is superior, that whatever the status of the planet may be Man is to be the seed of any intelligence to spread through the Universe.

It is this attitude that Lewis condemns. Although he uses the SF convention, he is almost an anti-science-fiction writer, partly perhaps because of his religious objective. In *Voyage to Venus* he refers to the space-travelling Professor who represents the Power of Evil, in these terms:

He was a man obsessed with the idea which is at this moment circulating all over our planet in obscure works of 'Scientification', in little inter-planetary societies of rocketry clubs, and between the covers of monstrous magazines ignored or mocked by the intellectuals, but ready if ever the power is put into its hands, to open a new chapter of misery for the universe. It is the idea that humanity, having now sufficiently corrupted the planet where it rose, must at all costs contrive to seed itself over a larger area: that the vast astronomical distances which are God's quarantine regulations, must somehow be overcome.[16]

However there is a strong school of SF writers which recognises Man's insignificance. This school portrays him usually on his own planet, as a specimen, a creature of alien whim or curiosity. A common treatment of this theme is to challenge the reader to decide whether the 'hero' is mad, victim of illusions, or is in fact the subject of some cosmic experiment. In Asimov's 'Breeds There A Man'[17] – a story with the interesting sub-theme that intelligence is of itself no guarantee of survival – the following exchange takes place:

Surely, said Doctor Blaustein, it is not possible that the sun can be turned up and down at will.

Why not? It's just like a heating element in an oven. You think bacteria know what it is that works the heat that reaches them? Who knows? Maybe they evolve theories, too. Maybe they have their cosmogonies about cosmic catastrophes, in which clashing light bulbs create strings of Petri dishes. Maybe they think there must be some benificent creator that supplies them with food and warmth and says to them, 'be fruitful and multiply!'

In 'The Squirrel Cage,[18] it is a compulsive author and his type-writer who are the 'subject' of the alien experiment, and in *The Cage*[19] humans are captured by other rational beings and put in a cage. They are at their wits' end how to persuade their captors that they are not just animals but intelligent beings. In an idle moment they themselves fortuitously capture and cage a small animal. Shortly afterwards they are released. 'What made them realise that we were rational beings?' . . . 'Only rational beings, he said, put other beings in cages.' 'Expendable'[20] is a clever story which could be either a study in paranoia, of a man who thinks that part of the insect world is out to destroy the human race and that another part is on our side, or, on the basis of the supposition that at some point in prehistory the precursors of Man and the ant world fought out a war on the earth's surface which reduced both of them to their present 'primitive' state in which they are trying to reassert mastery, an SF suggestion that the man's delusion is in fact reality. Again, in 'The Dark Door'[21] we find another SF paradox story. Is the hero mad and suffering from a persecution complex or is in fact the alien takeover which is subject of his apparent delusion actually happening? These stories serve a secondary role, common in SF, of warning the scientific community of the dangers of taking the desirability of their own experiments for granted, particularly in the biological sciences. The main purpose, however, is to try and make us look at ourselves as if through alien eyes.

Just as the sensational Sunday newspapers enjoy oscillating between scary stories of UFOs and poking fun at those who claim to have seen them as a bunch of cranks, the SF story, more seriously, tries to suggest that somewhere on the borders of what we commonly regard as madness there may in fact exist an alien kingdom which is not illusion but reality. The SF writer enjoys the advantage that his hypothesis is scarcely one that can be disproved and which seems to satisfy the need for a belief in an existence other than Man's own here and now. These may be just a substitute for traditional beliefs in immortality, but the fairies and demons of earlier centuries, which indeed feature in a good number of modern SF stories, seem to suggest some more deep-rooted cause. However intellectually sceptical one may be, it is wellnigh impossible to remain so emotionally detached on a dark and lonely night, for example. It may well be that we are merely giving shape to our deep-seated fears and anxieties in writing and reading about these 'alien' beings. But no amount of psychoanalysis seems to make them any less real or enduring.

When the aliens are on the earth, whether emasculating us with benevolence like Clarke's Guardians or terrorising us like Wells's Martians, our reaction is one of fear and suspicion. Because they have come here we assume too readily that they are of evil intent or consequence. When we ourselves go imaginatively exploring space, our conceit often assumes that our own collective intentions must be benevolent, if occasionally misunderstood by the aliens or opposed by an evil minority of men. Our self-confidence in the face of the universe is both stirring and risible. The outlook is typified by a character in Heinlein's children's story *Farmer in the Sky*[22] whose rather positive philosophy of colonising is that there is 'no such thing as natural environment – man creates his own environment' – and too bad if it does not suit other life forms. In space our inward-looking obsessions give way to a sense of adventure and above all curiosity. What will the aliens, if any, be like?

The orthodox Russian writer is in no doubt. Nowhere is the effect on SF of the limits imposed by Marxist theory more apparent than in the range of intelligent beings portrayed by Eastern and Western writers. In the work of the Western author intelligence, equal or superior to Man's, is found in a tremendous variety of forms, from abnormal known animals and strange galactic creatures to intangible, invisible forces. For almost every Soviet writer, nothing can be more intelligent than Man, indeed nothing but Man can be intelligent. Every intelligent being encountered in the cosmos is at most a slight variation of the human shape. The alien must have hands for example to conform to the Theory of Labour – a thesis argued at length in the Strugatskys' *Destination Amaltheia*.[23] One character recalls

the time long ago when it was still widely believed that thinking beings could exist in practically any form, that the structure of their organisms could vary greatly. That was when the survivals of religious prejudices induced even serious scientists to assume that a brain could develop in any body – just as men once believed gods could assume any physical form. Actually, however, the anatomy and physiology of man, the only creature with a brain capable of rational thinking on earth, were not the result of some accidental caprice of nature. On the contrary, they represented a maximum degree of adaptation to environment and corresponded to man's highly developed reasoning powers and nervous activity.

This argument is further developed as the cosmonauts speculate on the probable form of the aliens they will encounter. 'A trunk, too, is unnecessary for a being with hands and a human being must have hands.'[24] Again in *Stone from the Stars* Valentina Zhuravlyeva advances the thesis that intelligent life must be like Man. 'Without hands there can be no labour and it is labour that created man.'[25]

Man himself is assumed to be the climax of evolution by the orthodox Russian writer. 'Man was the only force in the Universe that was capable of acting intelligently, of overcoming the most formidable obstacles.'[26] 'The creatures of earth were like him, like this inhabitant of far-distant Mars. That meant that the super-rationality of evolution is narrow, for a rational being can only select similar forms.'[27] Statements like these abound in Russian science fiction, and not until the mid-1960s do one or two writers (S. Snegov is the most important of them) postulate non-humanoid life forms.

The attitude of Western SF writers was neatly put by Arthur Clarke in his Kalinga prize speech. 'Science fiction encourages the cosmic viewpoint; perhaps that's why it is not popular among those literary pundits who have never accepted the Copernican revolution, nor grown used to the idea that man may not be the highest form of life in the universe.'[28] Olaf Stapledon in *Sirius* chose a dog, despite its lack of hands and regretful admiration for manual work, as his creature of superior intelligence, because 'dogs excel in social awareness and only a social animal can make full use of its intelligence.'[29] – a theme we shall see touched on again in Russian SF. Not that the Western writer is without either hubris or unconscious irony. Asimov can say, 'Humanity was the natural climax of evolution on any world based upon a water/oxygen chemistry with proper intensities of temperature and gravitation.'[30] And in *Dreadful Sanctuary* Russell writes, 'The Martians therefore were white because they had to be white.'[31]

The concept of intelligent life forms in non-humanoid guise is the subject of frequent criticism in Russian SF.

> I'm quite sure that if octopuses were to come here from Mars there would be people who would come to an understanding with them. Perhaps they will now understand that it is not enough for a creature to do sums and solve problems in geometry to be considered a human being. They'll have to learn it requires something much more than that. Those scientists have grown very proud and can't see further than their experiments. But science isn't everything. In this century of amazing developments in science, one might conclude that science is all-powerful. But let us try to imagine that an artificial brain has been created which is far superior to the human brain, possessing greater capacity for work. Will a creature with a brain of this kind have the right to be called a human being? What really makes us what we are? The ability to count, to analyse, to make logical computations, or is it something else that has been bred by society, something to do with people's relations to each other and the attitude of the individual to a collective body?[32]

Or again: 'There cannot be any other entirely different thought process, just as man cannot exist outside a society and nature.'[33]

But these latter quotations are a variation on the theme of human superiority, and what constitutes human nature, with an interesting difference. These Russian writers are, it seems, arguing that it is our social relationships alone which make us human, that collectively we are clearly distinguishable as mankind; individually our status as Man is more in question. Unfortunately the Russian authors do not go on to examine the whole concept of collective intelligence which is the logical outcome of such a line of reasoning. Howard Fast is amongst the writers, albeit a Western one, who take their Marxism on to explore the possibilities of the social organism – the State – and the biological organisms of which it is composed – men – becoming merged into a single collective intelligence, both being and state. This is a world explored most successfully by the American writer, Theodore Sturgeon, who looks at it in evolutionary terms. He sees the development of new faculties, such as telepathy, leading to new forms of collective being, (Wyndham in Britain takes both this approach and that of the collective intelligence in alien form in *The Midwich Cuckoos*.)[34]

In 'To Marry Medusa'[35] Sturgeon wrote,

> Few humans would understand, but not many have made the effort to comprehend the nature of the hive mind – what it must be like to have such a mind, and further, to be totally ignorant of the fact that any other kind of mind could exist. . . . but so fused in its experience and comprehension were the concepts 'intelligence' and 'group' that it was genuinely incapable of regarding them as separable things.

He goes on to try and see mankind through the concepts of this collective intelligence:

> As a defence against thick concentrations of cosmic dust, these creatures had designed space-ships which, on approaching a cloud, broke up into hundreds of small, streamlined parts which would come together and reunite when the danger was passed. Could that be what humanity had done. Had they a built-in mechanism . . . . which would fragment the hive mind on contact from outside, break it up into $2\frac{1}{2}$ billion specimens like this Gurlick?[36]

This externalised approach leads to some delightful descriptions of the bizarre individualism of Man. 'It put out its fire by smothering it with its mink coat. It killed its rattle-snake by hitting it with the baby.'[37] But the story is unusual in that it suggests a number of positive and desirable attributes of the collective mind. Usually in Western SF this is treated as anathema, as a form of psychological totalitarianism.

Again in *More Than Human*[38] Sturgeon examines the theme of constructive collective intelligence, a kind of *homo Gestalt* which he sees as the next step in Man's own evolution, just as Wyndham does in *The Chrysalids*.[39] A more conventional view is expressed by one of the characters in Michael Bishop's *Funeral for the Eyes of Fire* when he says, 'a telepathic community would most likely centre either on thoroughly paranoic or a thoroughly homogeneous unit of individuals.'[40]

There are a number of good SF writers, like Bradbury and Zenha Henderson with her 'People', who bestow on groups of individuals some of the supposed faculties of a collective intelligence, such as telepathy, teleporting and so on. But somehow they are squeamish about accepting the total surrender of individual personality to such a collective being as a desirable and happy state. The psychological struggle involved in accepting such a surrender is well described in Samuel Delaney's *Babel 17*.[41] Creatures with different powers and qualities are moulded together not just to form the collective unified intelligence needed to control a spacecraft but to provide the physical composition of the vessel itself.

Although the writing is sometimes strained to the point of being unintelligible it does give the impression of an alien state in which the surrender of personality is, as in several Eastern religions, the ultimate release and achievement. Frank Herbert in *Hellstrom's Hive*[42] carefully isolates the 'collectiveness' of the hive as the only aspect of it we are likely to reject emotionally. All its other aspects, in theory at least, are laudable in conventional moral terms. Hellstrom himself, however, cannot abandon the very American concept of personal leadership.

Hoyle's story *The Black Cloud*[43] is interesting in that it postulates, largely successfully, a recognisable intelligence of a completely different order from Man's. The success with which this is done is such that the reader does not look on the cloud as 'alive' or intelligent much before the hero. Yet in retrospect the cloud's actions are all logically interrelated. Hoyle himself appears to reject what he at first suggests:

Because there is just one good way to construct a knee joint. Similarly there is just one logic, and just one way of designing the general layout of intelligent life.' ... 'It isn't the universe that's following our logic, it's *we* that are constructed in accordance with the logicale of the universe. And that is what I might call a definition of intelligent life; someting that reflects the basic structure of the universe.[44]

It would be wrong to think the Russian SF writer only capable of envisaging intelligence in quasi-human form, but in order to write of it he has to render it respectable by human derivation. A. Belayev's *Hoighty Toighty*[45] while apparently satirising the possibility of non-human intelligence by the device of transplanting a human brain into an elephant may in fact force the reader to consider whether intelligence could reside in non-human form. In the same way it implicitly ridicules the supposed absolute virtue of human anatomy, and in particular the possession of hands, by having the professor writing two theses simultaneously in different notebooks. It may be that this provocation is unintentional, a suspicion confirmed by the fact that Belayev is so much the orthodox child of his society that he thinks it necessary to explain to his reader that the Congo is in Africa. But by accident or design the effect is the same.

The Strugatskys can be more overtly heretical. In *Wanderers and Travellers*,[46] in which the SF element emerges slowly and convincingly, they examine the possibility that Man, even Marxist Man, is not the highest form of intelligence in the universe, while still refusing to accept that their aliens are *ipso facto* a proper subject for undue reverence by Man:

> We don't even know what to expect. We could meet them any moment, face to face. And, you know, they may turn out to be much superior to us . . . What I am afraid of is an unprecedented humiliation of mankind . . . To my mind the more superior they proved to be, the less chances there were of getting in their way. . . . They are still only a part of nature for us to discover and investigate, no matter how superior to us they might be . . . They are outsiders, and that's that.

The writers choose to endorse the orthodox position later in the story.

In 'An Emergency Case'[47] they take the old hydra-myth and give it a factual explanation, an explanation which necessitates the acceptance by the reader of an intelligent, non-hostile but non-human alien form. This kind of story is the exception to the confident domination of the universe by Man, the superior creature, which is usual in Soviet SF, but it *does* exist, notably in *Men Like Gods*, the Snegov trilogy. It may be that the reader sees more in these stories than their authors intended but perhaps that is why SF is such a dangerous enemy of all autocratic or dogmatic systems, as the editors of *Neues Deutschland* clearly saw in hammering poor Horst Müller's story referred to earlier.

The range of non-human intelligence in Western SF is, superficially at least, very extensive. However, many of these so-called aliens turn out on closer examination to be exercises in anthropomorphising in which only the externals have been changed. Some of these transpositions give rise to the most ludicrous imagery as when in *The Interpreter*[48] the usually sophisticated Brian Aldiss has two aliens 'linking eye stalks' in greeting. Many Western writers are as clearly circumscribed by their prejudices as the Russians by their dogma. In fairness, however, the difficulties of creating and conveying an alien species in human terms to human readers must not be minimised.

A practical limiting factor is the chemistry of life, the necessary elemental ingredients, as far as human science is aware, for any living organism. This does not restrict those writers who postulate non-organic intelligences, be they energy charges, wave patterns or any other physical phenomena; but for most writers some living creature is the essential basis for intelligence. In the Russian story 'The Heart of the Serpent'[49] some scientific ingenuity is displayed in constructing the idea of a planet whose oceans consist of hydrochloric acid, where plants break up hydrogen-oxide-accumulating carbohydrates and release free fluorine with the aid of the radiation energy of the system's luminary, as plants on earth break up water. Fluorine mixed with nitrogen is breathed by alien people and animals, who obtain energy from the combustion of the carbohydrates in fluorine, and must exhale carbon fluorine and hydrogen fluoride. The aliens when encountered closely resemble but are not the same as men, It is interesting that the inhabitants of this fluorine planet, in the opinion of the men who discover them, must be bound to conform to the socialist pattern at some stage.

In 1963 a paper at The British Association did speculate in non-fictional form about a world based on hydrogen peroxide or fluorine 'air'. It rightly recognised the difficulty of imagining silicon creatures breathing out silicon dioxide quartz crystals. The author settled in the end for fluorine breathing. In 1957 Poul Anderson in *Call Me Joe*[50] described 'a life using liquid methane as its basic solvent, solid ammonia as a starting point for nitrate synthesis; the plants use solar energy to build unsaturated carbon compounds, releasing hydrogen; the animals eat the plants and reduce those compounds again to the saturated form.'

Most SF writers create their alien planets much as their predecessors might have described or speculated on some recently discovered remote corner of the earth between the sixteenth and nineteenth centuries. They do not see them as totally different and coherent entities but as areas of this or that difference from the commonly known norm. This is not to say that a number of very good stories have not been written using this technique, the best usually dealing with a human attempt to survive or escape such conditions. But more satisfying are the stories where the world and its inhabitants are totally alien, where everything has a logic of its own, intelligible only by reference to the other characteristics of the creation and not to those of our own planet or people. Three Western writers in particular have excelled in this field: Hal Clement, in the creation of physically different worlds, James White in that of biologically and psychologically different beings and Colin Kapp in culturally and intellectually different societies which men strive to understand.

Hal Clement has a considerable gift for creating utterly alien but logical and plausible worlds. While humans do appear in his stories, they do not dominate. Indeed a central role is usually played by an alien being and Clement attempts to make us see the entire situation through these alien senses. He developed this technique steadily throughout the 1950s. In *Mission of Gravity* (1954)[51] he writes a story set on a disc-shaped planet with variations in gravity so great as to make one part of it virtually uninhabitable for creatures from another. At the centre the pull of gravity is fifty times that of earth and can only be survived by small creatures who take up minerals into their body structure for strength. (They are fascinatingly paralleled in this respect by the modern technique of microbial mining in which minute living organisms concentrate minerals metabolically in their bodies in sufficient concentration to be exploitable.)[52] There is a human character in this story but he soon finds he can only act through the agency of the aliens and in particular that of the merchant-adventuring insect-like creature who sails the seas of the high-gravity areas. Contact is by radio, but it is essentially the adventures of the alien which grip the sympathy of the reader; one almost comes to share his attitude to the human voice on the radio – to see Man from outside by this act of transference.

In *Cycle of Fire*[53] although human characters are actually physically present during some of the action we are again primarily interested in the actions of the native inhabitants. In this instance the world is one of extreme temperature variations on a cyclical basis. One form of life has to undergo an adaptive metamorphosis to make way for a second capable of surviving the opposite extreme of temperature. The abortive attempts to impose human ethical standards threaten the destruction of the species. They are well meaning but based on total misunderstanding. 'Dar Lang Ahn was not human, and the pictures which formed most of his thoughts, being shaped by an eyesight and cultural background drastically different from those of any human being, could never be properly translated to the mind of a person of Earth.'[54] The Western SF writer is at least prepared to recognise this fact. In this story for example when the human character eats meat which is cooked he is violently ill, having been perfectly all right when it was eaten uncooked. This is one of the ways in which SF inverts a situation to question the rationality of what we humans take for granted.

In *Close to Critical*, published in 1958,[55] we have two human children marooned in a space capsule on a planet whose environment is totally inimical to humans. Their survival depends on the outcome of a struggle between the indigenous creatures in which Man can again only play a second-hand role. In all of these three Clement stories the humans are not so much present to initiate and observe as to react and to be observed. Clement gives us an outside look at ourselves by writing so convincingly and excitingly about a coherent, logical and acceptable alien world that the reader temporarily identifies with their inhabitants and sees men as aliens. But where Lewis accomplishes this by a rather detached philosophic approach Clement operates on a less intellectual, more emotional level. Lewis made us think about Man as if we were alien professors of logic or sociology; Clement makes us feel as if we were ordinary aliens, makes us feel about men as they might feel.

Both White and Kapp, in their very different ways, make no attempt to exclude Man from their stories and are indeed quite happy to let a Man play the lead. Their object is not so much to get us to look at Man critically as to condition us to look at possible aliens sympathetically.

James White's approach in his novels and short stories about Sector General, the galactic hospital with patients and doctors of all races, is to see aliens as medical problems in the broadest sense. The hospital is constructed in various sections with different and mutually incompatible environments for the different creatures. But these are only the outward signs of much deeper differences in psychology and physiology between the patients which must be fully understood if the doctors are to effect a cure. The hero of the stories is a human doctor but he works as part of a medical team of several species whose different characteristics make them a formidable combination. There is Priliclla, for example, the delicate insect-like creature whose capacity for empathy is so highly developed that it is able to sense the reactions of patients with whom no other communication seems possible. These stories speculate on the satisfactions and difficulties of inter-specific co-operation. The doctors have to recognise that their pleasures and habits may cause revulsion to colleagues of other species on whose abilities they depend. White's ingenuity at creating different physiologies is considerable: 'Physically it was a large, fleshy doughnut which rolled continually because to stop rolling was to die – its ring-like body circulated while its blood, operating on a form of gravity feed system, remained still. Even the simplest medical examination or treatment necessitated the doctor rotating with his patient . . . .'[56] Or again in 'Vertigo'[57] he creates the planet Meatball on which the whole topology is biological. The psychological differences which White suggests are an even more stimulating part of his world. Diagnosis is assisted by the diagnostician absorbing medical data by tapes from direct electronic transfer to his own brain. With the information, he willy-nilly absorbs the feelings and conditioning of the patient's species. This deliberately accepted schizophrenia has disturbing effects on the diagnosticians who have to be strong and stable characters to endure it. Yet without this alien background, diagnosis and treatment would be impossible.

To a great extent White sees the problem of helping alien creatures as one of communication. They have to be made firstly to understand that help not harm is intended, and secondly to convey sufficient information about themselves and their reactions to enable the alien physician to take the correct action, often in the face of apparent and obvious contradictions to human logic.

Different is not wrong, only different and whatever the difference is between intelligent living species they have a responsibility towards each other. Ignorance breeds hostility, understanding amity, as when in the second novel about Sector General[58] an 'enemy's' attacks on the hospital are stopped on the verge of victory only by recognition of what its staff are trying to do for the sick and wounded both of their own species and of others, including the attacker's.

In White's stories the barrier to mutual understanding is failure to communicate on a face-to-face – if that is the right phrase – basis. In many of Kapp's the problem is a more abstract one, of understanding from the internal evidence of archaeology and engineering. Kapp will construct a complete, artificial environment with its own logic, as in *The Imagination Trap*[59] and then challenge his human protagonists, and readers, to crack the code of that logic by asking fundamental questions. 'Now what factors do control the size of things? Why is anything the size it is rather than a million times larger or smaller?'

In *The Subways of Tazoo*[60] he writes, 'The Tazoons were not even humanoid, and the probability is that neither their physiology nor their logic had anything in common with our own. It could be misleading if we attempt to interpret their actions by simple extrapolation of what we might have done in similar circumstances.' Or again,

> Alien! said Jacko in awe. The connotations of that word get lost by common usage. It doesn't begin to convey the mind-twisting sense that everything you know and believe has been scrunched up and re-sorted by a different kind of logic. These people had different values and different basics, and it makes the mind squirm even trying to readjust.

The opposite view is expressed by another of Kapp's archaeologist explorers:

> They didn't have different basics, said Fritz, they merely had a different emphasis on the relative values of the same old basics. We can't yet try to comprehend the culture, but when it comes to unravelling their engineering I think we shall find we have a great deal in common.

Like Fritz I find the distinction drawn between culture and science – which is surely a part of culture – a dubious one. Kapp seems to be trying to suggest that while metaphysical and sociological speculation about alien worlds may be fruitless in themselves through the artifacts of those worlds, and particularly those of engineering, we may arrive at some idea of their philosophy and social structure – provided always that we do not prejudicially circumscribe our imagination with our own scientific and technological concepts. In 'The Pen and the Dark'[61] one character tries to illustrate the gulf of understanding by analogy: 'even if they'd tried to tell us I doubt our capacity to have understood. Try explaining the uses and construction of a Dewar flask to an ant – and see who gets tired first.' In lighter vein in another story Kapp demonstrates that the gap can be bridged if we are prepared to explore any possibility – that a machine may in fact be an animal, fuel may be food and so on.

Kapp stories in general, unlike those of White and Clement, convey a sense not just of Man's universal insignificance but of his great loneliness, of our being cut off, by our inability to understand or to communicate, from all the other living beings of the galaxy. More optimistic writers speculate on what those common denominators to all living, sentient, intelligent beings might be which could form the starting point for communication between alien species.

Treatments of the problem differ widely. The Frenchman Claude Veillot in 'The First Days of May'[62] suggests that it is scarcely worth trying to communicate with the invading aliens.

> Imagine for a moment that in their eyes *we're* the ants. Would it bother you much to break up an ant hill with a few kicks? And did you ever think about negotiating in any way with the ants? They're intelligent and highly developed, too, undoubtedly, but in a way so different from ours that it doesn't pay to look for points of comparison.

In more humorous vein Alan Nourse suggests in 'Tiger by the Tail'[63] that when we try to communicate with an alien world we may in fact be treading on a limed twig. The hero of this story is consulted on a case of shoplifting in which vast quantities of metal materials seem to disappear into a very small bag. His theory is that another universe, short of particular metals, is pulling them from our universe by means of this bag. So our clever hero scientist thinks that he will catch whatever is on the other side by sticking a piece of metal into the bag attached to a huge winch, in the belief that the aliens at the other end will not be expecting such a move. The device is accordingly set up, but just as they think they have solved the problem and are drawing the other universe into ours, the metal rod begins to disappear *into* the bag again. The tiger of the title had thought of this particular trick first.

Katherine MacLean, in the excellent *Unhuman Sacrifice,*[64] warns most movingly of the dangers of one-way communication. This satire on religious and ethical proselytising and on the probability of misunderstanding other cultures and ways of life is an apt reminder that effective communication must be a two-way process. In this story earth men visiting another planet have with them a missionary. The natives of the planet hang the older adolescents up by the heels in what appears to be a barbarous initiation into adulthood. When the missionary dissuades the natives from pursuing their 'ungodly practices,' in fact all he does is to prevent them rooting their heads in the mud during the flood season and so turning into the plants during flood time which are their higher evolutionary form. The ironic conclusion, in which the devoted human ship's engineer plucks up the plant which he thinks was his native friend but which was in fact a quite different one, is most effective.

The risks inherent in the zeal of the missionary or the colonial administrator are well described in Bishop's clever *Stolen Faces*,[65] in which he uses Aztec-type names for the natives to help give a sense of alienness. As punishment for insubordination, the hero has been put in charge of a leper colony on an alien planet whose ruling race finds the lepers an embarrassment. 'The failure of the Tezcatil to regard the Muphomores as fundamentally human was not seriously put forward as a factor in the century long debate.' The real disease behind the apparent deformities of the leprosy is a cultivated self-denigration and lack of self-esteem which leads the Muphomores secretly to mutilate themselves in an annual ritual. The denouement is a typically depressing one of the 1970s SF. When the hero finds he cannot persuade the alien world's rulers to ameliorate the lot of the Muphomores he identifies himself with them by joining in their rites and fearfully mutilating himself. The only glimmer of hope is that perhaps this 'crucifixion' may bring one or two of the alien members of his own staff at least to recognise the underlying humanity of the Muphomores.

Another misconception is amusingly dealt with in Anthony Boucher's story 'Barrier'[66] in which an alien had prepared himself for time travel by studying the speech of earth, 'but made the mistake of thinking there was only one earthly speech, just as we tend imaginatively to think of Martian or Venusian as a single language.'

In many stories Pythagoras' theorem is used as the lowest common denominator for communication between completely alien species and intelligence. Very few of these stories, however, go on to develop the idea logically to the point at which all communication between species is mathematical, although some Russian writers do go a considerable way along this path. Another conventional trick for avoiding the necessity to explain the methods of inter-specific communication is to rely on thought-transference.

In an article in *Life*, 'A Serious Search for Weird Worlds,'[67] Ray Bradbury gave the most plausible hypothesis I have come across. He says that life would almost certainly be sustained by light from a neighbouring planet; 'therefore, any scientific civilisation would certainly seek to understand the nature of light which is the basis of their life. Once you understand the nature of light, you are led to the whole electromagnetic spectrum of which radio is a necessary part.' Since hydrogen is present throughout the universe then it is probable that the transmission of any signal designed to attract alien attention would be as close as possible to the frequency of the hydrogen band. By this means any alien could convey first algebraic symbols and then geometric figures – back to Pythagoras again. But supposing the aliens do not use our mathematical concepts? Perhaps in the end these questions become academic. If any being is so alien as to be even mathematically unintelligible then although his actions may affect us we shall, as with Kapp and Veillot's ants, never be able to communicate so as to alter those actions.

Russian writers in the main would subscribe to such theories as Bradbury's in so far as they suggest a common nature and form of intelligence throughout the universe. Most, but not all, of them believe we shall just discover more of what we know already.

Whatever the means of communication or the nature of the aliens, stories about them by Western SF writers reveal three things: an ineradicable instinct for colonisation, an insatiable curiosity about the nature of Man himself, and a great sense of loneliness. Some of the colonising stories are written from the point of view of the colonised, some from that of the colonisers but as Lewis suggested they all assume that Man, whether as subject or conquerer, villain or hero, has a destiny beyond the limits of his present planet. Most of the Western writers in this context are concerned that Man should behave in a civilised and humane way while sometimes fearing that, as in our own history, he may not. If we do ever make successful, peaceful contact with an alien race then I believe that SF writers will be able to take at least some of the credit for any open-minded approach which may be adopted. As Bradbury says in the article already referred to, 'Astronautical history may depend on those concepts of beauty and utility our men take along as unacknowledged cargo to the stars.'

SF about aliens may help us also to know our human selves better, to understand and therefore to a greater extent to control the foibles and virtues of mankind. Above all, however, I believe it reveals a sense of loneliness, however dignified, which is bound to descend on men without religion. This kind of writing is an expression of Man's longing to believe and discover that other beings share the burden of infinity.

Science fiction's concern with man's old deep seated fears in new guise and new settings is nowhere more clearly shown than in dealing with the medieval concept of the possession of Man by other forces. Indeed many modern SF possession stories would seem perfectly familiar to the reader of the Middle Ages once he had grasped that, in the religion of science, devils had been replaced by alien intelligences, and witches and sorcerers by irresponsible scientists. He would even have recognised that category of stories which deals with the possession of inanimate objects or their endowment, at least, with human characteristics, usually malevolent. We have already cited Sturgeon's *Killdozer* as a classic of this kind.[68] Another first-class story of the apparently animate machine can be found in Alistair Bevan's 'The Scarlet Lady'.[69] This describes a much sought after old motor car which holds an obsessive attraction for its owner whom it then seeks to destroy. The suddenly faulty brakes, the steering nut that drops off and all the other disasters could be just coincidence but . . . . The reader is left certain, however illogically, that the machine is actively motivated by destructive hate of the kind most wittily shown in Shel Silverstein's cartoon[70] of the television set which first tempts the solitary viewer to lean close to adjust the 'faulty' picture, then entangles him in the indoor aerial and finally gobbles him up.

The best philosophic argument for the animate nature of things as demonstrated by their animosity to Man is put forward by H. Chandler Elliott in *Inanimate Objection.*[71] This excellent story tells of the apparently mad major who argues that the hostility of inanimate objects is because in fact they are not inanimate but have a will to destroy the human race. He is, accordingly, locked up in a not unsympathetic mental hospital where he argues with his doctors to convince them he is right. As he says, 'Perhaps you will admit that any notion, however apparently fantastic, that has been held by many ages and cultures is worth scientific investigation, if only to explain it away.' Throughout the story we are left in doubt as to whether he is mad or in fact his theory is right.

All these tales of the possession of animate objects by forces inimical to Man have an absolute minimum of science in them. They count for their effect on that other ingredient of 'knowledge' fiction, their close association with recognisable everyday experience. Why does that particular step always make us stumble? Why do we kick and swear at the reluctant mowing machine as if it were alive? The fact that we do is enough to give substance to the implicit belief in the stories described. There is very little more scientific content in the tale of alien possession of a human or animal. A brief explanation of how the alien being – generally very small and parasitic in nature – arrived and spreads, or how it attempts to exercise control of human minds more remotely if it is not of the infective kind, is all the reader is generally afforded. Once this point has been established our writers are preoccupied with how the individual human or the human race can retain its freedom of action; how the invading alien can be repulsed; how in fact that other personality within us can be kept in its proper place. Typical, if better written than most, is Christopher's *The Possessors*[72] in which an alien 'spoor of intelligence' seizes one person in an isolated Swiss chalet and spreads to the others by that same compulsive desire to 'infect' their companions which is a hallmark of the destruction-bent drug addict, a common theme in tales of alien parasitic intelligence. Relatively early on the protagonists deduce what is happening – the reader earlier still – and it is the resistance to the ultimate prospect of a takeover of the entire human race which is the centre of interest.

There are literally hundreds of stories on this theme. Titles like *The Mind Worm, The Mind Parasites, Under Compulsion, The Sleep Eaters, The Silent Speakers* and *The Dream Master*[73] abound. The stories range from the sophisticated examination by writers such as Nourse and Ballard of what constitutes madness and therefore 'normal' intelligence, to straight horror stories. Ballard seems fascinated by those innate reflexes triggered by stimuli outside our control, which seem indicative of our lack of free will or at least of its great circumscription. Nourse looks the other way to the possible extension of our will through a Psi factor or telepathy and asks not only how far can we push the human mind and retain our sanity but how far ought we to push it even for national or racial survival.

A macabre subcategory of alien possession is that which suggests that our own small children are either themselves alien or are being used by aliens – a view to which an exasperated parent can occasionally subscribe. In 'Let's Play Poison'[74] one character says, 'Sometimes I actually believe the children are invaders from another dimension.' My favourite story in this group is the title story of the same Ray Bradbury collection, 'The Small Assassin'.[75] This is fiction of infinite possibilities – horrific and yet beautiful at the same time. In this story the baby is trying to kill its parents. Bradbury takes the real fears and feelings for a first born and twists and extrapolates them. He utilises our reluctant recognition of the repulsive, selfish hostility of the new-born child. 'If what you say is true, then every woman in the world would have to look on her baby as something to dread, something to wonder about.' And in the end the family doctor is compelled to this shocking conclusion and decides to ensure that the baby destroys itself. In 'My Friend Bobby'[76] Nourse writes about a five-year-old who can read, communicate and control the thoughts, first of all of his dog and then of his mother and father. He drives his parents out of the house but because of his immaturity does not realise that the dog cannot in fact look after him.

Possession, control or influence of one person's mind by another is more commonly treated in terms of adult humans. Such a takeover is often simple, old-fashioned and hostile as in Asimov's *Anybody Else Like Me.*[77] This is an odd-man-out story with the interesting difference that the two telepaths, a man and a married woman, eventually discover each other at a distance by mental contact. The man determines to have telepathic children. The woman, her husband away, resists this 'idea' frantically as the man gets nearer and nearer to her house. She finally finds and admits to herself her own telepathic powers only when he is as close as the far side of the road. Then she uses them to make him step in front of a car and so condemns herself to ask life-long the question of the title which had driven her would-be ravisher.

The problem of free will is more subtly deployed in a story like *The Dream Master*[78] where the takeover is for therapeutic purposes, rather as with James White's Sector General diagnosticians or in Walter Miller's story *Dark Benediction*,[79] in which the takeover does not diminish our free will but extends the range of our senses. The hero of Roger Zelazny's *Doorways in the Sand*[80] in the end willingly accepts the new symbiotic relationship with an alien intelligence, for while it sets him apart from the rest of mankind it opens up infinite prospects both for the hero and for the race. These writers are challenging us to ask ourselves whether in all circumstances the exercise of free will leads to the highest self-fulfilment. Finally, there are those stories where it is the human hero who takes over the alien body, whether parasitically or symbiotically the reader is left to decide, as in *Call me Joe.*[81] In this tale a native animal of a storm-swept ammonia planet is controlled by the mind of a man (a cripple) in a circling satellite because the planet itself is too deadly for human life yet needs to be worked for human purposes. During the course of the story the man becomes so identified with the animal as a result of this relationship that he is unable to survive when the animal can no longer survive.

In the 1970s a change takes place in the attitude of many writers towards the aliens in their stories. Of course, many of the old assumptions and tricks remain and nowhere are they more skilfully deployed than in *Doorways in the Sand.* [82] This is a rarity in SF both for its good writing and its strong characterisation. The existence of aliens is very gradually introduced, changes are incremental and gradual, and therefore hard to perceive. When the characters do become aware of change, their reaction of disorientation is quite traditional. 'Perhaps, deep down inside, I wanted us to be alone in the cosmos – to claim all of that for ourselves. Or any aliens encountered a little behind us in everything.'

The device of using an oddball perennial student, whose hobby is climbing the roofs and high buildings where much of the action is set, conveys a sense of both familiar objects and unfamiliar perspectives, which reflects Man's relationship with the aliens. But for all its unusual angles it reaches the usual conclusion of inferior Man nevertheless *feeling* in some ways innately superior; an attitude neatly explained by one of the minor characters. 'For all your talk of cultural relativism . . . the very act of evaluation automatically makes you feel superior to whatever you are evaluating, and you evaluate everything.'

Conventional, too, at first perusal, is Michael Bishop's *A Funeral For The Eyes of Fire* [83] in which an entertaining story is told (albeit sometimes clumsily) against the background of an ingeniously contrived and convincing alien culture, a culture which seems at first to be running the old trick of distributing distinct human qualities among different groups of aliens so that we can examine the way in which we resolve our own inner conflict in such matters. But gradually Bishop moves a little away from the conventional stance:

. . . we have created a society in which the miraculous is looked upon with all the grand and mighty suspicion of the intellect. Even that which appears momentarily worthy of the mind's dread and incomprehension has explanations and, paradoxically, derives from this fact a mystery of its own, becomes even more miraculous for having an empirical basis. If no answers now exist, one day they will.

The story moves on to adopt the backlash creed of the 1970s, and the totally rational ruling class is criticised for failing to see 'the abyss yawning under their uncomprehending homage to reason and science'. Bishop is in fact concerned with the conflict between the transcendental and rational longings of the different groups of characters. He seeks 'intersection of intellects and souls . . . transcendental convergence'.

In this latter attitude his story is indicative of that substantial body of work which no longer uses the difference or even the superiority of the alien to moralise or to improve Man let alone to demonstrate his innate invincibility. While many of the story lines remain the same, their tone suggests that the alien portrait is now shown to make us reject our humanity. Instead of writing about aliens so that we may more clearly understand what we are, we now write about them because we despair of what we are and desperately wish to be something else. In the *Ophiuchi Hotline*[84] the heroine asked of the human race, 'Was it going anywhere?' but the implied question, in this as in many other recent stories is, 'Has it anywhere to go?'

During the 1970s the nightmare of loss of personal identity suffered by most Western writers in considering the various ways in which increasing conformity is forced upon us took an even more monstrous shape. Animal experiments in cloning were soon extrapolated to create a world of human clones. The old technique for confronting oneself had been the standard paradox of time travel. The time 'loop' allowed the protagonist travelling to the past or future to meet another version of himself – or in the case of Heinlein's 'By His Bootstraps'[85] a whole series of himselves. An embarrassing alternative used with witty tristesse by James Tiptree[86] was to find yourself or your lover dead!

The effect of this is described by a character in Anthony Boucher's entertaining 'Barrier'.[84] 'She met herself, Brent explained. I think she found it pretty confusing.' The confusion is part of the deliberate but essentially humorous process of making the reader ask 'Who am I – really?' A variation was worked out by James Blish in 'A Work of Art',[88] which involved reincarnation. Now with the real prospect of human cloning the improbabilities inherent in the older literary devices have vanished, the smile has been wiped off and there is no escaping stark and serious confrontation with the old basic question. With a slight air of desperation many science fiction writers began to tackle this new manifestation of Man's identity crisis. The majority instinctively rejected the growing evidence of the extent to which our thoughts and actions are peer group conditioned by inviting our antipathy towards the clone group. We have already seen how Frank Herbert in *Hellstrom's Hive*[89] trapped us, as it were, into accepting that individuality and free will are paramount and that the collective virtues we have been persuaded to applaud in theory in the opening chapters can become repugnant if they can only be achieved at the cost of personal freedom. A similar reader response is evoked by Kate Wilhelm's *Where Late the Sweet Birds Sang*[90] or by *The Fifth Head of Cerberus*[91] by Gene Wolfe. I found the latter confusing in its complexity – a bit like trying to psychoanalyse a schizoid dream – but the attention it demands of the reader is rewarded by the speculation it prompts about the roles and relationships between species and the age old spirit–flesh antithesis. (It also has some nice satire on the obtuse logic of police states.) Kate Wilhelm's story is unconvincing in its analysis of the economic disasters which bring about the private creation of the eventually self-perpetuating clone group in a disintegrating world, but once the story is launched we are skilfully brought to share the author's revulsion at the individual sublimation demanded by membership of the psychically and physically interdependent clones.

All these American writers continue in their main-line tradition of rejecting the Gestalt solution offered by cloning, though with less traditional pessimism they seem to regard the ultimate displacement of variegated mankind by a few groups of superior beings as inevitable. Superman is, in a sense, the new Man-created alien of SF.

It remains for a British writer, also maintaining the national tradition of seeking salvation through personal evolution, even in the heart of disaster, to see things from the clone point of view – partially at least. *The Ophiuchi Hotline* states conventionally enough, 'our frontiers will be found not by trying to recapture the past but by looking within ourselves'.[92] It transpires, far less conventionally, that John Varley's use of the plural *ourselves* is deliberate, for he means our other selves as reflected in our clones. In keeping with the obsessive subjectivity of 1970s SF, he translates the traditional basic question of the alien story – 'Who, or what, are we?' – into a still more basic 'Who am I? or rather, what is the essential me?'

Notes

1. H. G. Wells, *War of the Worlds* (London: 1898).

2. Ibid.

3. C. S. Lewis, *Out of the Silent Planet* (Malacandra) (first pub. 1938; Pan, 1969), *Voyage to Venus* (Perelandra) (first pub. 1943; Pan, 1968), *That Hideous Strength* (first pub. 1945; Pan, 1969).

4. C. S. Lewis, *Out of the Silent Planet*.

5. Ibid.

6. Michael Bishop, *A Funeral for the Eyes of Fire* (Sphere, 1978).

7. Frederick Brown, 'The Last Martian', in *The Mindworm* (Tandem, 1967).

8. Lawrence M. Janifer, 'In the Bag', in *ABC of Science Fiction* (Four Square, 1966).

9. Howard Fast, 'The Large Ant', in *Fantastic Universe* (1960). He develops this theme further in his collection of stories *Beyond Infinity* (Hodder, 1975).

10. Robert Heinlein, *Revolt in 2100* (first pub. 1939; Digit, 1953).

11. [Details not available to the author.]

12. Clifford Simak, *Way Station* (first pub. 1963; Pan, 1966).

13. Ibid.

14. Ray Bradbury, 'The Strawberry Window', in *The Day it Rained for Ever* (Penguin, 1963).

15. Lloyd Biggle, Jnr, *The Fury Out of Time* (Sphere, 1968).

16. Lewis, *Voyage to Venus*. This theme is explored on a factual basis by Young, Silcock and Dunn in *Journey to Tranquillity* (Cape, 1970).

17. Isaac Asimov, 'Breeds There A Man', in *Earth is Room Enough* (Panther, 1960).

18. Thomas M. Disch, 'The Squirrel Cage', in *Under Compulsion* (Panther, 1970).

19. Bertram Chandler, *The Cage* (Mercury Press, 1957). J. G. Ballard, 'The Watch Towers' in *The Four Dimensional Nightmare* (Penguin, 1965) also treats of Man as a specimen.

20. Philip K. Dick, 'Expendable', in *Science Fiction Showcase* (first pub. 1959; Mayflower, 1968).

21. Alan Nourse, 'The Dark Door', in *The Counterfeit Man* (first pub. 1953; Corgi, 1965).

22. Robert Heinlein, *Farmer in the Sky* (first pub. 1950; Pan, 1967).

23. Arcady and Boris Strugatsky, *Destination Amaltheia* (Btk 491, 1960).

24. Ibid.

25. Valentina Zhuravleva, 'Stone from the Stars', *Tekhnika Molodyozhi*, No. 9 (1959).

26. Arcady and Boris Strugatsky, *Destination Amaltheia* (Btk 491, 1960).

27. Alexander Kazantsev, *The Martian* (Btk 387, 1963).

28. Arthur Clarke, Speech on receiving the 1963 Kalinga prize in Ceylon (27 Sept 1963).

29. Olaf Stapledon, *Sirius* (first pub. 1944; Penguin, 1964).

30. Isaac Asimov, *Pebble in the Sky* (first pub. 1933; Bantam Pathfinder, 1964).

31. Eric Frank Russell, *Dreadful Sanctuary* (first pub. 1953; Four Square, 1967).

32. Sever Gansovsky, *A Day of Wrath* (Btk 311, 1965).

33. Ivan Yefremov, 'The Heart of the Serpent', *Yunost*, No. 1 (1959) (Btk 367).

34. John Wyndham, *The Midwich Cuckoos* (first pub. Joseph, 1957). For another good British treatment see Keith Roberts, *The Inner Wheel* (Hart Davis, 1970).

35. Theodore Sturgeon, 'To Marry Medusa', in *The Joyous Invasions* (first pub. 1958; Penguin, 1967).

36. Ibid.

37. Ibid.

38. Theodore Sturgeon, *More Than Human* (first pub. 1953; Penguin, 1965).

39. John Wyndham, *The Chrysalids* (first pub. 1955; Penguin, 1969).

40. Michael Bishop, *A Funeral for the Eyes of Fire* (Sphere, 1978).

41. Samuel Delaney, *Babel 17* (Sphere, 1969).

42. Frank Herbert, *Hellstrom's Hive* (New English Library, 1974).

43. Frederick Hoyle, *The Black Cloud* (first pub. 1957; Penguin, 1960).

44. Ibid.

45. A. Belayev, *Hoighty Toighty* published in 1964 but written between 1930 and 1940 (Btk 136).

46. Arcady and Boris Strugatsky, *Wanderers and Travellers* (Btk 553, 1963).

47. Arcady and Boris Strugatsky, 'An Emergency Case', in *Path into the Unknown* (MacGibbon, 1966; Btk 491, 1960).

48. Brian Aldiss, *The Interpreter* (New York: Ace, 1960).

49. Ivan Yefremov, 'The Heart of the Serpent' (Btk 367, 1959).

50. Poul Anderson, *Call Me Joe* (Street & Smith, 1957).

51. Hal Clement, *Mission of Gravity* (first pub. 1954; Penguin, 1963).

52. Norman W. La Roux, *New Scientist* (25 Sept 1969).

53. Hal Clement, *Cycle of Fire* (first pub. 1957; Corgi, 1966).

54. Ibid.

55. Hal Clement, *Close to Critical* (first pub. 1958; Corgi, 1968).

56. James White, 'Blood Brother', in *New Writings in Science Fiction 14* (Corgi, 1969).

57. James White, 'Vertigo', in *New Writings in Science Fiction 12* (Corgi, 1968).

58. James White, *Star Surgeon* (first pub. 1963; Corgi, 1967).

59. Colin Kapp, 'The Imagination Trap' in *New Writings in Science Fiction 10* (Corgi, 1968).

60. Colin Kapp, 'The Subways of Tazoo', in *New Writings in Science Fiction 3* (Corgi, 1965).

61. Colin Kapp, 'The Pen and the Dark', in *New Writings in Science Fiction 8* (Corgi, 1966).

62. Claude Veillot, 'The First Days of May', in *A Century of Science Fiction* (Knight edn, Pan, 1966).

63. Alan Nourse, 'Tiger by the Tail', in *Beyond Infinity* (first pub. 1951; Corgi, 1964).

64. Katherine MacLean, *Unhuman Sacrifice* (Astounding, 1952).

65. Michael Bishop, *Stolen Faces* (Gollancz, 1977).

66. Anthony Boucher, 'Barrier', in *Spectrum IV* (first pub. Astounding, 1942; Pan, 1967).

67. Ray Bradbury, 'A Serious Search for Weird Worlds', *Life* (1960).

68. Theodore Sturgeon, *Killdozer*, in *Spectrum 3* (first pub. 1945; Pan, 1966).

69. Alistair Bevan, 'The Scarlet Lady', in *Impulse Six*, Vol. 1 6 (August 1966).

70. Cartoon by Shel Silverstein, in *The Best of Sci-Fi* (Mayflower, 1963, from *Playboy* (1960).

71. Chandler Elliott, *Inanimate Objection* (Galaxy, 1954).

72. John Christopher, *The Possessors* (Hodder, 1966).

73. Frederick Brown, *The Mind Worm* (Tandem Collection, 1967); Colin Wilson, *The Mind Parasites* (SFBC, 1968); *Under Compulsion*, Thomas Disch Collection (Panther, 1970); John Lymmington, *The Sleep Eaters* (Corgi, 1964); Arthur Sellings, *The Silent Speakers* (Panther, 1965); Roger Zelazny, *The Dream Master* (New York: Ace, 1966).

74. Ray Bradbury, 'Let's Play Poison', in *The Small Assassin* (first pub. 1948; Four Square, 1964). Cf. William Nolan, 'The Small World of Lewis Stillman', in *Impact 20* (Corgi, 1966).

75. Ray Bradbury, 'The Small Assassin', in *The Small Assassin* (first pub. 1948; Four Square, 1964).

76. Alan Nourse, 'My Friend Bobby', in *The Counterfeit Man* (Corgi, 1965).

77. Isaac Asimov, 'Anybody Else Like Me', in *The View from the Stars* (first pub. 1952; Panther, 1968). For a Russian example Cf. A. Mirer, *Wanderers' Home* (Moscow, 1976).

78. Roger Zelazny, *The Dream Master* (New York: Ace, 1966).

79. Walter Miller, *Dark Benediction* (first pub. 1951; Panther, 1966).

80. Roger Zelazny, *Doorways in the Sand* (New York: Harper & Row, 1976).

81. Poul Anderson, *Call Me Joe* (Astounding, 1957).

82. Zelazny, *Doorways in the Sand*.

83. Michael Bishop, *A Funeral for the Eyes of Fire* (Sphere, 1978).

84. John Varley, *The Ophiuchi Hotline* (Orbit/Fontana, 1978).

85. Robert Heinlein, 'By His Bootstraps', in *Spectrum 1* (Pan, 1964).

86. James Tiptree, 'For Ever to a Hudson Bay Blanket' (first pub. Astounding, 1941; in *10,000 Light Years from Home* (first pub. Astounding, 1941; Pan, 1977).

87. Anthony Boucher, 'Barrier', in *Spectrum IV* (first pub. Astounding, 1942; Pan, 1967).

88. James Blish, 'A Work of Art', in *Science Fiction Showcase* (first pub. 1959; Mayfair, 1968).

89. Frank Herbert, *Hellstrom's Hive* (New English Library, 1974).

90. Kate Wilhelm, *Where Late the Sweet Birds Sang* (Arrow, 1977).

91. Gene Wolfe, *The Fifth Head of Cerberus* (Gollancz, 1973).

92. Varley, *The Ophiuchi Hotline.*

8
The idea as hero

In SF, as Amis effectively argued over fifteen years ago, the real hero is an idea rather than a person. The development of the plot depends not on the subjectively motivated actions of a living 'hero' but on certain scientific or technological assumptions – the idea – possessing an intrinsic logic and coherence which makes them acceptable to the reader. But, it must be recognised that 'ideas are only important when explored and allowed to blossom into life, otherwise they remain dead, decorative notions'.[1] Or as we expressed it in our original definition in Chapter 1, a science fiction story is one in which the suspension of disbelief depends on the plausible development of a central technical or scientific idea or ideas.

It is probably more true to say that the hero of the SF story is often a question rather than an idea, but in either case the consequences to the writing are the same. As H. L. Gold wrote, 'The point at which specialisation of character becomes a narrowing and a weakening is reached much sooner in science fiction than elsewhere.'[2] So little trouble is usually taken with character drawing. The plot, aided by the detailed plausibility of the setting and of the scientific argument, is deemed sufficient to carry the narrative and the reader to its conclusion. But this can be an exhausting mode of travel, particularly in the hands of the less skilled writer whose quickly sketched protagonists often speak out of even such skeletal character as they possess in order to develop the central idea. Such authors often lapse into didactics, which seem more prevalent in SF than in any other type of fiction. But even the good writers find it difficult to sustain a pace which allows for no reflective pause for breath to explore the hero's purely subjective thoughts and feelings. We identify with the heroes of these literary sprinters on a racial not a personal basis.

Indeed it is even arguable that too much characterisation prevents the reader from putting himself in the protagonist's position, prevents him from seeing himself in the central dilemma. We are not meant to care how the central character copes with his problem but only to consider how we would cope in the same circumstances. It is because it is the idea-centred genre that SF is essentially the field of the short story. Even the greater length of the novel is generally used to pack in more ideas rather than to round out the characters. Who remembers the name of the hero of *The Space Merchants*[3] or of *Cat's Cradle*[4] or of any other SF classic? But any SF enthusiast can recall the themes and central ideas of these novels.

In SF you either have real people forced to do unreal things by the necessities of the plot and the central idea, or unreal people. The genre tends to settle for unreal people. Raymond Chandler, in describing why SF's cousin, the detective story, appeals, suggested that it creates a sense of fear, that 'Their characters lived in a world gone wrong, the world in which long before the atom bomb, civilisation had created the machine for its own destruction'.[5] The difference between SF and the detective story is that where the detective story uses things which we know go wrong, or events which do happen in every day life, SF relies on what we imagine might go wrong, or events which have never happened – yet. It is interesting that Asimov is one of the few writers, in his robot stories and 'mysteries', to have combined the detective and science fiction tale. Robots, and aliens, are almost invariably depicted as ideas not characters and it is rare indeed to come across a writer who distinguishes between one alien and another except in the most rudimentary terms of good and bad, friend or enemy.

Another explanation why people are subordinated to ideas was advanced by a character in Susan Cooper's *Mandrake*[6] who

> postulated the theory of a collective subconscious – not the Jungian variety, nothing so simple. He suggested that the unit of consciousness was not a mind, but an idea. That once conceived, the idea, whether or not it was expressed in any way, took on an existence of its own. That there exists . . . a world of ideas with which we are all linked, through our idea-forming minds. Which is therefore capable of influencing us all.[7]

One of the main dangers in working on this almost platonic level is that the fiction will totally disappear under the weight of the argument. Knight rightly says, 'I don't like to see science fiction degraded into a vehicle for anything. The story, I think, will always be more important than the idea; when the reverse gets to be true, you want an essay.'[8] But this presents us with a paradox for we have suggested that in most science fiction stories the hero is an idea, so we have to ask ourselves the question, 'Why write a story rather than an essay?' Perhaps science fiction is the essay in action, applied rather than pure science. Perhaps as Rackham argues in 'Computers Mate':[9] 'An idea has to have a visual analog before we can begin to grasp it.' The choice of the vehicle of communication is determined by the fact that readers are curious about what will happen, even to people of whose character they have no knowledge, as is evidenced by the crowd interest at the scene of an accident, a sporting contest or by the avid readership of newspapers. As the principal character in Kazantsev's *The Martian*[10] puts it, in extreme form, 'people are not interested in me but in what I do'. The writer who says 'Here are some stories about the future' will reach ten times as many readers as the one who says 'Here are some ideas about the future'. He will, more importantly, reach a kind and level of reader who would be untouched by the abstract approach – he will certainly communicate with far more people. One explanation for the high proportion of SF in Russia's limited fictional output is, I think, that the absence of flesh and blood heroes is almost welcomed. That the ideas are circumscribed by political necessity and prejudice may be a disappointment to the Western reader but is undoubtedly a convenience to the Russian writer, and enables his reader also to sniff safely at the heterodox.

The lack of characterisation in SF is frequently criticised by reviewers who have not grasped that it is a different if related branch of literature from that of the conventional novel or short story. A *New Scientist* critic, commenting on the not very effective *Doomwatch* television series fell into this trap:

Why, then, is the series so incredible? The reason is certainly not that it is mere science fiction; the best fictional material can create as deep and as genuine a chill as any fact-filled documentary. But to accept fiction of any sort one has to begin to believe in the humanity of its characters, and the scientists in *Doomwatch* have as much humanity as you would find in a month of Sunday supplements. They inhabit a two-dimensional world (the other dimension more often than not being sex) in which it is impossible to imagine personal relationships that are not constantly charged with high emotional voltage or a domesticity that has no insistent melodramatic overtones. If we ever caught Quist boiling an egg, it would probably blow up in his face.[11]

We are not in fact meant to be particularly interested in Quist, only in whether the egg may have been laid by an anarchist, or, as obvious explanations are usually eschewed in SF, by a dinosaur. However, it must be admitted that characterisation is sometimes unnecessarily sketchy or stereotyped in SF.

Certainly anything akin to characterisation in Russian SF is rare, for if the Soviet definition of intelligence is narrow, that of the hero is even narrower. Indeed it is hard to detect a personal hero, for the essential human role is usually given to a group. The leader and members of this group are endowed with the cold and comprehensive qualities of 'Soviet Man', who has a remarkable affinity with the American comic-strip Superman. When a major protagonist does die it is often by his own choice, as in *The Martian* referred to above; it is made clear that the fate of the individual in a Communist society is relatively unimportant. The individual has been made of no account, because the accumulation of scientific knowledge for Man, for the future, is what counts, so there can be no real tragedy. This is still largely true when the story revolves round an individual as in the work of the Strugatskys. Even here the human hero is primarily important as observer, catalyst or commentator. We do not much care what happens to him as an individual character but we do care what happens to him as the representative of mankind. The rare personal villain is as hollow as the hero – usually he is nothing more imaginative than an occasional ex-Nazi. Nowhere is this dearth of character more evident than in the labelling of the protagonists. If in the internationalised crews of future space craft the leading positive characters' names all stem from Russian roots, those of the villains and weaker characters sound English, Portuguese or German. While in a way an idea is also the hero of almost every Russian story, it is usually the same idea in each – Communism, or at least Marxism.

American writers are equally gauche where names are concerned and add to their shortcomings not just some astonishing conglomerations of supposedly alien consonants but the most terrible puns. Asimov's galactic human detective Dr Urth is I think the worst. One cannot help wondering why the SF writers cannot accept that the people of tomorrow may conceivably be called just John and Mary, unless one recognises that to most of them the people themselves

scarcely matter. In Western SF the individual as hero is less important than in other forms of writing since, as we have seen, the hero is
usually rather an idea; but in the Western story at least the impact of
the idea, even on whole societies, is almost always seen through the
eyes of a single person. Not that human relationships, particularly
between the sexes, flourish much in any nation's SF. The cosmos, it
seems, has a habit of daunting such trivial feelings. Nevertheless the
individual hero in Western SF is also capable of a far greater variety
of reactions and attitudes, many of them unpredictable. I think that
in general it is fair to claim that the British writers, Wyndham and
Christopher in particular, are less guilty of ignoring character in the
interests of plot than their American and Russian colleagues,
among whom Vonnegut, Sturgeon, Zelzany and the Strugatskys
deserve less stricture.

I have in the notes to this chapter included a random selection of
SF ideas which have appealed to me or which illustrate different
types of SF idea.[12] In all of them, whether taken from a full length
novel or a short three-page story, I found little difficulty in condens-
ing the core of the tale into one, two or three short sentences. This
emphasis on the central idea is both valuable and stimulating in the
way it compels the reader to look at things from a new angle, to
contemplate possibilities which would otherwise never have occurred to him. However, SF loses a number of important qualities as a
consequence of abandoning the carefully characterised hero or
villain. It usually lacks human romance, humour and the concept of
personal tragedy; compassion usually dies when we view Man, or
aliens, collectively rather than singly.

Asimov, in a pleasantly satirical poem ('The Foundation of SF
Success')[13] on the conventions of writing SF and its jargon, ad-
monishes his practitioner: 'Then eschew all thoughts of passion of a
man and woman/Fashioned from your hero's thoughtful mind,'
and pertinently praises his writer 'If all his yarns restrict themselves
to masculinity'. The almost exclusively male orientation of science
fiction does not appear to reveal any latent tendency toward
homosexuality among SF writers – indeed even the inter-specific
encounters on alien planets are essentially heterosexual – and in this
respect SF is less challenging than more conventional fiction. Nor
can I subscribe to the fanciful theories of Robert Plank[14] and Ednita
Barnabeu[15] who both see SF as symptomatic of a deeper psychosis.
'Deeper even than those which evoked the Demi-Gods, devils and
witches of other times.'[16] Both note the rejection of women,

whether as lovers or mothers, and Barnabeu even goes so far as to equate the imagery of space travel with expulsion at birth. While I agree that SF is the most sensitive social litmus precisely because it penetrates so far into the subconscious, I cannot accept their conclusions on the absence of women – conclusions which I do not find substantiated in the texts.

The explanation of the absence of women and romance is primarily the lack of characterisation in general. In addition we are dealing with a literature which largely reflects the attitudes and preoccupations of a particular section of society – the technically and scientifically orientated. However deplorable, this, in the West at least, is a section in which women are very much under-represented. It is interesting to note that even in the stories of the new influx of women writers, the central character is, in the great majority of cases, male. In Russian SF as in Russian society the balance of the sexes is more equal even if the absence of romance is as great. We are, moreover, frequently dealing with a fiction of action and a fiction of macrocosmic scale. Action and immensity in my experience tend in real life to leave one too tired, frightened or overawed for all but the smallest interest in sex! In the same way many of the stories are set in the working environment and since they are mostly written by men, who compartmentalise their domestic, emotional and working lives to a greater degree than women, the opposite sex tends to be switched off when the lab light is switched on. When women do appear, they are often seen as one character sees another who is introduced to the story as an 'expert' and turns out to be a woman. 'Her hair has square roots. If she condescends to listen to a wolf whistle, it's solely to study the Doppler effect.'[16] Even more regrettably rare than a normal woman in SF is any attempt to explore the disturbing possibilities of love, lust and reproduction between alien species. I can think of only very few stories[17] which treat this theme with sensitivity and originality – as opposed to on the basis of passing rapine for some galactic Viking. Ray Bradbury's sadly touching tale of the prehistoric monster lured from its lonely deeps by the love call of a lighthouse foghorn only to return to its deep sea retreat when the inanimate mate cannot respond to its thunderous caress[18] is one of the rare exceptions.

There are I believe two writers who deal consistently and convincingly with the relationships between the sexes in SF – Heinlein and Christopher. Both of them, in different ways, are much preoccupied with the theme of sexual jealousy. Christopher on the whole seems to present the loss of sexual exclusivity with a sense of regret even though usually, as in *Death of Grass*[19] and *Pendulum*,[20] for example, it is an involuntary loss through rape. The couple whose exclusive relationship is thus invaded are, at first, almost repelled by each other, but then pass on – with a touch of resignation? – to acceptance of the more important and fundamental aspects of their relationship, leaving sex behind as relatively unimportant. Such a bald analysis does not convey the skill with which Christopher makes his reader share that initial sense of loss and repugnance.

Heinlein is on a different tack. For him sex is much too important a thing to be jealous about and the hero has gradually to be educated to this point of view whether in swashbuckling style as in *Glory Road*[21] or over several hundred pages of social evolution as in *Stranger in a Strange Land.*[22] This latter story makes the reader share in the changing attitude of the principal human character from the outset, where he is most jealous of his mistress and other human beings, to the day when as a result of the influence of the Martian – the stranger of the title – he is a fully contented participant in group living and group sex, with his ex-mistress as happy in the Martian's arms as in his own and the hero himself not particularly disturbed by the situation.

The fact is that Man seldom likes to kiss before the uncurtained windows of infinity but perhaps more surprisingly he cannot often be brought to laugh at the infinite either. While SF is to a great extent deprived of the humour which springs from character or recognised characteristics – 'Have you heard the one about the Martian, the Venusian and the Earthman?' somehow sounds implausible – it can exploit the humorous situation, the funny idea. A convention which accepts time travel can, in Asimov's story 'The Immortal Bard'[23] return Shakespeare to a college class on Shakespeare and have him failed, with some entertaining digs at literary criticism. Space travel gives some original twists to the jokes of misunderstanding, as well as permitting SF writers to indulge their obsessive delight in puns. 'To Serve Man'[24] is a story of man trying to probe the motives of the pig-like aliens who come with considerable powers to earth and who appear to be benevolent. A significant role is played by the book, 'How to Serve Man', in convincing most humans of the good intentions of these visitors. It turns out in the end to be a cookery book! Another space-travel story 'Written in the Stars',[25] is one of the more ingenious and amusing SF stories I have come across. The alien visitors leave in a huff because one of our constellations accidentally forms a sign in their language which they take as an insulting message.

There is ample scope, too, for poking fun at Man's pretensions as in William Tenn's 'Null-P',[26] a story in which dogs supersede Man. 'Eventually, of course, the retriever civilisation developed machines which could throw sticks farther, faster, and with more frequency. Thereupon, except in the most backward canine communities, man disappeared.' Or in *The Sirens of Titan*: 'The discovery of the chrono-syncoasic infundibula said to mankind in effect: 'What makes you think you're going anywhere?'[27] We can, through laughing at others, be made to recognise the absurdities of some of our attitudes, as one character realises in Seaton McKettrig's witty satire on tough contemporary America, 'A World by the Tale.'[28] This story of inter-galactic publishing has a particularly nice observation by the native treated in the missionary hospital: 'The white witch doctor protects himself by wearing a little round mirror on his head which reflects back the evil spirits.'

But despite such exceptions there is often very little to laugh at in SF.[29] Apart from our general thesis on the consequences of lack of characterisation, this is probably due to the fact that many SF writers, but usually not the best of them, take themselves very seriously indeed and are consequently about as humourless and unself-critical as a minor Old Testament prophet.

Can a fictional genre which generally lacks characterisation, romance, humour, personal tragedy, contain works of any real literary value or distinction? Providing one remembers Amis's dictum that '90 per cent of SF is rubbish – but then 90 per cent of anything is rubbish',[30] I think an unequivocal 'Yes' can be given in answer to the question. A common view of SF is expressed by two of the characters discussing the genre in Clarke's *The Sands of Mars*:

'Yes, but it's no longer science fiction. It's either purely factual . . . or else it's pure fantasy. The stories have to go right outside the solar system and so they might just as well be fairy-tales. Which is all that most of them are.'

'So you don't consider that science fiction can ever have any permanent literary value?'

'I don't think so. It may sometimes have a *social* value when it is written, but to the next generation it must always seem quaint and archaic. Just look what happened, for example, to the space travel stories.'[31]

Certainly we have already recognised that one of the problems with science fiction is that the 'S' can become dated and the story apparently cease to be science fiction with the passage of time, but this is not strictly relevant to our argument as to its literary value. As well suggest that the novels of Elliot, Dickens or Gissing are unimportant because the social conditions in which they are set no longer prevail.

Amis has rightly warned us against 'too much nervous or complacent reluctance to invoke ordinary critical standards',[32] and adds, 'Science fiction is not ordinary fiction and cannot be judged as if it were, though we agree that it should be judged as rigorously.'[33] Lewis in his essay on science fiction[34] suggests that SF should receive the same treatment as 'fantastic or mythopoeic literature in general'. SF should not, therefore, be condemned for failing to achieve what it does not set out to do. Provided its objectives are not dismissed as totally trivial – a dismissal which I hope the preceding chapters have shown would be unfair – it is the performance of a writer within the limits prescribed by limited objectives which must determine whether his work has literary value.

SF is often strained and overwritten, but its range of vocabulary is very wide. This is not just due to the use of technical and scientific terms and similes, but to a willingness to explore ideas by means of exploring the full possibilities of the language. Delany in the essay referred to in chapter 3[35] suggested that while form and content can no more be separated in SF than in conventional fiction, SF has a particular, almost unique, way of using words and word associations: 'A distinctive level of subjunctivity informs all the words in an SF story at a level that is different from that which informs naturalistic fiction, fantasy or reportage.' It is true also that it is a cliché-ridden genre in the sense that there are endlessly repeated conventions – neuronic whips, hyperdrive, and so on – which serve as a kind of shorthand, a notice saying, 'Look, I'm writing science fiction', where some actual present-day equivalent would serve the interests of the story just as well. Unusual words are used in a way that Swift – who sometimes introduced non-existent words to make his reader go to the dictionary – would have appreciated. He might not always have cared quite so much for the bastard neologisms to which this word-coining gives rise. From four randomly chosen stories you come across pseudo-dactyls, capillotomer, contraterrene, sonolepsy and autopsychomymesis. Sometimes such words are used as pseudo-jargon merely to give authenticity, but they are more often used in an attempt to say something precisely. The SF writer is rarely inhibited from using difficult language if the complexity of his subject demands complex expression. He demands of his reader not only the uninhibited use of his imagination but a determined effort to understand precisely what the writer is trying to say.

SF can easily become *too* complicated. As in broadcasting to an audience for whom yours is a foreign language, nothing in the way of basically acceptable premises should be assumed. Or at least this is one doctrine. It is seldom sufficient to explain the central assumption then throw in minor ones in passing without explanation. The writer's difficulty in the complex situations of SF is to be consistent. Credibility can easily be destroyed by the inadequacy of even some quite small point of detail. The reader's imagination must, therefore, be captured so effectively as to avoid the risk of losing his willing suspension of disbelief by such slips. It has been contemptuously argued by some, who subscribe to the general pulp-rubbish image of SF which was prevalent at least until the end of the 1950s, that such low standards do not matter since SF is presumably intended for the less intelligent reader. But even if this were true, as Delany comments, 'It is the less skilled, less sophisticated reader who is most injured by bad writing.'[36]

If the weaknesses of SF lie in its lack of characterisation and emotion, its strengths lie in its tightness of plot, its descriptions of bizarre or unusual scenes and places and its capacity to blend argument and narrative imperceptibly into each other. It is, as we have already observed, a form of literature appealing to the intellect with little opportunity for wallowing in sensation. Its challenge to the imagination is so unbounded that imaginative writing has almost inevitably been produced from time to time. SF certainly has no novelist to compare with Dickens or Tolstoy, no short story writer to match Maugham, no playwright or poet of genius. It would be time consuming – and very expensive! – to demonstrate by quotation the abilities of the leading SF writers who are I believe generously represented in the ranks of the second division of literature. Anyone unfamiliar with the genre who was to read without prejudice, say, Bradbury's *Fahrenheit 451*, Vonnegut's *Cats Cradle*, Sturgeon's *More Than Human*, Miller's *Canticle for Liebowitz*, Heinlein's *Stranger in a Strange Land*, Christopher's *Death of Grass*, Wyndham's *The Chrysalids*, Ballard's *The Crystal World*, the Strugatskys' *Snail on the Slope* and Karp's *One*, or the best short stories of Asimov, Clarke, Bester and Simak, could not honestly deny that there is little as good, and probably nothing better, being written in any other branch of contemporary fiction.

Notes

1. Introduction to *Foundation* 11.
2. H. L. Gold, Editor of *Galaxy Science Fiction*, quoted in Kingsley Amis, *New Maps of Hell* (first pub.1961; New English Library, 1969).
3. Frederik Pohl and C. M. Kornbluth, *The Space Merchants* (first pub. 1953; Penguin, 1965).
4. Kurt Vonnegut, *Cat's Cradle* (first pub. 1963; Penguin, 1965).
5. The Preface to Raymond Chandler, *Pearls Are A Nuisance* (Penguin, 1966). Cf. p.192 for an interesting analysis of this effect in the works of Dorothy Sayers.
6. Susan Cooper, *Mandrake* (first pub. 1964; Penguin, 1966).
7. The same view was expressed by Louis Worth in his Preface to Karl Mannheim, *Ideology and Utopia* (Kegan Paul, 1936). Cf. ch. 10, note 17, below.
8. The Preface to Damon Knight (ed.), *A Century of Science Fiction* (Gollancz, 1963).
9. John Rackham, 'Computers Mate', *New Writings in Science Fiction 8* (Corgi, 1966).
10. Alexander Kazantsev, *The Martian* (Btk 387, 1963).
11. *New Scientist* (2 April 1970).
12. In John Baxter's story, 'Apple', *New Writings on SF 10* (Corgi 1967) the reader imagines himself as a human insect inside a huge apple and so uses a technique of size differential as old at least as Swift. In Simak's story, *The Night of the Pu-Udly* (Four Square, 1964), a laboratory experiment in making people's duplicates appears to have gone wrong. The duplicate itself plots cunningly to murder and replace his original. But the pay-off line, the usual SF twist, is a casual remark on the telephone letting the successful duplicate know that the duplicates of this batch have all been made with a 24-hour poison in their veins. In William Nolan's story, *The Small World of Lewis Stillman* (Corgi, 1966), in order to stop man going into space aliens have made the children destroy everyone over the age of six and this story is the story of the last adult. In 'The 'Final Solution', *New Writings on SF 8* (Corgi, 1966) R. W. Mackelworth writes an ironic little story in which two master races clash and the ultimate victor turns out to be a cannibal. As so often happens in SF we tend to react by saying, 'how clever' not 'how nauseating' or 'how beautiful', because ideas, the heroes, rarely provoke that response.

Bradbury is a past-master at spinning a story round a simple idea. In 'The Watchers' in *Fever Dream* (first pub. 1948, Sphere 1970) it is that flies might actually be the spies of the Deity. In 'Descending' (Thomas Dischin, *Under Compulsion*, Panther, 1970) an escalator just keeps on going down for ever. In 'A Scent of Sarsaparilla, in *The Day it Rained Forever* (Penguin, 1963), an attic is in fact a time machine because of its spectrum of memory-provoking flotsam. In 'The Dust of Death' *Asimov's Mysteries* (Panther, 1969), the simple fact that platinum black is a catalyst which will cause hydrogen to explode is the basis of an intriguing SF detective story. Again, in a story like 'The Three-Cornered Wheel', in Poul Anderson's *The Trouble Twister* (SFBC/Gollancz, 1969) we are asked to imagine a society in which it is blasphemous to use, think of or make a wheel. A small boy and an old man overcome the evil of fear which is behind this. This, too, is a surprisingly moving story, a rarity in SF. In *The Disaster Area* (Panther, 1967) Ballard takes the simple and quasi-scientific starting point of the growth of birds to man-size as a result of crop-growth sprays to study the way in which on this occasion his genuine characters might behave in a bizarre environment. Such a list could go on forever but I think this purely random selection of SF ideas indicates how far the imagination of the SF writer is prepared to range.

13. Isaac Asimov, 'The Foundation of SF Success,' in *Earth is Room Enough* (first pub. 1957; Panther, 1967).

14. Robert Plank, 'Lighter Than Air; But Heavy as Hate; an essay in space travel', *Partisan Review* XXIV (Winter 1957).

15. Ednita Barnabeu, 'Science Fiction; A New Mythos;' *Psycho-analytic Quarterly* XXVI (October 1957), from Eric Frank Russell, *Dreadful Sanctuary* (first pub. 1953; Four Square, 1967).

16. Robert Heinlein, *Podkayne of Mars* (first pub. 1963; New English Library, 1969).

17. Kirill Stanukovich, *The Golub Yavan*; Philip José Farmer, 'The Lovers'; *Startling Stories* (Aug. 1952); Mikhail Vasilyev, 'Flying Flowers' in *Destination Amaltheia*; John Rankine, 'Six Cubed Plus One', and William Temple, 'Coco-Talk', both in *New Writings in Science Fiction 7* (Corgi, 1966); Theodore Sturgeon *The Wonderbirds* and *Green Monkey*, and the relationship between the dog Sirius in Olaf Stapledon's story of that name and his human mistress.

These are the few love stories, either inter- or intra-specific, other than those mentioned in the text, which I have encountered in my reading.

18. Ray Bradbury, 'The Foghorn' in *The Golden Apples of the Sun* (first pub. 1951; Corgi, 1964).

19. John Christopher, *The Death of Grass* (first pub. 1956; Penguin, 1970).

20. John Christopher, *Pendulum* (Hodder, 1969).

21. Robert Heinlein, *Glory Road* (Four Square, 1965).

22. Robert Heinlein, *Stranger in a Strange Land* (New York: Avon, 1961).

23. Isaac Asimov, 'The Immortal Bard' (1957), in *Earth is Room Enough* (Panther, 1967).

24. Damon Knight, 'To Serve Man,' in *The Mind Worm* (first pub. 1950; Tandem, 1967).

25. Robert Young, 'Written in the Stars', in *The Worlds of Robert F. Young* (Panther, 1968).

26. William Tenn, 'Null-P', in *Spectrum 1* (Pan, 1964).

27. Kurt Vonnegut, *The Sirens of Titan* (first pub. 1950; Hodder, 1967).

28. Seaton McKettrig, 'A World by the Tale', in *Analog 3* (Panther, 1966).

29. *Humour Section*

Isaac Asimov, 'The Message', in *Earth is Room Enough* (Panther, 1967). Humorous time travel story of a page and a half based on that most simple of all graffiti 'Kilroy was here'; Peter Phillips, *Dreams Are Sacred* (Astounding, 1948); John Novotny, 'A Trick or Two', in *A Decade of Fantasy in Science Fiction* (Corgi, 1964); A poem by James Kirkup, 'Love in a Spacesuit', in *Frontier of Going*, an anthology of space poetry selected by John Fairfax (Panther, 1969); John Wyndham, *Jizzle* (first pub. 1954; Four Square, 1962), a good example of malicious humour; Richard Matheson, 'Doll That Does Everything' in *The Shores of Space* (first pub. 1954; Corgi, 1965); John Anthony, 'The Hypnoglyf', in *A Decade of Fantasy in Science Fiction*, (Corgi, 1964); Clifford Simak, 'Frying Jag', in *The Night of the Pu-Udly* (Four Square, 1964); Theodore Sturgeon, 'The Wigget, the Wagget and Boff' in *The Joyous Invasions* (first pub. 1955; Penguin, 1967); Harlan Ellison, 'Shatterday', *Gallery* (Sept 1965), a typical but ingeniously handled doppelganger story. The hero telephones his flat by accident and finds himself answering; Bob Shaw, *Tomorrow Lies in Ambush* (Gollancz, 1973); the psychotic washing machine that 'cracks' and swims out to sea in Ron Goulart's, *What's Become of Screw Loose* (New York: Scribners, 1971); *Crackpot* and *Nemo* (New York: Doubleday, 1977). Norman Spinrad, 'A Thing of Beauty' in *No Direction Home* (first pub. 1969–1974; Fontana, 1977). Japan is the dominating commercial power and the United States a backward tourist spot selling off its past for souvenirs. A Japanese businessman actually buys the Brooklyn Bridge; K. Bulychov, *Fault on the Line* (Fantastika, 1969/70), a wrong number story in which wires are crossed between 1967 and 1667.

30. In a radio interview with the author and doubtless in several other places as well (1962).

31. Arthur Clarke, *The Sands of Mars* (first pub. 1951; Pan, 1964).

32. The Foreword to Kingsley Amis, *New Maps of Hell* (first pub. New English Library, 1969).

33. Quoted in the preface to *Spectrum 1* Kingsley Amis and Robert Conquest (eds.), (first pub. 1961; Pan, 1964).

34. C. S. Lewis, *Of Other Worlds: Essays and Stories* (New York: Harcourt Brace, 1966).

35. R. Delany, 'About 5175 Words', in *The Disappearing Future* (Panther, 1970).

36. Ibid.

9
Retreat from reality

For a short time in the late 1960s, as if détente affected even the world of letters, Western and Russian SF seemed to belong to the same genre. In the years leading up to the first moon landing Western SF retained a certain optimism in Man's ability to deal with the new problems he was identifying. In Russia a new sense of enterprise inspired SF writers as they openly recognised problems they had previously been obliged to close their eyes to. Most hopeful of all, both groups were not only recognising the same problems but recognising that they were common problems affecting the whole of mankind and not confined to one political system or another. It was not to last. The 1970s saw a profound change, particularly in the West.

In the preceding chapters we have cited many Western SF stories exemplifying a great variety of attitudes, but with one or two exceptions the Russian writers discussed have reflected the orthodox attitudes of their society. We have had to gauge their real hopes and fears by the risky process of negative inference. In the 1960s this diffidence gradually disappeared and much more conventionally Western stories were written (though these remained Russian in flavour). The work of the Strugatsky brothers and of S. Snegov show the most exciting evidence of the new heterodoxy, but plenty of other writers were at least flexing their muscles even if not striking out as vigorously. The number of original Russian titles was still fairly restricted[1] but there was a great increase in the publication, in Russian, of Western SF. Although this did not include any 'new wave' writers and still concentrated on such politically neutral authors as the old favourite Bradbury, it did cover the far less safe stories of Asimov, Sheckley, Bester, Vonnegut, Simak, Clarke, Wyndham and Stanislav Lem, Russell, Heinlein and James White, Tenn, Harrison and Leiber.

Among the most noticeable thematic changes was the willingness of Russian writers to travel in time and space no longer constrained by the demand that all future societies be basically communist and all alien life forms humanoid and friendly. In A. Mirer's *Wanderers' Home*,[2] small bullet-shaped crystalline intelligences prepare to shoot themselves into every mind on earth and in *Hunting Expedition*[3] M. Pukhov tells the tale of human hunters of rare galactic creatures who are turned unwittingly into a stalking horse for an alien invasion. Hostility and conflict had hitherto been seen as exclusively capitalistic elements. Now even many of the capitalist societies portrayed are not the Dickensian slum worlds of earlier Russian SF but affluent, socially quite benevolent societies afflicted with the ills of excessive materialism: greed, boredom and inertia. The picture drawn is not so very different from the one being shown simultaneously by Western writers. The Donomaga of Varshavsky's story 'Cockroaches'[4] would be readily recognisable to any inhabitant of New York or London and the hero's conclusion that so much responsibility for their own work and lives had been taken from ordinary people that they might as well 'Go and race cockroaches' finds its echo in the work of Vonnegut or Bester.

The Russian time traveller is still inhibited in the extent to which he can interfere in the inevitable processes of history – an inhibition self-imposed by many Western writers to increase the tensions set up by time-travel paradox. He can, however, eliminate geniuses born ahead of their time,[5] get conservationally involved with dinosaurs,[6] ensure that his scientific discoveries are not abused in the future,[7] and bring back from the future the deathday of everyone on earth.[8] A variation of the time-travel theme puts the hero of *Lebensraum*[9] literally on the spot. He can travel temporally but the living-space to which he is confined gets smaller and smaller.

None of these themes is in itself particularly novel to the Western reader but, compared with what preceded them, they indicate an increase in what the Russian SF writer dared to speculate about typical of the more challenging and sceptical approach of many Russians in other walks of life in the decade of dissidence. Under the very thin disguise of 'Fascist' settings, dictatorship and bureaucracy are attacked sharply[10] and even that relatively orthodox figure, Ivan Yefremov, had a last, rather boring, fling against Stalinism from the safe retrospect of 1970.[11]

But if we accept that the 'capitalist' societies satirised in such tales may have been intended, by inference, to reflect the shortcomings of the Soviet Union, we must also be open to the possibility that much more overt attacks on Russian bureaucracy and oppression, in the Strugatskys' work for example, may have been aimed at a world-wide rather than a national disease.

Much of the credit for the major breakthrough in Russian SF writing must go to the editors of the Leningrad magazine *Ellinskiy Sekret*, who not only brought out in 1966 the first part of the Strugatskys' remarkable *Snail on the Slope*[12] but, in the same year, part one of Snegov's panoramic space opera *Men Like Gods*.[13] Parts two and three appeared in 1968 and 1974. Alan Myers has compared the work as a whole to Asimov's celebrated *Foundation* trilogy.[14]

Men Like Gods starts off with modest heresies only; there are other intelligent creatures in the Galaxy but they are inferior to Man and there is some debate before the people of earth (communist era year 563, of course) decide to risk their own extinction by defending them from cyborg Destroyers. The analogy is very much that of the Soviet Union intervening to protect the Third World from the menace of imperialism. The other menace, that of moral indifference, is embodied in the Galactics. In part three the reader finds himself fairly far down the path of heresy when he discovers that these erstwhile enemies have become allies. Man, Galactics and Destroyers unite to form an expedition to contact the Ramirs who in trying to fulfil their objective of reversing entropy threaten our Galaxy. The space fleet is just an irrelevance to the Ramirs, who neutralise it in a reverse time-loop. The leader of the expedition (still Man, be it noted) argues with the Ramirs that biological intelligence has its place in the universe too, and that they should be freed from the reverse time-loop in which they are imprisoned. Implicit in the plea is the recognition that biological intelligence may not be, even in the future, the most powerful intelligence in the universe.

There is still much to alarm a Western reader in this story, most of all, perhaps, the all-seeing, all-knowing computer 'Great Academic' which watches over each individual and intervenes to 'protect him' if he shows even the first clinical signs of mental breakdown. The author's evident approval is indicative of the difference that still remains between the two systems in the balance they strike between the demands of the collective good and individual freedom. The trilogy remains, too, an optimistic paean to the future of a Marxist mankind, but it is also quite unlike anything else in Russian SF in the quality of characterisation and writing and in the scope, not just in length, but in the range of permitted topics.

In a reversal of the process by which they usually failed to recognise the irony in supposedly orthodox tales, the official critics felt obliged to explain the unorthodoxy of this Wellsian romance by references to an irony which it does not contain. To be fair to the critics, it is Myers' view that Russian SF criticism has become much more sophisticated in recent years.[15]

Undoubtedly the most remarkable of Soviet SF writers are the brothers Strugatsky – Arcady, a linguist, and Boris, an astronomical mathematician. Their early work was relatively conventional, though it already showed signs of their recognition that utopianism is an unreal state of mind. They described this conflict as 'the conflict between the good and the better'.

That accomplished Polish SF writer, Stanislav Lem, has condemned the Strugatskys because they have failed 'to break out of the great socio-critical tradition of Russian literature' and because they 'have tried very hard to turn their books into a kind of instrument of righteousness.'[16] The fact is that they do not want or need to break out of that tradition. They are, after all, attacking those endemic failings of the Russian rather than the Soviet tradition which attracted the humorous scorn of a Gogol or a Pushkin. Lem seems, for example, completely to have misunderstood *Roadside Picnic*,[17] which he says shows 'an extreme example of contempt for humanity' because the 'visitors' 'treat humankind like parasites or noxious insects'. To my mind, the nub of the story is not that we have been oppressed but that we probably had not even been noticed by the alien visitors. In this case it is our insignificance not our vulnerability to which the Strugatskys are drawing attention. What the Strugatskys do show contempt for is the unwillingness of the great majority to do anything about the abuses to which they are subjected.

> Noonan went on chatting but thought as he looked at those two horrors born of the zone: My God what else? What else has to be done to us before we understand? Isn't this enough? But he knew it wasn't. He knew that millions upon millions of people knew nothing and wanted to know nothing, and even if they found out would ooh and aah for five minutes and then go back to their own routines.

Such a view may be élitist and thus unorthodox in that it supposes the necessity for each individual, for the hero, consciously to resist the forces of evil even if they do appear to have the strength of historical inevitability behind them.

If there is one consistent theme running through the Strugatskys' work it is that of interference. Should we interfere in the lives of others? If so, when should we interfere and how much and with what consequences? Pepper and Kandid, the two heroes of *Snail on the Slope*, long for the understanding which will give them the answer to the question. They seem to represent respectively the two apparently irreconcilable aspects of Man in a modern technical society so long ago identified by Olaf Stapledon in *The Philosophy of Living*[18] as the dichotomy between 'moral protest and mystical acceptance'.

In *Hard to be God* (1964),[19] the most popular SF book to be published in the Soviet Union, they face the dilemma fairly directly but in a safe and relatively superficial way by placing the protagonist on a backward feudal planet where failure to interfere would result in barbaric regression rather than in a 'correct' evolution towards an advanced (Soviet?) society. There can be no doubt even in the most orthodox reader's mind – the hero must intervene. But the Strugatskys have sown the seed that they are to nurture carefully in future works; non-interference is a tacit acquiescence in evil, whether on an alien planet or in the Soviet Union or in the world at large. The Western horror of cultural interference, its belief that non-involvement equates with tolerance, is implicitly rejected by the brothers as a decadent abrogation of personal responsibility. They do not exempt exceptional characters from taking exceptional action because they do not believe that the masses left to their own devices will behave well. 'If there had never been the visitation there would have been something else. Pigs always find mud.'[20]

In *The Final Circle of Paradise*[21] (1965), otherwise known as *The Predatory Things of our Time*, such interference in a clearly capitalist setting is with the approval of wider authority (the hero, though Russian, works for the UN). We deplore with him the hedonist society – 'souls which had been devoured by affluence' – seeking pleasure at all costs through hallucinogenic drugs and even through the direct stimulation of the pleasure centres of the brain.[22] But there is not much sympathy either in *The Final Circle* for strait-laced conservatism, whose orthodox views are put in the mouths of the least sympathetic characters, nor for the revolutionary violence of power-hungry rebels. There is a nice satire, too, on the paranoia of the Soviet-type man with a KGB-complex. Real bitterness, however, is already reserved for the hopeless apathy of the ordinary man when he discovers, like the workers in Vonnegut's *Player*

Piano, that he is superfluous in modern automated society. 'Nobody really needs you, not even your own wife and children, if you examine it honestly.' The Strugatskys demand, like their hero, 'When would you learn to rescue yourselves?' Yet the Soviet authorities have found the text unexceptionable. It is, after all, clearly a capitalist-type society which is being satirised and the Strugatskys could not be held responsible for any other parallel which might be drawn.

But in *Snail on the Slope* we have a very different animal, openly turning to bite the hand that doled out its shchi and kasha. Published in 1966, this is in my opinion one of the most satirically biting yet mystical SF works to be written in any of the three countries whose SF we have examined. It bears favourable comparison with the best of Vonnegut, Bester or Sturgeon, and the way in which Kandid and Pepper, in their different ways, allow themselves to be subsumed into the very environments against which they struggle echoes Ballard in his most self-immolatory mood. No wonder it was only published furtively in two separate parts, the chapters concerning Kandid on their own in *Ellinskiy Sekret* and the more direct satire of the Directorate chapters, again on their own, in the Siberian journal *Baikal* in 1968.

Structurally it is a relatively simple work. There is a Forest of jumping trees, trance-bound villagers, hostile robbers and zombie-like 'deadlings', miasmas and mystical meres and superwomen. In antithesis we have the Directorate whose purported function is to exploit the Forest and to eradicate its various inhabitants.

The Forest (jungle might be a more atmospheric word for the translation) is 'somehow familiar, a resemblance somewhere, but profoundly alien. The hardest part was to accept it as alien and familiar at the same time.' 'A man could easily have guessed at its existence if only because of the simple existence of the Directorate.' Let the reader draw what analogies he will; that freedom must exist by inference from the necessity for a system of repression, that the corollary of tyranny is injustice; of stupidity, waste – the onion goes on peeling layer after layer. At its simplest level the chapters on the Directorate (they alternate in the full version with the Forest chapters but have never been published in this book form in the Soviet Union) are a satire of Kafkaesque frustration on the follies of self-perpetuating bureaucracies. For all the effect the Directorate has on the luxuriant, bizarre world at the foot of the cliff on which its ever-expanding buildings are perched, it might as well not exist. The two worlds impinge on each other only psychologically, in the effect they have on their respective inhabitants' behaviour and that of the two protagonists, Kandid, stranded almost literally mindlessly in the forest, and Pepper struggling to escape from the mindless world of the Directorate. The two heroes never meet or even know of each other's existence, but the tragedy of the one is the mirror-tragedy of the other.

Gradually the satire on the Directorate builds up. 'There's only one thing they lack – understanding. They always substituted some sort of surrogate for understanding, be it faith, disbelief, indifference or neglect.' 'The Directorate has no need of goodness and honour to function properly. Pleasant, desirable, but by no means essential. Like a knowledge of Latin to a bath house attendant or biceps on an accountant.' The Director, on whom Pepper has called to beg to be allowed to leave – though, fascinated by the Forest into which he is not allowed to go, he half wishes to stay – discusses a work of art. 'The original, naturally, has been destroyed as a work of art, not permitting ambiguous interpretation. The first and second copies were also destroyed as a precautionary measure . . . .'[23] As Pepper says, '. . . it will all be strange and, therefore, meaningless to us, or at any rate for those of us who still can't get used to lack of meaning or accept it as the norm.' Eventually he finds that he himself has been made Director by some bizarre quirk of fate. At first his protesting soul hopes to turn over the whole crazy system by getting the staff to laugh at its absurdities.

> No, they wouldn't laugh at him. They'd cry, complain . . . to . . . Monsieur Alas. . . . they'd kill each other. But not laugh. That was the worst part of it, he thought, they didn't know how to laugh, they didn't know what that was or the reason for it. People, he thought, people and little people and little people. Democracy's what's wanted, freedom of opinion, freedom of criticism. I'll get them all together and tell them; criticise! Criticise and laugh. . . .

Pepper quickly realises the futility of such a gesture and surrenders by accepting the *status quo* and going along with the bureaucratic momentum. Even his last ironic gesture of contempt at the system to which he has acquiesced backfires on him. Since he must issue directives – that is what directors are for – he issues one for the internal security team, the eradicator branch, to go out and eradicate itself by suicide. His mistress/secretary, advocate of the *status quo*, takes him literally and regards this as a stroke of genius; so, even, does the chief eradicator who will have to carry out the order!

As Pepper travels with perverse logic from sanity to lunacy, so Kandid in the Forest makes a very different odyssey by coherently illogical steps from neurological mindlessness to a kind of mystical, other-worldly sanity. It is a sanity which must make him opposed to forces of history which the authors' society has so often insisted are both inevitable and ultimately beneficial, by however bloody a route they travel:

> ... worst of all, historical truth, here in the forest, is not on their side, they are relics condemned to destruction by objective laws, and to assist them means to go against progress, to delay progress on some tiny sector of the front. Only that doesn't interest me, thought Kandid. What has their progress to do with me, it's not my progress and I call it progress only because there's no other suitable word . . . Here the head doesn't choose. The heart chooses. Natural laws are neither good nor bad, they're outside morality. But I'm not . . . If I'd learned the women's language, everything would have sounded different to me: enemies of progress, gluttonous stupid idlers . . . Ideals . . . Greater aims . . . natural laws of nature . . . and for the sake of this annihilate half the inhabitants! No, that's not for me. In any language that's not for me.

It's a heart-rending plea for humanity in an inhumane world, but it is a plea which protagonists and authors alike expect to go unheard: '. . . now it understands with absolute clarity what before it only guessed at; that there is no freedom, whether doors are open before you or not, that everything is stupidity and chaos, there is loneliness alone . . . .' *Snail on the Slope* is indisputedly a pessimistic book, though not without its glimmer of hope, and not, I believe, by any means primarily intended as an anti-Soviet work. The overwhelming impression is of a painfully experienced *Weltschmerz*.

Whatever its intentions, it clearly upset the Soviet publishing authorities, for no further novel from the Strutgaskys was to appear for five years and then only the relatively harmless *The Inhabited Island* in 1971.[24] They did in the interim manage to have a number of stories published in magazine form, including *The Second Martian Invasion*,[25] with its original notion that the only weapon the invaders would require to conquer our greedy planet was the supply of corrupt information. This difficult period also saw the appearance of the amusing and satirical 'The Tale of the Triumvirate',[26] in *The Inspector-General* tradition, on a commission which, set up initially to investigate the plumbing, finds itself taking power by the same inescapable lunatic logic we came across in the Directorate.

The Strugatskys apparently found it difficult to acquiesce in emasculation as the condition of the lucrative form of publication in novel form through the State publishing house, for their next (and virtually last) work returns to the scathing attack on the corrupting effects of a bureaucratic approach to science. *Roadside Picnic* is a clever analogy. The hero asks a sensitive scientist acquaintance what he makes of the alien visitation which has left behind it a small zone in which the natural laws as man knows them do not apply and from which officials and poachers find riches and disaster:

'What do you think about the Visitation?'
'My pleasure. Imagine a picnic.'
Noonan shuddered.
'What did you say?'
'A picnic. Picture a forest, a country road, a meadow. A car drives off the country road into the meadow, a group of young people get out of the car carrying bottles, baskets of food, transistor radios, and cameras. They light fires, pitch tents, turn on the music. In the morning they leave. The animals, birds, and insects that watched in horror through the long night creep out from their hiding places. And what do they see? Gas and oil spilled on the grass. Old spark plugs and old filters strewn around. Rags, burnt-out bulbs, and a monkey wrench left behind. Oil slicks on the pond. And of course, the usual mess – apple cores, candy wrappers, charred remains of the campfire, cans, bottles, somebody's handkerchief, somebody's penknife, torn newspaper, coins, faded flowers picked in another meadow.'
'I see. A roadside picnic.'
'Precisely. A roadside picnic, on some road in the cosmos. And you ask if they will come back.'

Roadside Picnic is full of the multi-level symbolism which by its ambiguity allows the Strugatskys a disclaimer of intended heresy while permitting their more sophisticated readers to enjoy some fairly heretical thoughts. A passage such as this is totally orthodox.

The hypothesis of God, for instance, gives an incomparably absolute opportunity to understand everything and know absolutely nothing. Give man an extremely simplified system of the world and explain every phenomenon away on the basis of that system. An approach like that doesn't require any knowledge. Just a few memorised formulas plus so-called intuition and so-called common sense.

Substitute Marxism–Leninism for God and the passage would find an echo in many a dissident heart. But while it is tempting to read analogies into passages such as this, it must be recognised that as creative artists the Strutgatskys are basically expressing the human predicament as they see it rather than specifically castigating any particular example of it. The themes in *Roadside Picnic* are general to the Strugatskys' work and echo their contemporaries in the West. 'We know that everything changes, we're taught from childhood that everything changes, and we've seen everything change with our own eyes many a time, and yet we're totally incapable of recognising the moment when the change comes, or else we look for the change in the wrong place.' In a state of flux, where linear direction is unpredictable, flexibility, of which the right and readiness to make mistakes is an essential part, is crucial.

A million years from now our instinct will have matured and we will stop making the mistakes that are probably integral to reason. And then, if something should change in the universe, we will all become extinct – precisely because we will have forgotten how to make mistakes, that is, to try various approaches not stipulated by an inflexible program of permitted alternatives.

The enemy, therefore, is the deadly and powerful alliance of technology and administration and the vested interest in conformity of those whose material comforts are derived from this irrelevant power structure. The most potentially dangerous thought in the Strugatskys' work, from the point of view of any autocratic regime such as the one under which they live, is that collective responsibility, collective action, is a myth; that reliance on it is simply an excuse for avoiding individual responsibility and action. The ordinary man dissociates himself in bewilderment from the meaningless ritual dances expressed in the conduct and relationships of the members of a hierarchy of scientists and bureaucrats. In so doing, the Strugatskys suggest, they are asking them to dance on the grave of humanity. Knowledge is not the essential ingredient. Understanding is what we need, and in particular understanding of the not always obvious relationships between cause and effect. 'The violation of the law of causality is much more frightening than a stampede of ghosts.' As far as the Strugatskys are concerned we cannot rely on the average man to be brave or willing enough to meet this challenge on his own.

> But the whole problem with that is that the average man – the one you have in mind when you talk about 'us' and 'not us' – very easily manages to overcome this need for knowledge. I don't believe that need even exists. There is a need to understand, and you don't need knowledge for that.

For this we need heroes and in the Strugatskys' tales we find them; men (significantly, perhaps, never women) who are prepared to resist the orthodox and the inevitable if it denies not only the value of the individual in the Western sense, but also the ultimate responsibility of every individual for the mental and physical well-being of every other on whom his actions impinge. It is after all this second element which gives theoretical communism such strong instinctive appeal. The Strugatskys are not afraid to ask the unnerving question, 'In these strange times, what *is* evil?' and come up with their own unequivocal answer. They have been dubbed pessimists. If they are, they are only tactical pessimists. Strategically they still hope for mankind.

> 'You ask me what makes man great?' he quoted. 'That he re-created nature? That he has harnessed cosmic forces? That in a brief time he conquered the planet and opened a window on the universe? No! That, despite all this, he has survived and intends to survive in the future.'

The hopeful ambivalence of Russian attitudes to the thought-provoking work of the kind described above is implicit in the fact that while the centralised Soviet publishing system would not countenance the novels of the Strugatskys, their work did appear in journals throughout the Soviet Union. The depressing thing is that, as far as I know, apart from one story in 1976 the brothers have had nothing published since *Roadside Picnic*. There has been no major work from Snegov and the spate of enterprising short stories of the late 1960s and early 1970s has also dried up. It could be that this is more apparent than real, the result of the perpetual information-famine regarding unorthodox work in the Soviet Union. Or it could be a sign of an increasingly repressive attitude by the Soviet authorities, conscious that they have become, or are rapidly becoming, the greatest power in the world and need no longer take any notice of what the rest of the world thinks of their conduct. This shift in attitudes has coincided with an equally severe *loss* of confidence in the United States, also anticipated by many of its SF writers. After America's military defeats in Vietnam and the tacit acceptance in the negotiations and accession to the SALT agreements that they could no longer win the arms race, imperial confidence has evaporated to the point where the United States is no longer prepared to confront Russian expansionism in any quarter of the globe – nor, many of its allies suspect, in the final analysis even in Europe. The SALT treaties recognise Russia's parity of power at the very least, and the Soviet success by proxy in Africa and Afghanistan have shown there need be no limit to her inherited imperial amibitions. In a supposed state of military equilibrium, Russian leaders are confident that their moral standpoint (at least they have one, even if we might regard it as immoral) will assure them of ultimate victory and the world dominance of their system of thought.

Notes

1. Cf. It is interesting to note that in Britikov's bibliography only 38 titles are referred to before 1917 and a further 80, with such noticeable omissions as Zamyatin's *We*, up to 1930. To be fair, passing critical reference is made twice to *We* in the lengthy and tedious historical section which precedes the bibliography. There are in all only 861 titles given, including collections and critical works of which there are proportionately far more than in Western SF.

2. A. Mirer, *Wanderers Home* (Moscow, 1976).

3. M. Pukhov, *Hunting Expedition* (Fantastika, 1967).

4. Ilya Varshavsky, 'Cockroaches' (Leningrad, 1967). 'Donomaga' is an anagram of Magodon – the concentration camp region.

5. A. Balubakha, 'Appendix' (Fantastika, 1967).

6. V. Mikhailov, 'Deep Minus' (Fantastika, 1966).

7. V. Mikhanovsky, 'Fialka – The Violet' (NF 12, 1972).

8. Olga Larionova, 'The Kilimanjaro Leopard' (NF 3, 1965).

9. M. Chudnova, 'Lebensraum' (Fantastika, 1969/70).

10. Cf. A. Sharov, 'Pirrow Island' (*Fantastika* 1965); V. Kakhnov, *When the Sun Went Out, Fantastika* (1968).

11. I. Yefremov, *The Hour of the Bull* (Moscow, 1970).

12. Arcady and Boris Strugatsky, *The Snail on the Slope* (501, Leningrad: 1966). Translation by A. Myers due at the time of writing to be published by Bantam.

13. S. Snegov, *Men Like Gods* (3 vols Leningrad, 1966, 1968, 1974). No English version yet available.

14. Alan Myers, 'Some Developments in Soviet SF Since 1966', an article due to appear in *Foundation* 17 (1980). I am indebted to a bibliographical note by Darko Suvin appended to a critical essay on the Strugatskys due to appear in *Foundation* 17 for most of the Russian publishing details of their work in these notes.

15. Ibid. Myers cites Nudelman, Revich, Cherpysheva and Brandis, Kagarlitsky, Dimitryevsky, and Britikov. Nudelman has since emigrated to Israel.

16. An interview in *Foundation* 15 (January, 1979).

17. Arcady and Boris Strugatsky, *Roadside Picnic* (first pub. 1970–72; Gollancz, 1978).

18. Olaf Stapledon, *The Philosophy of Living* (Pelican Books, 1939).

19. Arcady and Boris Strugatsky, *Hard to be God* (first pub. 1964; New York: Seaburg, 1973).

20. Strugatsky, *Roadside Picnic*.

21. Arcady and Boris Strugatsky, *The Final Circle of Paradise* (first pub. 1965; Daw, 1976).

22. They quote Amis with approval.

The contemporary English writer and critic Kingsley Amis, having learned of the experiments with rats, wrote: 'I cannot be sure that this frightens me more than a Berlin or a Taiwan crisis, but it should, I believe, frighten me more.' He feared much about the future, this brilliant and venomous author of *New Maps of Hell*, and in particular, he foresaw the possibilities of brain stimulation for the creation of an illusory existence, just as intense as the actual, or more intense.

23. The German Marxist critic, Walter Benjamin, in *The Work of Art in the Age of Mechanical Reproduction* (1933) suggests that the alienating qualities which he sees in a traditional work of art are removed by mechanical mass-reproduction. This enables a multiplicity of viewers to respond, he contends, to the work in a time and place of their own choosing. Thus there may be a still further layer of satire in this scene to be appreciated by the reader versed in Marxist literary criticism.

24. Arcady and Boris Strugatsky, *The Inhabited Island* (Moscow, 1972). (In German only: Schroeder, 1972.)

25. Arcady and Boris Strugatsky, *The Second Martian Invasion* (first pub. 1968; Pan, 1971).

26. Arcady and Boris Strugatsky, 'The Tale of the Triumvirate', *Angara* 4 and 5 (1968).

10

Tomorrow has been cancelled

The Western science fiction of the past decade bears little resemblance to what has gone before. The difference has been not so much one of technique or approach as one of tone. When I first started to re-read SF extensively again after a lapse of a decade I thought it might be that the genre had simply rejoined the mainstream of literature, in which it had flowed in the days of Wells, Huxley and Verne. Certainly a number of critics[1] were suggesting that it had or almost had, and others, like Watson,[2] had likened the process to the obsolescence of the Stone Age axe when better instruments for the splitting of metaphysical skulls were invented, and welcomed the change. The borderlines between SF and mainstream literature were less clearly defined, with non-SF authors, such as Castenada and Marquez, Lyal Watson and Pirsig, even conventional novelists like Muriel Spark, producing work which, while not claiming to be SF, had elements characteristic of the genre. Certainly SF writing in turn was much more personalised and subjective, but, nevertheless, I detected that there was still a distinctive genre with many works fulfilling the requirements of our earlier definition of SF.

Other superficial changes were also quickly apparent. There had, for example, been a dramatic change in the proportion of women to men among the writers. Pamela Sargent, Vonda McIntyre, Doris Piserchia, Kate Wilhelm, James Tiptree Jnr and others had joined the female regiment and were all writing good SF stories. But although the driving force behind the entry of these writers into the field may have been the Women's Liberation movement and the widening area of acceptance of women's unrestricted role, I did not feel the stories in general to be essentially feminine in outlook. Indeed, it seemed rather that they were simply well-justified assertions of woman's right to enter yet another man's world. One new writer, Dr Alice Sheldon, had gone so far as to enter it in the pseudonymous male guise of James Tiptree Jnr, with a prose and story style which was aggressively masculine. She wrote well and entertainingly on all the standard themes, with a little extra bite which led me to conclude that she might well be sending up the whole genre – in itself no bad thing, but perhaps indicative of a wider lack of confidence in its ability to deal seriously and effectively with serious themes. One line in 'I'm Too Big But I Love to Play'[3] gave me a clue as well as echoing a recurring theme in the work of the Strugatskys. 'You can understand why a system would seek information – by why in hell would it *offer* information? Why do we strive to be understood?'

The advent of sexual equality among SF writers coincided with an even greater alienation between the sexes within the pages of SF itself. Certainly the taboo on sex had vanished but the sex in SF, as in society, had become both promiscuous and aggressive, an emphasis on the differences and the impermanence of all relationships rather than a means of communication. In the crude and rapacious embraces of SF in the 1970s it seems as if Man had forgotten how to reach out to Woman with anything but his prick.

There was clearly no shortage of new talent in the field, not only among the women writers but in the work of Priest, Shaw, Wolfe, Bishop, Varley and others. But none, I felt, seemed likely to attain real stature. In many cases this appeared to stem not from lack of talent but from lack of will, lack of confidence, not only in the genre but in Man's ability, even his need, to tackle the kind of problems with which SF had traditionally dealt. SF was becoming escapist with a vengeance, but from what was it escaping and was this only to be observed in the work of newer writers? It was clearly also necessary for me to review the recent work of the well-established writers as a control group.

Some seemed content to repeat what they had always done. Ray Bradbury still displayed his own remarkable brand of originality, but was basically taking the old SF tricks he used to get us to sympathise with blacks or Indians, to gain sympathy for the new underdogs – in *Long After Midnight*,[4] for instance, for a suicidal transvestite. He still cannot be predicted in detail and if he occasionally feverishly overwrites, it is at least the burning fever of imagination. Frederik Pohl[5] was still venturing away and Philip Dick[6] playing games (with religion). On the British side of the Atlantic John Brunner's *Shockwave Rider*[7] inspired by Alvin Toffler's

Future Shock,[8] asked a number of pertinent questions: 'What in the modern world could be identified as evil, an abomination, wrong?' By implication he suggests that for most people the answer is already nothing, or rather nothing except that which militates against the subject's survival and even comfort. This new morality has a dehumanising effect. 'The subject exhibited a pain response. But not, under any circumstances, we hurt her.' Or again: 'In this age of unprecedented information flow people are haunted by the belief that they're actually ignorant . . . because there is literally too much to be known. . . .' In *The Sheep Look Up*[9] he sadly deplores the inefficiency of the good and the obtuseness of the efficient and is, in short, a much less optimistic writer than he was in the 1960s. Sturgeon, Bester and John Christopher, among other old hands, seem to have stopped writing altogether (or at least I never *saw* the obituaries) or have turned their pens elsewhere. Even some of the newer luminaries such as Barry Malzberg and Alexei Panshin have foresworn SF. The gradual disillusionment of SF writers with the role of science in society, observable at least since the 1940s, had accelerated sharply. A closer look at the work of two Western writers, one American, one British, illustrates this process.

Kurt Vonnegut, once the scourge of American materialism and of the debasing effects of machine-produced affluence, has lapsed into a kind of self-indulgent cynicism, continually digesting and regurgitating his own work. Because he is Vonnegut he does it with wit and many a detailed, penetrating insight, but gone is the burning indignation. It is almost as if he had regressed into childish attention-seeking in desperation that the message of his earlier works was not getting through. There is the same tongue-poking puerility, sexual obsession and lavatorial humour which is sometimes found in the later Ballard. Why has this jouster turned jester? There is a revealing passage in *Breakfast of Champions*:

> As I approached my fiftieth birthday, I had become more and more enraged and mystified by the idiot decisions made by my countrymen. And then I had come suddenly to pity them, for I understood how innocent and natural it was for them to behave so abominably, and with such abominable results: They were doing their best to live as people invented in story books. This was the reason Americans shot each other so often: It was a convenient literary device for ending short stories and books.
> Why were so many Americans treated by their government as

though their lives were as disposable as paper facial tissues? Because that was the way authors customarily treated bit-part players in their made-up tales.

And so on.

Once I understood what was making America such a dangerous, unhappy nation of people who had nothing to do with real life, I resolved to shun storytelling. I would write about life. Every person would be exactly as important as any other. All facts would also be given equal weightiness. Nothing would be left out. Let others bring order to chaos. I would bring chaos to order, instead, which I think I have done.

If all writers would do that, then perhaps citizens not in the literary trades will understand that there is no order in the world around us, that we must adapt ourselves to the requirements of chaos instead.

It is hard to adapt to chaos, but it can be done. I am living proof of that: It can be done.[10]

It is interesting to compare this with a passage from *Zen and the Art of Motor Cycle Maintenance*, a work written at the same time (1973–74) that has undoubtedly had much influence on SF writers since, in which Pirsig tries to explain how this state of chaos has come about.

The major producer of the social chaos, the indeterminacy of thought and values that rational knowledge is supposed to eliminate, is none other than science itself. And what Phaedrus saw in the isolation of his own laboratory work years ago is now seen everywhere in the technological world today. Scientifically produced antiscience – chaos.[11]

For Vonnegut, the confusion between Man, the product of nature, and the machine, the product of science and technology, has become absolute. 'I had come to the conclusion there was nothing sacred about myself or about any human being, but we were all machines, doomed to collide and collide and collide.' It is always dangerous to infer a skilled writer's views from those of one of his fictional characters, but Kilgore Trout is special. So, is Vonnegut simply accepting what Stapledon, fifty years earlier, had called 'the disease of robotism, of purely mechanical living',[12] or is he hoping we will find his approach so risible that we will perceive the deliberate fallacy of its assumptions? It is difficult to tell, but the danger of considering people as conditioned machines is that there can be no moral implications in how we treat them.

My example from the established British writers, J. G. Ballard, extends this hyper-detachment from humanity to the point where it includes even ourselves. Ballard's work in the 1970s underwent a metamorphosis as extensive as that of any of his early worlds. From drastic change in the world at large he moved, on one tack, towards minor changes in a specific urban environment; a tower block, a traffic island, a motor car or cars; and, on the other, to a highly egotistic, almost hedonist, realisation of self, not now through sublimation of a nirvanistic kind, but through physical masochism and sadism. *Crash*[13] was an aberration from the standard usually set by his remarkable talent, though he himself described it as 'a cautionary warning against the brutal, erotic and over-lit realm that beckons more and more persuasively to us from the margins of a technological landscape'. My personal opinion is that it seldom rises above the level of pseudo-sociological pornography. But in *Concrete Island*[14] and *High Rise*[15] and his short story collection *Low Flying Aircraft*[16] he returns to writing the powerful science fiction of which he is capable. The sexuality and cruelty, still sometimes gratuitous, remain but the challenge to ask ourselves questions about the relationship between Man and his environment returns once more. In particular he attacks the dehumanising aspects of modern technology while questioning the dogmatic rejection of all technology which typifies so much of the backlash literature of the 1970s. Where many writers have been able to see and depict the horrors of contemporary urban society and its artifacts, Ballard is able to see the new beauty of them also. Holloway, the hero of 'Ultimate City',[17] sings a paean to industrial waste which is, even as we reject his values, exciting and poetic. Ballard uses the SF writer's mirror-image technique to sharpen our awareness: 'it's a living, urban structure, not a film set. We've got traffic problems, inflation, even the beginnings of serious crime and pollution.'

In 'Low Flying Aircraft', the title story of the same collection, he again confronts us with our easy assumptions about the future of Man. In a drastically depopulated world, ninety-nine per cent of the births are of deformed babies who are got rid of. The hero and his wife decide to keep their child, recognising that what we are witnessing is evolution not detrimental mutation, that mankind is inviting its own disappearance by pursuing the wrong set of values.

The values pursued – or rather acquiesced in – by the protagonists of *High Rise* and *Concrete Island* are certainly abnormal and by contemporary standards aberrant. In *High Rise* he describes the new world we are making and the new moral, or amoral, code appropriate to it – not quite what Paul Johnson had in mind, I suspect, in his *New Scientist* article referred to above.

A new social type was being created by the apartment building, a cool, unemotional personality impervious to the psychological pressures of high-rise life, with minimal needs for privacy, who thrived like an advanced species of machine in the neutral atmosphere. This was the sort of resident who was content to do nothing but sit in his over-priced apartment, watch television with the sound turned down, and wait for his neighbours to make a mistake.

People who were content with their lives in the high-rise, who felt no particular objection to an impersonal steel and concrete landscape, no qualms about the invasion of their privacy by government agencies and data-processing organisations, and if anything welcomed these invisible intrusions, using them for their own purposes. These people were the first to master a new kind of late twentieth-century life. They thrived on the rapid turnover of acquaintances, the lack of involvement with others, and the total self-sufficiency of lives which, needing nothing, were never disappointed.

Alternatively, their real needs might emerge later. The more arid and effortless life became in the high-rise, the greater the possibilities it offered. By its very efficiency, the high-rise took over the task of maintaining the social structure that supported them all. For the first time it removed the need to repress every kind of anti-social behaviour, and left them free to explore any deviant or wayward impulses. It was precisely in these areas that the most important and most interesting aspects of their lives would take place. Secure within the shell of the high-rise like passengers on board an automatically piloted airliner, they were free to behave in any way they wished, explore the darkest corners they could find. In many ways, the high-rise was a model of all that technology had done to make possible the expression of a truly 'free' psychopathology.

From this picture he draws a depressing conclusion:

Even the run-down nature of the high-rise was a model of the world into which the future was carrying them, a landscape beyond technology where everything was either derelict or, more ambiguously, recombined in unexpected but more meaningful ways. Laing pondered this – sometimes he found it difficult not to believe that they were living in a future that had already taken place, and was now exhausted.

Ballard turns away from what might be regarded as conventional SF because he seems to feel that it no longer is capable of offering solutions to problems which can have none – or rather, problems which themselves change so rapidly in nature and impact that by the time solutions are devised they are no longer relevant. A war can carry on for years, but, the odd Vietnam apart, it cannot make the headlines for more than a few days. The multiplicity of simultaneous, multi-locational problems is brought home by the media in a way which makes all problems seem like second-hand video tapes. Like Vonnegut, he concludes that we now live in a fictional world, conduct our lives like characters in some piece of escapist literature. The distinction between image and reality has vanished.

Ballard's new obsession is with the need to dominate our unusual and unnatural urban environment, instead of being subsumed into the general environment – the obsession in his earlier books. This is strongly evident in *Concrete Island*, yet it is played in paradoxical counterpoint with the hero's wilful desire, psychotherapeutic rather than masochistic, to inflict suffering and isolation on himself so as to come to terms with himself.

In radio interviews and articles he has explored these notions in non-fictional forms:

The marriage of reason and nightmare which has dominated the 20th century has given birth to an ever more ambiguous world. Across the communications landscape move the spectres of sinister technologies and the dreams that money can buy. Thermo-nuclear weapons systems and soft-drink commercials coexist in an overlit realm ruled by advertising and pseudo-events, science and pornography. Over our lives preside the great twin leitmotifs of the 20th century – sex and paranoia. In addition, I feel that the balance between fiction and reality has changed significantly in the past decade. Increasingly their roles are reversed. We live in a world ruled by fictions of every kind –

mass-merchandising, advertising, politics conducted as a branch of advertising, the instant translation of science and technology into popular imagery, the increasing blurring and intermingling of identities within the realm of consumer goods, the pre-empting of any free or original imaginative response to experience by the television screen. We live inside an enormous novel. For the writer in particular it is less and less necessary for him to invent the fictional content of his novel. The fiction is already there. The writer's task is to invent the reality.[18]

In adopting this shift to the right – if anarchy can properly be called a right-wing position – he appears to welcome the 'sacred violence to come', the 'sense of renascent barbarism', for which we are heading in place of the feudal order and simplicity so beloved of earlier British science fiction writers. His pessimism is reflected in his imagery and in particular in his fascination with the detritus of modern society, broken glass, condoms, and excrement. Ballard has despaired and doesn't care.

Nor is the attitude of the new writers any more hopeful – or caring. It is perhaps summed up by Norman Spihrad in his collection of short stories aptly entitled *No Direction Home*:[19] 'dark mystical insight filled Cardinal McGavin's soul with terror, a harsh illumination of his existential relationship to the Church and to God; they couldn't both be right, but there was no reason why they couldn't both be wrong. Apart from both God and Satan existed the void.' And again in the same collection: 'There is no basic reality. I thought they taught that in kindergarten these days . . . nothing is where we are *really* at.' This existential nihilism pervades a great deal of recent SF writing and stems from what Helmut Kuhn has called[20] 'the gradual destruction of traditional shelters and barriers, the progress towards catastrophe, the emancipation of man from kindly illusions, and his issuing forth into his terrible freedom.' If the picture drawn by the science fiction writers is correct, we have indeed been seeking freedom in chaos and have found, as Gottfried Keller warned us we should, that the ultimate triumph of freedom is barren. While the committed existentialists may reject certainty and believe that 'the more worthy intellectual task is to learn to think dynamically and relationally rather than statically',[21] the ordinary man longs for concrete points of reference. Mannheim may well have been right when even before the last World War he was saying, 'our uncertainty brings us a good deal closer to reality than was possible in former periods which had faith in the absolute',[22] but it seems fairly clear that today's citizen of the Western world, if his electoral behaviour in 1979[23] is anything to go by, is seeking less reality, in the sense of personal responsibility, and more absolutism. The science fiction writer in attempting to reconcile order and freedom is no longer anticipating popular trends but appears to be opposing them. Or it may be that he simply is not offering the right solutions.

Some writers have tried to explore the idea of spatio-temporal disorientation, to work within the terms of an intellectual uncertainty principle in which time and space, being and knowledge, understanding and believing are eternally divergent co-ordinates in life. The point of truth which would be marked by their intersections simply does not exist. The new wave writers offer only one escape from our dilemma – transcendence.[24] Unfortunately the routes to that state which they recommend are no easier than they are in real life. The kind of escapes from linear concepts of time and three-dimensional space offered by, for example, Priest in *Indoctrinaire* or Shaw in *Others Days, Other Eyes*,[25] make good stories but unreassuring philosophies. No more hopeful are the tales of hallucinogenically-induced transcendence of one kind or another. Even the writers who have tripped on LSD[26] and similar drugs to see their visions condemn such transcendence as escapism and no substitute for spiritual trips through time and space in search of ourselves.

Another route to transcendence offered by present day SF writers is that of violence. Death and destruction are seen as the ultimate high, on the grand scale of a world eagerly embracing nuclear holocaust as in Spinrad's *The Big Flash*[27] or in the lovingly grotesque detail of Priest's 'Fire Storm',[28] in which the central character reconstructs a captured city so it shall be in a state of perfection to be totally destroyed by his nuclear attack. Other less brutal but equally illogical roads to transcendence are offered in a variety of novels and stories[29] but they all smack of magic rather than science. SF seems to have become bogged down in a morass of total subjectivity. We are left trying to navigate through life without landmarks entirely by the gyro compass of self for which we know neither the polarity nor the deviation. The hero of Priest's *The Inverted World*[30] decides 'that I would make what I could of what I saw and not rely on the interpretation of others'. Priest and his fellow new wave writers challenge – or rather abandon us – to do the same. Thomas Disch, a writer of the old school, distinguishes between his work and that of the new writers by a comparison with Ian Watson. 'Watson wants to *believe* in his ideas, while I am content to entertain mine.' It is this longing to believe in miracles which perhaps distinguishes much modern SF from what preceded it, but the verdict of such an approach must surely be that brought in by Bob Shaw: 'My principal objection to the new wave is that it asks me to accept as true things that are clearly untrue.'[31] How has the fiction of reason managed to arrive at the lunatic state where it resolves its dilemmas by abandoning reason for magic? Has science fiction given up the idea as hero or have the ideas simply become increasingly dotty? And how far does this state of affairs reflect the state of the world and its immediate prospects?

To answer such questions we need to return to the element which distinguishes SF from other fiction – science as the catalyst for the plausible development of the plot. It may well be that we have all along been approaching SF with the false premise that science is purposeful, is going somewhere specific. But it is not. Science, the scientific method, is a process of development. It is evolutionary in a Darwinian sense. It is not going *to* anywhere, it is coming *from*. There are no more goals than there are absolute truths, only puzzles to be identified and puzzles to be solved. In as much as SF is really, like the detective novel, a puzzle-solving rather than an ontological genre, it truly reflects the activity in which it is based. Of course, it will be no more successful than the detective novel in solving the problems of the age – these can be tackled only by action not in books – but it can make it fairly clear that there are no answers. We have been conditioned by the thought processes asociated with science and the scientific method to recognise that there are no material verities, no guaranteed unchanging constants and by analogy we have come to suppose that there are, therefore, no such constants in the metaphysical or even in the moral world. The logical inference is that progress as traditionally defined is unimportant. 'We ain't going nowhere', just running from the last place. That being the case we inevitably seek rules to maximise satisfaction in the short run, indeed the instant – tomorrow we die. Not even rules, simply the minimum of rationalisation necessary to disinhibit us to pursue instant gratification at whatever cost not only to others but to ourselves. The addict knows the heroin is killing him and doesn't care, not because of his physical addiction, but because he sees no alternative to nothingness anyway. In a world plagued by a plethora of faintly discerned but rarely even partially understood miracles of science we long for a world outside the limitations of scientific probability. It may be that the lurch towards the fantastic in science fiction is an oblique recognition that it is only the supranormal aspects of human capacity which can now present not only the most fruitful source for rational scientific exploration but the best hope of transcending the morass of moral and intellectual confusion in which we also find ourselves.

The process was well analysed by Pirsig.

But what's happening is that each year our old flat earth of conventional reason becomes less and less adequate to handle the experiences we have and this is creating widespread feelings of topsy-turviness. As a result we're getting more and more people in irrational areas of thought – occultism, mysticism, drug changes and the like – because they feel the inadequacy of classical reason to handle what they know are real experiences.[32]

Forty years earlier Mannheim had been aware of the same developments.

Today, however, we have reached a stage in which this weapon of the reciprocal unmasking and laying bare of the unconscious sources of intellectual existence has become the property not of one group among many but all of them. But in the measure that the various groups sought to destroy their adversaries' confidence in their thinking by this most modern intellectual weapon of radical unmasking, they also destroyed, as all positions gradually came to be subjected to analysis, man's confidence in human thought in general. The process of exposing the problematic elements in thought which had been latent since the collapse of the Middle Ages culminated at last in the collapse of confidence in thought in general. There is nothing accidental but rather more of the inevitable in the fact that more and more people took flight into scepticism or irrationalism.[33]

That we are still struggling with the same problem might be taken as a hopeful sign that it has not beaten us yet. But if contemporary Western SF is any guide, the prognosis is not hopeful. Ours is recognised as the age of corporatism – in business, trade unions, politics and government. The group, not as a collection of individuals but as an abstraction with its own non-human dynamic has become paramount. This all-consuming collectivism has pervaded the world of science – how often do you see a paper with only *one* name under the title? – and the arts and recreation; in jazz as the collective creation of music, in impromptu theatre in which the actors improvise together round the skeleton of a plot, in team games and mass spectator sports. Even much of the writer's and musician's creativity has become a collective effort in television and cinema or in the studio and electronic engineer's laboratory. Nowhere does it seem to be accepted that the individual by personal, isolated effort can influence or even much contribute. To the extent that this illustrates man's capacity for co-operation it may be interpreted hopefully. But in as much as it reflects the refusal of the individual to rely on his own judgement or to obey his own conscience it marks the beginning of the end. All over the world, East and West alike, the ordinary man is surrendering his responsibility for what happens to his fellow man. He pays people to undertake his personal relations – the housemother, the social worker, the counsellor, the old people's home – in a kind of emotional prostitution. He expects the mysterious 'them' to educate his children, doctor his ills, fight his enemies and worst of all tilt the supposedly endless cornucopia of material goods ever more steeply in his direction. As his technical power to communicate with his fellow man doubles every two or three years so his intellectual ability to communicate is at the same time fast disappearing altogether as we progressively debase and devalue the coinage of language.[34] In other words, unity and consistency of thought seem to be inversely proportional to volume of information. I am thus, like every other writer, faced with the paradox that the very book I write in order to elucidate will simply add to the general confusion. Yet to adopt that point of view is to surrender to a mindless fate, to indulge in that betrayal of thought against which Mannheim warned us almost half a century ago: 'The widespread depreciation of the value of thought on the one hand and its repression on the other hand are ominous signs of the deepening twilight of modern culture. Such a catastrophe can be averted only by the most intelligent and resolute measures.'[35] Night has come on apace since then.

The Dark Ages were not so much an epoch as a state of mind. The physical impact of the ruthless insensitive invasion of invigorating barbarians was certainly devastating, but its most profound effect was on the outlook and mental attitudes of the conquered. The

16. J. G. Ballard, *Low Flying Aircraft* (Cape, 1976).

17. 'Ultimate City', ibid.

18. Introduction to the French edition of *Crash*. Pirsig put it thus a few months later:

> Now the stream of our common consciousness seems to be obliterating its own banks, losing its central direction and purpose, flooding the low-lands, disconnecting and isolating the highlands and to no particular purpose other than the wasteful fulfilment of its own internal momentum. Some channel deepening seems called for.

and Louis Wirth in the preface to *Ideology and Utopia* said forty years before:

> A society is possible in the last analysis because the individuals in it carry around in their heads some sort of picture of that society. Our society, however, in this period of minute division of labour, of extreme heterogeneity and profound conflict of interests, has come to a pass where these pictures are blurred and incongruous. Hence we no longer perceive the same things as real, and coincident with our vanishing sense of a common reality we are losing our common medium for expressing and communicating our experiences. The world has been splintered into countless fragments of atomized individuals and groups.

19. Norman Spinrad, *No Direction Home* (first pub. 1969–74; Fontana, 1977).

20. Helmut Kuhn, *Encounter with Nothingness* (Methuen, 1951), recommended as an outline of the Existentialist position seen critically but not unkindly from a Christian viewpoint.

21. Karl Mannheim, *Ideology and Utopia* (Kegan Paul, 1936).

22. Ibid.

23. Recent elections in Britain, Canada, Australia, and even Italy all showed a marked shift to the right.

24. As Stableford put it in his *Notes Towards a Sociology of SF* . . . : 'resulting in fascination with images of transcendence. A new vocabulary of ideas, concerned with social, psychological and transcendental "answers" to story-predicaments has grown up to displace (to a very large extent) the traditional vocabulary of technological "answers".'

25. Christopher Priest, *Indoctrinaire* (first pub. 1970; Pan, 1979). Cf. Priest, *Real Time World* (NEL, 1974), and Bob Shaw, *Other Days Other Eyes* (Pan, 1974).

26. E.g. Philip Dick in the Preface to *A Maze of Death* (Gollancz, 1972).

27. Norman Spinrad, 'The Big Flash', in *No Direction Home* (first pub. 1969–74, Fontana, 1977).

28. Christopher Priest, 'Fire Storm', in *Indoctrinaire*.

29. E.g. Paddy Chayevsky, *Altered States* (Hutchinson, 1978) and Frederick Turner, *A Double Shadow* (Putnam, 1978). Brian Stableford by

contrast is one of the few new writers who does not allow his characters to 'cop out' in this way.

30. Christopher Priest, *The Inverted World* (Faber, 1974).

31. *Foundation* 7 and 8.

32. Pirsig, *Zen and the Art of Motor Cycle Maintenance.*

33. Mannheim, *Ideology and Utopia.*

34. Ibid. Mannheim warned us:

the absence of a common apperception mass vitiates the possibility of appealing to the same criteria of relevance and truth, and since the world is held together to a large extent by words, when these words have ceased to mean the same thing to those who use them, it follows that men will of necessity misunderstand and talk past one another.

And Bacon more succinctly long ago in *The Advancement of Learning*: 'words are formed at the will of the generality, and there arises from a bad and unapt formation of words a wonderful obstruction to the mind.'

35. Mannheim, *Ideology and Utopia.*

Index